Albrecht Altdorfer
Four Centuries of Criticism

Studies in the Fine Arts: Criticism, No. 9

Donald B. Kuspit

Chairman, Department of Art
State University of New York at Stony Brook

Kenneth S. Friedman, Ph.D.

Consulting Editor

Other Titles in This Series

No. 1   Champfleury: The Realist Writer as Art Critic   David A. Flanary

No. 2   The Critics of Abstract Expressionism   Stephen C. Foster

No. 3   Art Critics and the Avant-Garde:
New York, 1900-1913   Arlene R. Olson

No. 4   In/Stability: The Shape and Space
of Claudel's Art Criticism   Lynne L. Gelber

No. 5   Cubist Criticism   Lynn Gamwell

No. 6   Félix Fénéon and the Language of
Art Criticism   Joan Ungersma Halperin

No. 7   The Metaphor of Painting: Essays on
Baudelaire, Ruskin, Proust, and Pater   Lee McKay Johnson

No. 8   Roger Fry and the Beginnings of
Formalist Art Criticism   Jacqueline V. Falkenheim

No. 10 The Formation of a Legend:
van Gogh Criticism, 1890-1920   Carol M. Zemel

Albrecht Altdorfer

Four Centuries of Criticism

by
Reinhild Janzen

umi
RESEARCH PRESS

Produced and distributed by
UMI Research Press
an imprint of
University Microfilms International
Ann Arbor, Michigan 48106

Library of Congress Cataloging in Publication Data

Janzen, Reinhild.
  Albrecht Altdorfer, four centuries of criticism.

  (Studies in fine arts : Criticism ; no. 9)
  Bibliography: p.
  Includes index.
  1. Altdorfer, Albrecht, 1480 (ca.)-1538. 2. Donauschule.
I. Title. II. Series.
N688.A55J36   709'.2'4   80-22780
ISBN 0-8357-1120-X

To the Memory of My Father
Dr. phil. Kurt Kauenhoven
1888 - 1975

Contents

List of Plates   *viii*

Acknowledgments   *x*

Foreword   *xi*

Introduction: The History of Altdorfer Criticism as a Case Study
in *Rezeptionsgeschichte*   *1*

Part I
Altdorfer Criticism from the
Sixteenth to the Nineteenth Century   *7*

Chapter 1
Albrecht Altdorfer's Life and Work   *9*

Chapter 2
Romanticism Rediscovers Altdorfer:
From Raselius to Schlegel   *23*

Chapter 3
Nineteenth Century Altdorfer Criticism:
The Beginning of Art History as an Academic Discipline   *39*

Part II
Altdorfer Criticism in the Twentieth Century   *53*

Chapter 4
Image Makers   *55*

Chapter 5
Altdorfer and Ideologies   *61*

Chapter 6
The Quest to Identify Altdorfer's
Intellectual and Spiritual Position   77

Chapter 7
The Eye of Darius: Altdorfer Interpretations in
Kokoschka and Other Modern Artists   91

Chapter 8
Conclusion   103

Notes   109

Appendix A
Friedrich Schlegel's Essay
on Albrecht Altdorfer's *Battle of Alexander*   143

Appendix B
Oskar Kokoschka, "The Eye of Darius"   145

Plates   149

Bibliography   163

Index   169

List of Plates

Following page 148.

Parenthetical numbers within the text refer to the illustrations which follow the appendices. The source of the illustrations is given in parentheses. The following abbreviations were used in referring works by Albrecht Altdorfer to their numbers in Franz Winzinger's three-volume catalogue raisonné:

W.Z. — Franz Winzinger, *Albrecht Altdorfer, Zeichnungen,* 1952.
W. Gr. — Franz Winzinger, *Albrecht Altdorfer, Graphik,* 1963.
W. G. — Franz Winzinger, *Albrecht Altdorfer, Die Gemälde,* 1975.

Plate 1
Albrecht Altdorfer, *The Two Sts. John*

Plate 2
Albrecht Altdorfer, *Birth of the Virgin*

Plate 3
Albrecht Altdorfer, *Standard Bearer*

Plate 4
Albrecht Altdorfer, *The Battle of Alexander*

Plate 5
Albrecht Altdorfer, *The Beautiful Mary*

Plate 6
Albrecht Altdorfer, *Susanna's Bath*

Plate 7
Albrecht Altdorfer, *The Dead Pyramus*

Plate 8
Albrecht Altdorfer, *St. George*

Plate 9
Max Ernst, *The Last Forest*

Plate 10
Otto Dix, *St. Anthony in the Forest*

Plate 11
Pablo Picasso, *Recovery of the Body of St. Florian*

Plate 12
Pablo Picasso, *Kneeling Woman,* after Altdorfer, 1953
lithograph

Plate 13
Albrecht Altdorfer, "Darius," enlarged detail from the
Battle of Alexander

Plate 14
Oskar Kokoschka. *Thermopylae,* central panel

Acknowledgments

I wish to thank Professor Erik Larsen of the Department of the History of Art, University of Kansas, for his continuing encouragement and help during the writing of this study. Similarly, I am grateful to Professor James Connelly and to Ted Coe, Director of the Nelson-Gallery of Kansas City, for their constructive advice and support of this project. The research was made possible through a grant from the University of Kansas to study at the Art History Department of the University of Bonn, Germany, during the academic year 1976-77. While in Germany incisive and expert judgment on the particular direction of this project was given to me by Professor Franz Winzinger, today's foremost authority on Albrecht Altdorfer; by Dr. Wolfgang Pfeiffer of the Städtische Museum of Regensburg; by Dr. Giselda Goldberg, Landeskonservatorin at the Dörner Institute in Munich; by Wolfgang Kehr of the Akademie der Künste in Munich. I am grateful to Professors Helmut Huelsbergen and to Frank Baron of the Department of Germanic Languages and Literature at the University of Kansas for contributing valuable information. I thank Rosalie Neufeld for her excellent work in shaping the manuscript.

My mother, Edith Kauenhoven, deserves special recognition for her support in every way and so does my husband, whose assistance in all aspects of this study has been crucial.

R.J.

Foreword

The role of the art critic is paradoxical. He makes the first, and presumably the freshest, response to the work of art, grasps it when it is still new and strange, and gives us a preliminary hold on its meaning. Yet his response is not comprehensive, for it is inexperienced: the work has not yet had a history, a context of response to give its "text" density. When the critic encounters it as a contemporary product, it lacks historical "bearing." Indeed, part of the critic's task is to win it a hearing at the court of history. This is why, as Baudelaire says, the critic is often a "passionate, partisan observer" of the work, rather than a detached judge of its value. As its contemporary, he plays the role of advocate, knowing the case only from the viewpoint of the work itself. For the sensitive critic the work will always remain a surprise, and he will always be its enthusiast. He will leave it to the future historian to engage in that dissection of art which presupposes a settled opinion of its significance.

Yet—and this is the paradox—the temporary opinion of the critic often becomes the characteristic one. The critic's response is, if not the model, then the condition for all future interpretation. His attention is the work's ticket into history.

A sign of the critic's power, in modern times, is his *naming* of new art. Louis Vauxcelles' labels "Fauvism" and "Cubism," for instance, have had an enormous influence on the understanding of these styles. Through such names art assumes an identity for future generations. And an understanding which begins as no more than a "semiotic enclave," to use Umberto Eco's term, becomes a whole language of discourse, creating an entire climate of opinion. Clearly, the responsibility is awesome. Clement Greenberg once wrote that the best moment to approach a work of art critically was after the novelty had worn off but before it became history. Yet it is at just that moment that the work is most unsettled and vulnerable, when the critic's swift "decision," in the form of an impromptu name, can seal its destiny forever. In so seemingly trivial an instance as naming we can see criticism's enormous power of determination.

Criticism, then, as Oscar Wilde wrote in "The Critic as Artist," is vital to art. Criticism grasps and preserves, cultivates and exalts. The history of art criticism is the history of different generations' responses to the art. No doubt the interests of the generation determine what is interesting about the art. As

Reinhild Janzen tells us in her study of Altdorfer criticism, the assumption of *Rezeptionsgeschichte*—the history of critical response to an art—is that "a work of art is a piece of dead matter until it is drawn into a dialectic, dynamic relationship with an observer," and the interests of the observer obviously influence the nature of the relationship. The history of art criticism is both the record of such relationships and the demonstration of their significance to the work of art. This insight underlies the Janzen study as well as the other volumes in this series.

At stake in the encounter between art and its observer is ideology or, in H. R. Jauss' words, the "recipient's . . . horizon of expectation." That ideology both conditions the recipient's response to the work of art and is itself affected by the encounter.

At the same time, as Janzen says, the recipient's horizon of expectation leads to the differentiation between "primary and secondary types of reception. The first is the original experience or encounter with a work of art." The second is influenced by "knowledge of preceding, traditional interpretations." In Janzen's study, Friedrich Schlegel's essay on Altdorfer's *Battle of Alexander* is an example of primary reception and Oskar Kokoschka's later interpretation of the same painting illustrates secondary reception. Clearly, from the viewpoint of *Rezeptionsgeschichte,* there are no absolute criticisms of art, for even the primary reception is determined by the interests of the critic, and thus is dialectical. Indeed, as Janzen implies in her endorsement of Herder's concept of criticism, the recognition of the dialectical character of criticism that *Rezeptionsgeschichte* forces upon us is an antidote to "aesthetic historicism's static view of history," i.e., its concept of the aesthetic finality of the work of art.

This series of titles selected from dissertation literature exemplifies *Rezeptionsgeschichte* in a variety of ways. First, it shows us the history of the reception of artists whom we have come to regard as "major," in particular Altdorfer (in the Janzen volume) and Van Gogh (in Zemel's study). The authors discuss both how these artists moved from minor to major status and the meaning of the move for the culture in which it was made.

Second, the series offers us the history of individual critics' reception of a variety of art. We trace the development of a characteristic view of art in Baudelaire, Ruskin, Proust, and Pater (in the Johnson work), in Champfleury (Flanary), and in Claudel (Gelber). Sometimes, as in the case of Champfleury and Claudel, we are dealing with figures whose primary identity does not seem connected with the visual arts. At other times, as in the cases of Baudelaire, Ruskin, Proust, and Pater, even when the figure is associated with the visual arts, the ideology is grounded in larger cultural issues as well as other, usually literary, arts. The perspective of such a mind often leads to unexpected insights and lends fresh significance to the work of art.

Third, the series addresses the critical response to whole movements of art, in particular Cubism (in the Gamwell treatise) and Abstract Expressionism (Foster). We learn how an art that seemed aberrant came to seem central and how critical response created a unified outlook on a highly differentiated group of artists.

Fourth, we have portraits of figures—Félix Fénéon by Halperin and Roger Fry by Falkenheim—who are more or less exclusively art critics. As professionals their horizons of expectation developed in close encounters with art. And their outlooks are also shown to involve larger cultural orientations—the ideology that makes their responses to art dramatic, part of a larger dialectic, dynamic relationship with their culture.

Finally, Olson's treatise examines the development of journalistic criticism in New York. We see *Rezeptionsgeschichte* as it enters a new, democratic, populist phase. Journalistic critics spearhead the advance of culture for the masses in which the encounter with art is there for the asking by anyone.

These five genres of *Rezeptionsgeschichte* demonstrate the richness and complexity of art criticism as an intellectual and cultural enterprise. They also make clear that there is no such thing as neutral, ideology-free criticism. Indeed, the very meaning of criticism is to put information to a larger use, to subject it to an *Aufhebung* or mediation which makes it truly telling—truly revelatory of the art. Art criticism, as it is examined in these volumes, is neither description nor evaluation of art. It is a means of entry, through art, into a study of the complex intentions that structure the life-world, and a demonstration of art's structural role in the life-world that produces it.

In concluding, let us note some particulars of the volumes in this series, especially the ways in which they tie in with broader cultural issues. Janzen makes clear that Altdorfer's reputation hangs on the familiar North/South—Northern Romantic/Southern Classical—conflict. Altdorfer's slow acceptance corresponds to the reluctant acceptance of Northern irrationality or abnormality and Southern (Italianate) rationality and normativeness. In her study of Van Gogh Zemel shows that at issue in the reception of Van Gogh's art was the artist's temperament or emotionality, as the foundation of his creativity. Van Gogh came to be accepted when it was recognized that emotions were a major component of creativity. Van Gogh's art became the proof of this assumption.

Johnson shows us that the art criticism of Baudelaire, Ruskin, Proust, and Pater demonstrates the growth of bourgeois individualism. The "poetic" individuality the critic can achieve through the art becomes emblematic of bourgeois self-possession and integrity in the eyes of the world. Their art criticism is also caught up in the shift from the concept of art as a (romantic) depiction of nature to the idea of art for art's sake. Art for art's sake is another means whereby individuality is achieved and refined.

In her work on Claudel, Gelber offers us a new perspective: modern art seen in a religious context. Claudel is haunted by the possibility of a modern religious, specifically Christian, art. Gelber shows how one well-formed ideology, even if based more on non-art than art encounters, can lead to a powerful analysis of art. Flanary makes a similar point in his study of Champfleury, although here the ideology is secular rather than sacred. Champfleury's sense of the importance of realism and Claudel's sense of the importance of Christianity as comprehensive *Weltanschauungs* shape their perspectives on art.

In Gamwell's volume on Cubist criticism and Foster's on Abstract Expressionist criticism we see the way in which complexity of meaning can interfere with an understanding of art. In these studies we have a sense of how much an art can deliver, and how uncertain we finally are about what is delivered. Yet, we sense that the art is aesthetically important because it has become a stylistic idiom for many.

Halperin's work on Fénéon offers us a study of a critic's language. In Falkenheim's book we learn the historical background of Roger Fry's formalism, which became a major ideology as well as an empirical mode of analysis of 20th-century art. Olson acquaints us with critics who claim to represent the masses in their encounter with art—popularizers of criticism as well as of art. All three studies show us criticism in a practical as well as theoretical light. Criticism can be a short, sharp look as well as a considered opinion, a way of dealing with a newly given object as well as with a standing problem.

These volumes demonstrate the versatility and subtlety of art criticism. Whether we accept Robert Goldwater's notion that criticism is a "provisional perspective" on art and so implicitly journalistic, or Pater's notion that it is a means to profound spiritual experience and self-discovery, or Claudel's view that criticism is the study of art in the light of a dominant *Weltanschauung,* art criticism displays a unique range of methods for the investigation of art.

Donald B. Kuspit
Series Editor

Introduction

The History of Altdorfer Criticism as a Case Study in *Rezeptionsgeschichte*

> A work of art requires an intelligent spectator
> who must go beyond the pleasure of the eyes to
> express a judgment and argue the reason for
> what he sees.
>
> —Lucian[1]

The aim of this study is to establish the history of the impact and criticism of Albrecht Altdorfer's (ca. 1480-1538) art over the span of four centuries. By criticism is meant every kind of response to the artist's work, but this study will investigate the professional-scholarly criticism rather than the popular. Albrecht Altdorfer, illuminator, draftsman, printmaker, painter, architect, municipal politician, and diplomat was the foremost artist of a regional style commonly referred to as the Danube School. Today's scholarship would agree that he may best be characterized as Dürer's antipode.

A critical survey of the body of responses to and receptions of Altdorfer's art is necessary for several reasons: first, it has never been studied;[2] second, it may be justified by Altdorfer's importance as a major catalyst of German sixteenth century graphic art and painting; third, from his death to the present, Altdorfer's art has been subject to divergent, sometimes contradictory criticism and to oblivion. Interpretations of his art have evoked comparisons with Bavarian folk music; with Bach, Beethoven, and Bruckner; with Leonardo, Giorgione, Tintoretto, and Rembrandt; with Homer, Shakespeare, Goethe's *Faust,* Eichendorff, and Thieck. Attempts to discern the spiritual and intellectual determinants of Altdorfer's work have been equally varied, and the categorizing of his art into any particular period style—Medieval, Gothic, Mannerist, Baroque—has also produced disparate judgments.

During his lifetime Altdorfer did well for himself with his art and with his art he also helped the economy of his town. Today he is profitable again, his art is marketable, popular then as now. A five-thousand-piece puzzle of a blown-up detail of the *Battle of Alexander* is sold in toystores throughout Germany; a poster of the same painting appeared as a centerfold in a pharmaceutical magazine, as well as a calendar of a paper-producing firm; color reproductions of Altdorfer's oeuvre may be had to suit any size of pocketbook or bank account. But between then and now the curve of appreciation for Altdorfer dipped very low. An eighteenth century travel book described the *Battle of Alexander* as Dürer's accomplishment.

This inquiry into the history of the *reception* of Altdorfer's work by its critics—and every single response to the work is a critique—hopes to shed new light on the complex nature of Altdorfer's art. By recognizing the relativity of aesthetic judgment, it hopes to establish a degree of objectivity. The goal then is to understand *why* Altdorfer criticism took its particular profile.

The basic presupposition of such a study, and of this one, is that a work of art is a piece of dead matter until it is drawn into a dialectic, dynamic relationship with an observer. This research will, accordingly, trace this dynamic relationship comprehensively in the case of Altdorfer's art. In German this method of historical and critical inquiry is called *Rezeptionsgeschichte,* meaning the history of how a work of art has been received, acknowledged, and criticized at a particular time. There seems to be no equivalent term in English art historical literature. However, the operational concepts do exist in English under the term criticism. Of the variety of approaches to the visual arts, *Rezeptionsgeschichte* may be classified as one of the extrinsic perspectives.

The term and the concept originated in literary criticism where it can be traced to antiquity.[3] The 1975 edition of the first novel devoted to an artist (*Künstler-Roman*) in Germany, W. Heinse's *Ardinghello* (1787) may be cited as a recent example of the application of *Rezeptionsgeschichte* to elucidate the original intention of the work.[4] Today *Rezeption* in its general usage means the total realm of human cognition, including the analysis of tradition. Transferred to art, *Rezeption* means reproduction, adaptation, assimilation, and critical judgment of a work of art with or without considering its larger context. "*Rezeption* may be spontaneous or reactionary, adaptive or critical, naive or scientific."[5]

In the context of this study it is interesting to note that the theory of *Rezeption* received a "Copernican" impetus by Johann Gottfried Herder's insight into the relativity of taste, its dependency on and relationship to "education, climate, mode of living and frame of mind (world view)."[6] This happened during the same period of time as Friedrich Schlegel's rediscovery of Old German painting, as described in his essay on Altdorfer's *Battle of Alexander.*

In the twentieth century, culture critic Walter Benjamin (1892-1940) was an influential advocate of *Rezeption* in the history of the visual arts, particularly in his research in the sociology of art and mass culture. Benjamin's vantage point as a critic was that of dialectic historical materialism. He claimed

"All attempts to understand a work of art are in vain unless its historical context is approached by a dialectic perception" [my translation].[7] In his essay on "The Work of Art in the Era of Mechanical Reproduction"[8] he developed his notion of the *aura*, the unique nimbus that surrounded an original work of art. It was the special sense of the here and now giving authenticity to the work. This unique aura of a genuine work of art could not be preserved once the art was reproduced. Therefore, Benjamin distinguished between *Rezeption* in the era of mechanical reproduction and traditional *Rezeption* prior to mass production of art. According to Benjamin, traditional *Rezeption* responds to the cult value of the work of art; postindustrial *Rezeption* responds to the exhibition value of the work of art.[9]

Benjamin also acknowledged the historical element of the aura of a work of art. He contended that "the authenticity of a thing is all that is transmissible from its beginning, ranging from its substantive duration to its testimony to the history which it has experienced."[10] And, in the same essay, he stated an idea crucial to the present study, namely that the "uniqueness of a work of art is inseparable from its being imbedded in the fabric of tradition,"[11] an idea which Wölfflin had expressed and, before him, Burkhardt.

In Benjamin's reflection on "Eduard Fuchs, Connoisseur and Historian"[12] he presented Fuchs as a pioneer of the dialectic-materialist approach to knowledge of art. Fuchs recognized early the necessity to supplement, even to overcome, aesthetic historicism's static view of history with a dialectic approach to the history of the reception of a given work of art. Fuchs had criticized the neglect in art history of the question of a piece's "success." The discovery of the real causes for the relative success of an artist, the reasons for the duration of his success as well as the opposite, is one of the most important problems connected with art criticism.[13]

Benjamin stated that for the dialectical historian, works of art integrate their pre-history as well as their post-history, a post-history which reveals also the work's pre-history as continuously changing. Works of art teach the historian how their function survived their creator and surpassed his intentions; how the reception by their contemporaries is an integral part of the impact which they exercise on us today; and how this impact results not only from the encounter with the work of art but also through the encounter with that history which allowed it to endure to the present. If art is understood as concretized history, then any image of the past, any work of art vanishes irrevocably unless each present recognizes itself in that image.[14]

Problems of *Rezeption* and *Rezeptionsgeschichte* constituted the central issue of a collection of essays edited by Martin Warnke (University of Marburg, Germany) on "The Work of Art Between Science and Ideology" (1970).[15] The introduction postulated the necessity of critical inquiry into the reception of a work of art as the object of ideological interests or as the victim of an ideologically-oriented reception. It was suggested that *Rezeptionsgeschichte* as a method could discover the authentic instrinsic value (Gehalt) of the work of art by analyzing the relationship between it and the given "receiving" ideology. This becomes pertinent in the case of Altdorfer's reception during the Third Reich in Germany.

Wolfgang Kehr, lecturer at the Academy of Fine Arts in Munich, uses *Rezeptionsgeschichte* in his work as a politically conscious pedagogue. He understands this method to have its scientific roots in semiotics. So far, Kehr is the only scholar who has applied the method of *Rezeptionsgeschichte* to the analysis of Altdorfer's work in his efforts to mount a didactic exhibition about Altdorfer's *Battle of Alexander*.[16]

While these three applications of *Rezeptionsgeschichte* have endeavored to understand the popular reception of a work of art and are guided by a sociological orientation, the present research adopts rather the goal and the methodology of an aesthetics of *Rezeption* as they are spelled out by the leading contemporary proponent of literary *Rezeption,* H.R. Jauss.[17] The intention is to bridge the gap between historical and aesthetic knowledge (*Erkenntnis*) by researching the recipient's perception (*Adressaten-Rezeption*) which in itself constitutes a historical force (*geschichtsbildende Energie*). Jauss proposed the following procedures for analysis which are to safeguard the desired objectivity: the study of the reception of a work of art by a given observer must elucidate the "recipient's . . . horizon of expectation" or at least the knowledge (*Vorwissen*) which he brings to the work of art; it then must follow the analysis of the recipient's *description* of his *Rezeption* whether such a description takes the form of paraphrase or reproduction, whether it is argumentative, judgmental, or exploratory; this must be followed in turn by an analysis of the *concepts* used in a given form of *Rezeption*.[18]

The study of *Rezeption* distinguishes between primary and secondary types of reception. The first is the original experience or encounter with a work of art. In this study, F. Schlegel's essay on Altdorfer's *Battle of Alexander* constitutes an example of a primary reception of a work of art. The secondary type of reception is exemplified by Kokoschka's interpretation of the same painting because he brings to his encounter with it knowledge of preceding, traditional interpretations of the work.

This study presupposes a certain body of evidence, namely the ready availability of Altdorfer's oeuvre as it has been established since M. J. Friedländer's first monograph on Altdorfer (1891), the works of the present leading Altdorfer scholar Franz Winzinger, and the comprehensive Altdorfer exhibitions and related scholarship on Altdorfer in the context of the Danube School in Munich (1938) and in Linz and St. Florian (1965). The major body of criticism, of "reactions" to Altdorfer, is German, including Swiss and Austrian. Not counting general art historical works, dictionaries, or encyclopedias, Altdorfer interpretations by non-Germans are rare. The exceptions are Sturge Moore, Kenneth Clark, Picasso, Nicolo Rasmo and the Americans Charles Talbot, Craig Harbison, and Jack Spalding.[19]

Criticism views art as knowledge. Therefore it is the duty of the critic to understand, not to judge. The original verb "to criticize" in Greek meant to cut, to distinguish, to analyze.[20] "The subjective elements in criticism can be objectified by being related to their objects and viewed in a larger perspective. . . ."[21] The study of *Rezeption* and its method proposes to do just that.

Part I

Altdorfer Criticism from the Sixteenth to the Nineteenth Century

Albrecht Altdorfer's Life and Work

1528 Wahl Eines Statt Cammerers . . . Crucis ist
h. Albrecht Altdorfer, Maler, Burger des Innern
Raths von den verordneten Wehlern durch
ordentliche Wahl . . . zu einen Statt-Cammrer
erwehlet worden. Nu hat sich aber gemelter Herr
Altdorfer berürt Cammrer Ambt anzunemen,
zum Höchsten verwidert und desshalb etliche
seine Ehehoften und unter andern diese
ursachen angezeigt: Er hette iezo ein sonders
werkh dem durchleuchtigen Fürsten, meinen
gnädigen Herrn Herzog Wilhelmen in Bayern zu
uerfertigen ganz genöttig unter Handen und
solchs zum ehisten zu vollenden seiner Frstl.
Gnaden versprochen, das auch Ihme doran
merkhlich gelegen wer, mit höchster Bitt, Ihm so
uferlegter bürd des Cammrer Amts günstiglich
zu erlassen.

—From the records of the Regensburg City Council[1]

Altdorfer's life ran its course between the burning of Savonarola and the founding of the order of the Jesuits, between Dürer's *Apocalypse* and Michelangelo's *Last Judgment,* between an eager growth of students and schools and a decline of the universities.

In 1505 the name of Albrecht Altdorfer entered the records of history when "Albrecht Alltdorffer painter from Amberg" acquired the rights of citizenship in Regensburg upon paying the amount of two florins on "Pfinztag nach Judica."[2] There are no documents which pertain to the date and the place of Altdorfer's birth. Citizenship could be obtained as early as the age of 16 in Regensburg, so that there is no compelling reason to assume a birthdate earlier than 1488. That year was indicated as Altdorfer's birthdate in a newspaper report of 1840 about the discovery of fragments of Altdorfer's tombstone.[3]

He was of the same generation of Martin Luther and less than a generation younger than Dürer, Granach, Grünewald, and Holbein. Like those of his
famous contemporaries, Altdorfer's formative years coincided with the reign
of the "Last Knight," the Emperor Maximilian I, whereas the years of
maturity of all of these artists were affected in various ways by the upheavals of
the Reformation.

From 1505 until the time of his death on February 12, 1538, Altdorfer's
life was closely interwoven with that of the town he chose for his home, the free
imperial city of Regensburg. Dürer, on the other hand, had written from
Venice in 1506 that he felt like a stranger in his native Nürnberg.[4]

Regensburg's location on the confluence of the Regen and Danube rivers
in Bavaria and on a major trade route had contributed to the city's economic
and political importance. This trade route allowed for direct connections with
Hamburg to the north; Nürnberg, Cologne and Antwerp to the west; and
Salzburg and Venice to the south. In Venice, Regensburg merchants were
leading representatives in the Fondaco dei Tedesci.[5] Trade products in
Regensburg and its environs were wax, linen, woolen cloth, Netherlandish
sheep, yarns, lard, iron, tallow, as well as Dutch, English, French and domestic
cloths.[6] Major manufacturers depended on the work of specialized artisans
such as the dyers, weavers, shearers, carders, tailors, and hosiers.

From the latter part of the fifteenth century and continuing into the next
century, Regensburg suffered a decline of culture and commerce because of
political unrest, continuous feuding, crime, and violence. The city's judicial
system sought to deter the high rate of robberies, murders, forgeries, and
political rebellion by meting out cruel and draconian forms of public punishment. An average of twenty decapitations, burnings, or hangings per annum
were considered quite normal by the chroniclers. Relatively minor offenses
were punished by blinding, the cutting off of ears or hands, or banishment into
exile by literally beating the victim out of town.[7] Citizens complained
vigorously about the lack of public safety. At night hardly anyone dared to
leave his private dwelling. Noisy carousers were locked into an iron cage, called
a "fool's house," in front of City Hall for the remainder of the night.[8] Justice
could be bought for money, and it was not beyond the City Council to hire
clandestine henchmen to silence potential as well as existing troublemakers.[9]

In the countryside as well, daily life was accompanied by the constant
threat of danger. Altdorfer recorded an armed robbery in a woods and a
confrontation between a knight and a foot soldier in two drawings of journalistic immediacy of observation (W.Z. 4 and W.Z. 30). Ulrich von Hutten wrote
from his family's estate to Willibald Pirckheimer in Nürnberg on October 25,
1518:

> . . . we can never leave the castle unarmed. We dare not go hunting or fishing unless we
> are clad in our armour . . . anytime and anywhere we may be ambushed and attacked to
> be sold to our enemies. . . .[10]

There are accounts of destructive mass hysteria, as when the Jews were expelled from Regensburg in 1519, and accounts of religious hysteria surrounding, for example, the feverish cult of the Beautiful Mary.

On the other hand, the Regensburg chronicles report on the city's exemplary welfare services for the sick and the poor as well as for gifted students.[11]

Economic decline developed in the wake of the discovery of new sea passages to Asia and the Americas. Trade gravitated to the Atlantic seaports of northwestern Europe and took economic leadership from the old Hanseatic cities as well as from Venice. Moreover, unlike Nürnberg and Augsburg, Regensburg was bypassed by the major south-north, east-west arteries of commerce, and by 1508 the city's trade relations with Venice had deteriorated because of strained political relations with the Emperor. The cost of city government in Regensburg rose steadily and heavy tax burdens had to be put on the citizens as well as on foreign trade goods.

The political crisis in the Empire had its roots in a tripartite conflict between the Emperor, the landed aristocracy, and the municipal democracies. The particular difficulty and challenge which city governments such as Regensburg's faced lay in the task perpetually to mediate the demands of the clergy, the commercial and professional guilds, the artisans organized in brotherhoods, and those of the Emperor and the Duke of Bavaria.

Despite these difficult circumstances and its relatively small size of 15,000 inhabitants (as compared to Augsburg's 50,000, or nearly 90,000 in Florence), Regensburg was counted among the foremost towns in Europe during Altdorfer's life time.[12] This is attested to by its inclusion as a sizable dot on the first printed map of Europe in Hartman Schedel's *Pictorial World History*.[13]

Further, two woodcuts of Regensburg were in print at the turn of the century. One covered two half-pages of a folio in the same *Pictorial World History*. The beholder sees a large fortified town on the banks of the Danube, a river busy with cargo-bearing boats. Inside the walls rise church steeples and the numerous towers of the houses of old patrician families, symbols of wealth and prosperity. While this prospect of the city affords an understanding of Regensburg's prosperous mercantile socio-economic situation, the other woodcut shows the intellectual climate of German humanism prevalent in the cities which housed scholars benefiting from Maximilian I's patronage. The woodcut was published in 1502 in Konrad Celtis' *Quattuor libri amorum*. The author was Maximilian's poet laureate, founder and leader of the humanist movement issuing from Vienna, the *Sodalitas Danubiana*.[14] The book's protagonist relates amorous adventures in Krakau, Regensburg, Mainz, and Lübeck. Each city represents and personifies one of the four cardinal points of the compass which are brought into relation with the seasons of the year, the four ages of man, the four humors, the four times of day, the temperatures, the elements, and the primary colors. Each of the four chapters of the book pays homage to the number nine, in honor of the nine muses. The second chapter of Celtis' *Quattuor Amores* takes place in Regensburg, the city chosen to symbolize the age of adolescence, the choleric temperament, and the color red. The corresponding woodcut shows a bird's eye view of the prosperous city as seen in Hartman Schedel's *World History,* but surrounding it are fields being harvested, woods, valleys, mountains, and neighboring towns. The central motif also shows an appreciation for nature: young lovers meet in a garden.

Contrary to the reader's expectations fostered by the philosophical and cosmological framework of the book, the plot develops on a realistic and popular level rather than on an abstract or speculative one. A lovers' quarrel ensues over the mistress' indulgence in luxurious clothes and drink.

The themes which emerge in the book and the accompanying illustrations are ever-present in the chronicles of the time and in Altdorfer's life and art: the close relationship to nature; the respect for her laws and awareness of how these affect the fate of man; the many city ordinances against extravagant dress; the concern over each year's wine harvest rather than over matters of politics and religion; the awed acknowledgments of strange appearances in the skies; Altdorfer's ownership of two vineyards and a second house with a large garden on the outskirts of the city; and his highly individualistic adaptations and interpretations of humanist thought, tinged with a homely flavor.

Even though the city of Regensburg suffered one financial crisis after another, the documents give evidence of the City Council's continuous effort to improve the town's cultural life and spiritual growth. As early as 1430 the Council had exhibited a painting of the Virgin of Orléans. Books were printed in town from 1486.[15] During the pre-Lenten season, municipal soldiers performed sword dances, students produced comedies, the furriers acted out carnival plays in their beer halls, and people participating in the merry-making wore masks.[16] No expenses were spared to celebrate the feast days of the Church with splendor and to lend magnificence to the joyous *entrées* of the Emperor and of princes or their emissaries. Jousts were staged. Artists were commissioned with preparations for these festivities, a fact which reflects a high degree of tolerance for the ephemeral on the part of the patrons, the public, and the artists.[17] The stained glass windows of St. Peter's Cathedral and the rich vestments worked by the many embroiderers provided more permanent forms of art.

Another important concern of the municipal authorities was the institution and support of schools. In addition to the traditional monastic schools, the city of Regensburg employed and supervised four so-called German school masters whose instruction was designed to meet the needs of the sons of merchants and craftsmen who would follow their father's occupation and not prepare for the university.[18] The curriculum consisted mainly of the rudiments of reading and writing and Latin. Altdorfer himself probably attended either this kind of school or a traditional monastic school, which did not differ greatly in the basic course of instruction. But by 1503 the city sought to expand secular education by adopting the model set by Nürnberg's city schools in which the curriculum consisted of the classical authors as well as the introductions to university subjects.[19] The City Council of Regensburg approved the application of the humanist Dr. Joseph Grünpeck, formerly the Emperor Maximilian's private secretary, to institute a *Gymnasium Poeticum* in Regensburg.[20] Grünpeck was a renowned philologist, astrologer, physician, and author. His school in Regensburg was probably inspired by the College of Poets which the Emperor had newly created as a fifth faculty in Vienna. Grünpeck's school was located in a private home near the Augustinian monastery, which continued the school after Grünpeck's departure, in the same vicinity as Altdorfer's first house.[21] There was probably a closer link than geographic proximity between Grünpeck and Altdorfer: the painter furnished the illustrations for the scholar's work *Vita Frederici et Maximiliani.* Johannes Stabius, another humanist linked to the circle of the *Sodalitas Danubiana,* also lived and worked in Regensburg during the later periods of his life.[22] Altdorfer must have been in contact with him through his illustrations for Emperor Maximilian's *Triumphal Arch,* the Latin text of which Stabius composed. Stabius, whose most significant contributions were in mathematics, geography, and astronomy, led the College of Mathematics in Vienna instituted by Maximilian as an auxiliary to his College of Poets.

In view of the presence of these German humanists in Regensburg during Altdorfer's residence there, it is not surprising that his early dated graphic work treats such humanist themes as those of the muses, personifications of the planets, and allegorical figures of virtues and vices. The rise of German as written language also influenced Altdorfer's Regensburg. For the first time instruction in all subjects in the schools could be obtained in German.[23] A parallel development in literature was inspired by Ulrich von Hutten's polemic against the evils of a Latin-dominated education, at a time when he self-consciously abandoned Latin poetry-writing for German poetry. Johannes Aventinus (Turmair) (1477-1534), who was Bavaria's own historian and who spent the latter part of his life in Regensburg, contributed to the creation of German prose and German national consciousness with the German version of his *History of Bavaria.* This development in language—in the popular appeal, the absence of formalism, immediacy of expression—must have affected Altdorfer's art.

When Altdorfer came from Amberg to Regensburg in 1505 he was but one of many painters, cartographers, letter-writers, and illuminators who had come to earn their living there (thirty-two were entered between 1470 and 1506 in the burgher-books of Regensburg).[24] Among them was a painter, Ulrich Altdorfer, who is listed in the documents as a citizen of Regensburg between

1478 and 1491, at which time he left the town because he was completely impoverished. It is generally assumed that he was Albrecht's father. No trace of his work exists. Albrecht and his brother may have been apprenticed initially to their father.

The question as to where and to whom Altdorfer was originally apprenticed remains an unsettled one. The answers have been as divergent and as manifold as there were painters in Franconia, Bavaria, and Upper Austria during the last decades of the fifteenth century. Since lack of documents shrouds Altdorfer's artistic beginnings before 1506, the year of the first signed and dated drawings and engravings, only stylistic analysis can suggest the specific nature of his schooling.

As Max J. Friedländer was the first to observe, Altdorfer's early miniature style reflects neither influences of Dürer nor of Bavarian panel painting. Instead, the choice of the small format and the unprecedented predominance of landscape motifs as well as the incidental treatment of the human figure may be linked to miniature painting. See for example Altdorfer's *Satyrfamily* in Berlin, the Bremen *Nativity,* the *St. George* in Munich. At the close of the fifteenth century miniature painting was held in such high esteem that the illuminators formed a separate guild in several cities. Regensburg and Nürnberg were the principal centers for this art.[25] The miniature painter Berthold Furtmayr, who was active in Regensburg from 1476 until 1501, has been suggested as a direct influence on the early development of Altdorfer's art.[26] A comparison between Furtmayr's miniatures in his missal for Bishop von Rohr of Salzburg and some of Altdorfer's own miniatures for Maximilian's *Triumphal Procession* bear a striking stylistic resemblance.[27]

During the years around 1500, book illumination declined in favor of woodcut illustrations for handwritten or printed books. Indeed, the earliest proofs of Altdorfer's creative activity are thirteen diminutive tinted woodcuts of saints, which date from around 1500 and were intended to be pasted into handwritten prayerbooks. These woodcuts were created for the Benedictine monastery at Mondsee where Altdorfer probably worked for some time during his extended, obligatory journey at the close of his apprenticeship. There he also came to know Michael Pacher's monumental altarpiece in the church of St. Wolfgang, an experience which found its most poignant expression more than a decade later in Altdorfer's own monumental altarpiece in the Augustinian monastery church of St. Florian.[28]

What significance might be hidden in the fact that Altdorfer began signing his graphic work only after he had become a citizen in Regensburg? Only then do the first signed and dated paintings appear. In 1508 further rights of citizenship were granted to him, such as the use of a personal seal.[29] From that year forward, the records of his life as have been preserved in the municipal archives of Regensburg convey Altdorfer's increasing professional and public success.

The first recorded instance of the city's patronage of Altdorfer dates from the year 1509 when the City Council contributed ten *gulden* toward the installation of one of his paintings in the choir of St. Peter's as part of a number of preparations for a religious celebration.[30] The next entry of Altdorfer's name in the municipal records occurred in 1522 when he was paid sixteen *pfennig* and two *wiener* for having delivered the design for a gold coin. The reverse shows the image of St. Peter and the obverse the two crossed keys on a shield which were the arms of Regensburg.[31] In 1517 Altdorfer was commissioned to paint a curtain for a reliquary shrine and a banner to be carried in a procession.[32]

The year 1519 was to be of crucial consequence in Altdorfer's life. He had just completed what was to be his last monumental religious work. With Maximilian's death, an era had come to an end. The voices of the Reformation became more and more urgent. Altdorfer had reached the third stage of a man's life, the years of maturity. He was elected to the city's Outer Council. This was the beginning of nearly twenty years of public service.

His first political activities in this same year were to be reflected in his artistic activities. As a member of the Outer Council he was immediately involved in the expulsion of the Jews from Regensburg.[33] A warning was issued that the Synagogue was to be destroyed within two hours, and the destruction was fast and furious. Soon afterwards Altdorfer etched its interior and the portico of its school from memory. These etchings bear dates and inscriptions in Latin and were very likely intended as souvenirs.[34] The chroniclers remarked with astonishment on the Synagogue's antiquity, vaulted ceilings, and structural solidity. The subject was at once artistically challenging, topical, and profitable.

In the same year (1519) the Council sponsored the erection of a provisional wooden chapel to be built on the site of the destroyed synagogue and dedicated to an old venerated image of the Beautiful Mary. Labor was donated by the populace from near and far. Instantly this chapel became a popular shrine attracting thousands of pilgrims.[35] The cult of the Beautiful Mary involved Altdorfer once more in his double role as artist and politician. The story of the cult as such is one of a mixture of money, politics, art, and religion. Art was used to stimulate religion, which in turn was expected to prompt generous votive-offerings—even donated clothing could be washed and resold—which kept the municipal budget from threatened collapse.[36] Altdorfer was commissioned to paint for the bell tower a banner carrying the image of the Beautiful Mary and the arms of Regensburg; to design a pilgrim's coin; and to illuminate the initial letter of a papal indulgence with the image of the Beautiful Mary.[37]

The city's last recorded commission to Altdorfer for a painting was also intended for the promotion of the cult of the Beautiful Mary. This painting, now lost, was about a miracle concerning a woman suspected of several incidents of arson in the Austrian village Persenburg. She acknowledged these crimes in a confession and was condemned to death by drowning. The woman was sewn into a sack and thrown into the Danube. For a long while the executioner forced the sack to the bottom of the river with his long pole. Nevertheless, the sack surfaced again and floated to the little town of Ips. There the waves washed the sack ashore and the crowd pulled it up from the water and freed the woman. She ran directly to Regensburg to thank the Beautiful Mary for having saved her life. She impressed the clergy with her innocence and they urged the City Council to commission Altdorfer with a depiction of this miracle. He was paid eight *gulden* for his efforts, an indication that the painting must have been fairly large and elaborate. The panel was hung in the chapel of the Beautiful Mary next to a printed story of the miracle.[38]

In addition to the city's commissions for this cult, Altdorfer created numerous variations of the motif of the Beautiful Mary in each technique of his art.[39] Whether these were motivated by a desire for profit or by a personal religious involvement, or by both factors, is difficult to discern. The last recorded instance of the city's employment of Altdorfer's services as a painter dates from 1520 when he decorated the city's artillery with Regensburg's armorial device. This was done in anticipation of a visit by the Emperor Charles, who was traveling through on his way to Austria.[40] During the same year Altdorfer was honored with an additional public office, that of presiding in the *Hansgrafenamt*.[41]

There are no further entries concerning Altdorfer in the city's records until 1526 when he was nominated to the Inner Council as well as to the office of superintendent of municipal buildings. From that time Altdorfer referred to himself with his official title of *Baumeister*.[42] That this office was not contingent on the incumbent's training in a related craft can be deduced from an entry in the minutes of the Council meetings. In 1513, a saddlemaker named Peuchel had been a member of the Council and had held the office of superintendent of municipal buildings for a "long time."[43] Both of these high honorary offices Altdorfer held actively until the year of his death. All four of the buildings erected or remodeled under his supervision are still standing in Regensburg today, as are parts of the four fortifications of the city's walls built as a defense against the impending danger of a Turkish assault. These improvements of the walls were Altdorfer's responsibility immediately following his completion in 1528 of the *Battle of Alexander* for the Duke William IV of Bavaria.[44] In 1528 Altdorfer's success as an arbitrator added to his already high reputation and he was voted to be mayor for the three months preceding Christmas. He declined this honor, however, on the grounds that he had promised the Duke he would soon deliver the *Battle of Alexander*. This resignation from high office has been interpreted to mean that Altdorfer's first devotion was to his art. Another explanation is equally valid in the light of Altdorfer's sympathetic leanings toward endeavors to reform the Church. In his capacity as city council member he was present at two of the three interrogations *cum* torture of the influential Anabaptist Würzlburger during May of 1528. He perceived that it would have been his duty as mayor to follow through with the execution of Würzlburger as demanded by Bavarian government authorities, and so he used his excuse of work for the Duke to avoid having to commit to death a man for his religious conviction, a man whom Altdorfer respected.[45] The amount and range of Altdorfer's civic duties had made it necessary for him to keep a horse for which the city provided the oats.[46]

In 1533, a decade after the feverish cult of the Beautiful Mary had waned, the city officially adopted Protestantism. Altdorfer's name appeared among those members of the Council who complied with the citizens' request to search for a Protestant pastor.[47] This change of official religious confession caused continuous friction between the municipal authorities and the clergy, and in order to exert firm control in religious as well as fiscal matters the Council placed two wardens with the city's monasteries. Altdorfer was assigned additional duties as warden of the Augustinians in whose church his wife had been buried the previous year.[48] These involvements in the city's change to Protestantism have been cited as evidence of Altdorfer's personal religious convictions in favor of the Reformation. This question will be examined in another context, but it is certain that Altdorfer was not fervently outspoken for the Protestant cause. Had he been other than moderate in his views, he would not have been sent on a diplomatic mission to King Ferdinand in Vienna in 1535 to apologize for two Augustinian monks who were sympathetic toward Luther's reform movement. Altdorfer completed this mission successfully[49] and brought back a benign letter from the King's Chancellery to the city of Regensburg. The involvement of an artist as a leader in his community was not unique to Altdorfer. Tilman Riemenschneider served as mayor of Würzburg in 1520-21,[50] and Jörg Ratgeb died a martyr for the cause of the peasants as he negotiated between the warring parties.

Altdorfer's active concern for his community may perhaps be explained as an outgrowth of the guild system's traditional emphasis on commitment to the welfare of its members as well as to that of the poor and the needy. The members were bound to "show brotherly love and kindness . . . to practise Christian and fraternal charity. . . ."[51] The guilds were represented in town government either directly through their respective leaders or through an elected member. Altdorfer must have risen to his high position through the artisan-guilds; his view of the artist's role in society was the traditional one of the artist-craftsman and was not influenced by the Renaissance conception of the artist as gentleman scholar or even genius, an attitude adopted by Dürer in nearby Nürnberg.

The charter-book (*Freiheitsbuch*) of the city of Regensburg contains a miniature from the year 1536 which bears testimony to a social situation which permitted artists to rise to the city's highest honorary offices. Merchants, craftsmen, patricians, and the guilds were the upholders of culture, and as such they equaled the Church and the princes in ways they had not before 1400 and would not after 1550. The miniature shows a chamber in the City Hall where the Inner Council is assembled. The margin of the page is decorated with the arms of the members, among them Altdorfer's.[52]

Considering the possible scope of Altdorfer's travels, the only journey which is documented was the diplomatic mission to Vienna in 1535. Other travel is suggested by circumstantial evidence in his work. Certain landscape drawings of sites along the Danube indicate that Altdorfer repeated his apprentice-journey eastward to Austria in 1511 and again in 1518 when he had to put the finishing touches on the altarpiece in St. Florian.[53]

Because of his knowledge of Italian art, it has been suggested by several scholars that Altdorfer traveled at least once to Northern Italy, to Verona, and to Venice. Altdorfer's use of Renaissance architectural motifs in such paintings as *Susanna's Bath,* the St. Sebastian altarpiece, and the *Holy Night* in Vienna suggests direct contact with North Italian architecture, but there is no evidence.[54] A journey to the Netherlands has been suggested as well.[55]

Altdorfer's workshop must have been fairly large. Numerous copies of his paintings and drawings were done under his supervision, probably on commission by private collectors. His house was equipped to accommodate at least two apprentices. His workshop had grown after 1511; that is, after the commission for the St. Florian altarpiece and during a time when he was kept busy with the work on the *Triumphal Procession* for the Emperor Maximilian. During these years an apprentice executed the Regensburg altarpiece which was completed in 1517.[56]

What is known about Altdorfer is revealed through the legacy of his work as an artist, as a supervisor of public buildings, through the documents of his work as a politician, and through his earthly possessions as they were itemized at the time of his death. No personal written records from his own hand are known, but an inventory which specifies three boxes containing letters is evidence of Altdorfer's connections beyond the limits of Regensburg.

The 20 pages of his will, dictated on the day of his death on February 12, 1538, have sometimes been interpreted as a key to his personality.[57] The phrasing, however, is that of the notary; the document states that Altdorfer is weak of body but sound of mind and continues elaborately acknowledging the vanity of this world and emphasizing the right way to die.[58] Sentences pertaining to these themes reflect the writings of Gailer von Kaisersberg and such works as his book of the good death (*Das Buch vom guten Tode*) in which he stresses, among other things, the generous giving of alms. Gailer's published sermons were very popular at the time, so much so that they were plagiarized frequently. He preached reform within the Church and chastized its corruption long before Luther.[59]

The most direct revelation of Altdorfer's religious conviction is contained in his explicit rejection in the will of the customary mass for his soul after his death. In lieu of paying the money for such a mass, he ordered that his wedding present to his wife, a silver goblet with a gilded lid decorated with *welsche Angesichtlen,* be given to the general fund for the poor. This provision indicated his sympathy with the new faith and it also constituted an extraordinary change in religious custom. Only two other wills preserved in Regensburg archives made the same provision, one in 1533, the other in 1539.[60] The art of Cranach and Dürer, and particularly their graphic work, reveal an actual conversion of religious faith, but no such conversion is to be detected in the iconography of Altdorfer's oeuvre.[61]

The inventory of Altdorfer's two houses evokes the picture of comfortable, even wealthy, surroundings. In addition to black and green curtains and clothes including one red waistcoat, the inventory lists copper utensils, brass candleholders, silver cutlery, 19 books, several trunks containing prints and paintings, art books, weapons, and paintings on linen which had just recently become fashionable in Venice. There was also a collection of at least 10 luxurious goblets of gold and silver, and nine rosaries fashioned of precious materials such as gold, silver, coral, pearls, and bone. Sermons, police regulations, and popular sayings of the time make it clear that rosaries were often used like the jewelry and the rings Altdorfer owned, that is, as signs of wealth and for personal adornment rather than as signs of piety and religious devotion. A person's status was judged by the kind of rosary he carried.[62]

Altdorfer was buried next to his wife in the church of the monastery of St. Augustin. The inscription on his tombstone, a fragment of which is preserved in the city museum of Regensburg, refers to him as "master-builder."

It may be an accident of history that nothing is known of Altdorfer's appearance, and that he is the only one of the major artists of the time about whom this is true. Altdorfer was not self-reflective or introspective, as was Dürer, and has left no personal evidence of himself either in written testimony or self-portraits. His whole oeuvre as it is known today contains only three portraits.[63] But as it was common practice for artists to include themselves disguised as bystanders in major works involving important Christian themes, it is plausible to suggest that Altdorfer may have done so as well.

One of the panels of the altarpiece at St. Florian shows the handwashing of Pilate. A bystander watches intensely as water is poured from a precious vessel whose spout is shaped in the form of a dragon. The head of this bystander has strongly individualistic features and in that respect it differs significantly from the otherwise rather typecast actors in the religious drama. The physiognomy and expression of this head are strikingly similar to Joachim von Sandrart's drawing of Altdorfer after a now lost Altdorfer portrait,[64] and on the basis of this similarity it has been suggested that the man watching Pilate declare his innocence is indeed a disguised self-portrait of Altdorfer. Stronger support for this hypothesis may be found in examining the question as to why Altdorfer would identify himself with this particular event in the Passion story.

The episode of the handwashing occurs in only one of the Gospels, in Matthew (27:24-25). Thus Matthew seems to exonerate Pilate and places the full blame for the death of Jesus on the Jews.[65] This interpretation started a process which led to embellishments of Pilate's character in the apocryphal writings. He emerges rather as a hero and even as a Christian. In view of the general hostility toward the Jews and the persecution of them in Altdorfer's time, this scene assumes pertinence. Only one year after the completion of the altarpiece Altdorfer was involved in the expulsion of the Jews from Regensburg. The scene becomes even more pertinent in view of the fact that some historians have seen Pilate as a skillful and successful politician[66] and administrator, a role Altdorfer played in Regensburg. A third circumstance strongly supports the thesis that Altdorfer included himself as a bystander in the scene of the handwashing of Pilate and that the artist had personal reasons for doing so. The man whose gaze is fixed on that fanciful ewer was himself a designer and collector of luxury objects.[67] The one in this scene is identical with one of Altdorfer's own design. This threefold coincidence between the implications of Pilate's act, the vessel used in the scene, and Altdorfer's own situation could hardly have occurred by chance.

The range of Altdorfer's creativity was vast, both in terms of the techniques he employed and also in terms of the media and art forms he mastered. His work included miniature painting and diminutive engravings; designs for doors, tombstones, sculptured altarpieces; monumental frescoes for the so-called Emperor's Bath in the bishop's residence in Regensburg. Nor does his productivity seem to have suffered from Protestant theology or Luther's position on idolatry, as did Dürer's.[68] Yet despite this productivity and range in Altdorfer's work, much of it was destroyed within less than three centuries after his death. The destructive waves of iconoclasm between 1522 and 1537, from which Regensburg itself was protected, took place in lootings and burnings of the castles and monasteries in the countryside.[69] Works commissioned by landed aristocracy and monasteries could likely have been destroyed at this time. It was in the next century, during the Thirty Years' War, that the art of Altdorfer's time was dispersed, lost, or destroyed.[70] Further losses of his work occurred during the Counter-Reformation and the Baroque redecoration of churches, and in Napoleon's entry into Regensburg, which was accompanied by looting of art and the burning of a third of the city.

Subsequent chapters will evaluate the impact of Altdorfer's diminished oeuvre in the light of these depredations of history, and the ideas in terms of which it was received.

Table of Correspondences Between Life and Work of Albrecht Altdorfer

1505	Obtains citizen's rights in Regensburg	*Early period* of small format: Bremen Nativity, Berlin Diptychon, Berlin Satyr-family
1509		Commission for the St. Sebastian Altarpiece in St. Florian
1510	Possibly a first journey to Italy	Munich St. George, Berlin Rest on the Flight to Egypt
1511	Journey along the Danube toward Passau, Salzburg, Linz	Drawings of Landscape Portraits
1513	Purchase of first house with tower and court	Woodcut cycle of the Fall and Redemption of Man, *middle period* of the large panel paintings: The Two Sts. John, Christ's Leavetaking
1515		Work on commissions for Emperor Maximilian's Triumphal Procession
1518	Purchase of second house	Story of Life of St. Florian
1519	Election to the City Council	Work on numerous commissions for the city of Regensburg, such as for the promotion of the cult of the Beautiful Mary
1520	Possibly a second journey to Italy	Potrait of a Canon, private collection. Birth of the Virgin, Munich
1522	Sale of second house	Madonna and Child in Glory, Munich
1526	Election to the Inner Council of the city of Regensburg and to the office of municipal architect	Suzanna's Bath, Munich; Calvary, Nürnberg; Crucifixion, Berlin
1528	Several cases of successful arbitration, attends trials against anabaptists	Commission by Duke William IV of Bavaria for the Battle of Alexander
1529	Work on city's fortifications, Turkish armies near Vienna	*Period of late works* Portrait of a Woman, Castagnola
1530	Purchase of vineyard	
1531		Painting of a Proverb, Berlin

Table of Correspondences Between Life and Work of Albrecht Altdorfer

1532	Purchase of house with large garden, death of his wife	Wall paintings for the Emperor's Bath in the Bishop's Palace in Regensburg
1533	Votes in favor of a protestant pastor for the city	
1534	Responsibility as Warden of the Augustinian monastery	
1535	Diplomatic mission to King Ferdinand in Vienna on behalf of the city, supervision of construction of the market tower	
1537		Lot and his Daughters, Vienna
1538	February 12, he dictated his will and died on the same day.	

Romanticism Rediscovers Altdorfer: From Raselius to Schlegel

Ein köstliches Gemälde ist nicht ein Paragraph
eines Lehrbuches, den ich, wenn ich mit kurzer
Mühe die Bedeutung der Worte heraus-
genommen habe, als eine unnütze Hülse liegen-
lasse. Vielmehr währt bei vortrefflichen Kunstwerken der Genuss immer, ohne Aufhören fort.
Wir glauben immer tiefer in sie einzudringen,
und dennoch regen sie unsere Sinne immer von
neuen auf, und wir sehen keine Grenze ab, da
unsere Seele sie erschöpft hat. Es flammt in
ihnen ein ewig brennendes Lebensöl, welches nie
vor unseren Augen verlischt.

—W. H. Wackenroder[1]

Albrecht Altdorfer's art was not honored in writing by brilliant comments of contemporaries, such as Erasmus' *laudatio* on Albrecht Dürer. The documents preserved in Regensburg's archives do not reveal qualifying adjectives in conjunction with records of Altdorfer's activities as a painter and draftsman.[2]

A first—if brief—criticism of Altdorfer's art was written by the chronicler Raselius (1536-1602). It was published in a topography of Bavaria in 1644, more than 100 years after Altdorfer's death. Raselius described the painting of *St. John the Baptist and St. John the Evangelist* (ca. 1513, W. G. 27) (Plate 1): ". . . there [in St. Emmeran] is a beautiful, jolly (*lustig*) and artful panel painted delicately (*artig*), inclusive of a beautiful landscape, painted by Albrecht Altdorfer who was a City Councilman here."[3] The painting dates from Altdorfer's middle period, from the time between 1513-1515. In terms of artistic achievement this largest panel painting by Altdorfer has been ranked by Winzinger next to the *Battle of Alexander*.

The key word in Raselius' description is the adjective *lustig,* for which there is no modern English equivalent. In the modern sense *lustig* would translate as "amusing" or "funny," but in sixteenth century usage the meaning of the word *lustig* is quite different. Luther used it to express a positive frame of mind, a determination to act positively in the sense of "wanting or feeling prepared to do something." But mainly *lustig* was used in the visual sense, especially in connection with the description of particularly lush, green, pleasant landscape or countryside. Aventinus as well used the word *lustig* frequently to distinguish, for example, fertile, hospitable soils from rough, infertile terrains, or to describe the paradisiacal beauty of a garden "as if God Himself had planted it."[4]

The fact that Raselius used the word *lustig* in his description of Altdorfer's painting of the *Two Sts. John* reveals Raselius' receptivity and responsiveness to its landscape, abundant with lush vegetation, rather than to the portrayal of the saints who are painted as if they were of the same matter as the moss, the flowers, the trees, and animated by the same lifegiving force. Raselius' brief description represents the first, if indirect and unselfconscious, acknowledgment of a crucial Altdorfer characteristic. That is an ambivalence in the representation of traditional subject matter or rather, his fusion of subject categories.

Raselius concluded his remarks by mentioning Altdorfer's social position as a member of the City Council. His reputation as a prominent, influential citizen was held in at least as high an esteem as his artistic contributions.

By 1651 this emphasis on Altdorfer's political role seemed to lessen somewhat. In that year, Georg Abraham Peuchel, a citizen of Regensburg, presented the City Council with a bound volume of woodcuts, engravings, and etchings by Albrecht Altdorfer. For the first time Altdorfer was introduced on the title page as a "highly famous" (*hochberühmt*) painter and only secondly was a reference made to his past political role.[5] In addition to this bound collection of prints, Abraham Peuchel also gave the Council a painted panel by Altdorfer in the hope of receiving a favorable position with the Council. These gifts were recorded in the city's books; there, too, the quality of the panel painting was praised and only then was added a comment on Altdorfer's membership in the city's government.[6] Testimony to Altdorfer's popularity at this time are the copies of about 1650 which were made after certain of his paintings, such as that of the *Birth of the Virgin* (municipal museum of Regensburg).[7] But by 1663 a historical poem of Regensburg described the original *Birth of the Virgin* as Dürer's work (Plate 2).[8]

The first professional art critic to discuss Albrecht Altdorfer was Joachim von Sandrart (1602-1688).[9] Like Alberti and Vasari before him, he belonged to those critics who are active artists themselves. Sandrart had trained with the engraver Aegidius Sadler in Prague and then with Gerhard Honthorst in Utrecht. He had furbished many a cathedral, parish church, and monastery in Munich, Eichstatt, Salzburg, Brunn, and Vienna with colossal altarpieces, portraits, and historical paintings in the style and in the service of the Counter-Reformation. Princes and lords honored him, and the Doge of Venice made him a knight of St. Mark's. Toward the close of his life he wrote his *Teutsche Academie der edlen Bau-Bild-und Mahlerey-künste,* published in Nürnberg in 1674. This work constitutes primarily a collection of biographies of artists, but it also conveys a clear idea of its author's aesthetic views. Sandrart's principal contribution to art history was his discovery of the identity of Mathias Grünewald.

Sandrart, himself trained as an engraver, knew best Altdorfer's graphic work and on this basis classified Altdorfer as one of the "Little Masters." As a collector, Sandrart owned an Altdorfer drawing, but of the circumstances of Altdorfer's life Sandrart knew very little.[10] However, Sandrart's characterization of what he knew of Altdorfer's art remains pertinent:

> . . . he painted best small narrative scenes, put much thought into them and much diligence, and in all of these one feels a spirited inventiveness and an uncommon strangeness for which he deserves special praise, for, even though his works seem a little wild—because according to the taste of his time that which is distant is represented with equal clarity as that which is in the foreground—one finds profundity of thought, especially in his large Jerome, in the Crucifixion and in others. Also very delicate in his large woodcut of the Banner Carrier, also his Pyramus, Thisbe, Abigail[11] and Passion which reveal very beautiful effects. Engravings and woodcuts are all to be held in esteem, and, together with the books, are classified with the little engravings or masters, all of which convey very well his productivity, diligence and subtle thoughtfulness [intellect].[12]

In each of his biographical sketches Sandrart tried to single out the special, distinguishing qualities of the artist. In the case of Altdorfer we see that he admired the artist's "spirited inventiveness," his "extraordinary strangeness," and his "subtle intellect" more than diligence and craftsmanship. (Sandrart used the expressions *tiefsinniger Verstand* and *sinnreicher Verstand.*) He recognized and appreciated Altdorfer's highly personal, original vision. Sandrart placed priority on the idea in the mind of the artist rather than on rules and verisimilitude, qualities stressed by the French Academicians.

Sandrart's own baroque taste is reflected in his selection of the works which he enumerated in his book as representative of Altdorfer's style. *Standard Bearer* (W. Gr. 84, 1514-18; Plate 3), *Pyramus and Thysbe* (W. Gr. 22, 1513), and the cycle of woodcuts of the *Fall and Redemption of Man* (W. Gr. 25-64, 1513) are dramatic compositions, full of contrasts of scale, of movement along diagonal axis into deep spaces, of moments of climactic action and of pathos. All of this Sandrart meant when he spoke of "beautiful effects."

In view of subsequent Altdorfer criticism until Friedländer (1891), it is noteworthy that Sandrart does not speak of Altdorfer in terms of a dependence on Dürer, nor does he use Dürer's art as a touchstone for Altdorfer's achievements. In Sandrart's eyes Dürer was "world famous" and "incomparable," but despite these superlatives accorded to Dürer, Sandrart was able to recognize in Albrecht Altdorfer a creative talent of a very different nature. Quite possibly Sandrart was acquainted with the treatise of Longinus on the Sublime which propagated the doctrine of genius and placed personal originality and "expression" above "order" and the golden mean.[13]

The attitude in Germany in the eighteenth century toward the value of its own culture, present and past, was perhaps best summed up by Goethe when he asked: ". . . and our aevum? He has renounced his genius and has sent our sons about to gather foreign plants—to their detriment. . . ."[14] The eighteenth century seems to have ignored Altdorfer's art and nearly forgotten his name, even in his home town of Regensburg. The historian Johannes Paricius published a history of Regensburg in 1753 in which Altdorfer's name does not appear once, even though Paricius described at length public buildings, churches and their tombstones, and monasteries which had borne witness to Altdorfer's activity in Regensburg.[15] In the seventeenth and in the eighteenth centuries the arts in Regensburg served the needs and the tastes of an international aristocracy, assembled there for the Imperial Assemblies, and the court of the princes Thurn and Taxis. Paintings of heroic landscapes and portraits of high society were favored; Italian opera and French comedy and the dramatic productions of the Jesuits furnished entertainment.[16] The *communis opinio* of the Enlightenment seemed to agree with David Hume (1711-1762) who had condemned the Middle Ages as "barbaric, ignorant times."[17]

An entry in a travel journal of 1729 is indicative of a general amnesia when it came to sixteenth century German painting, except for the name Albrecht Dürer. Johann Georg Keyssler described Altdorfer's *Battle of Alexander,* mistaking it for a painting by Dürer. This traveler took delight in the realistic representation of detail; he ignored, or perhaps did not understand, the allegorical, symbolic significance of Altdorfer's *Battle of Alexander.*[18]

In Germany, the appreciation of the German artistic past was rather negative, particularly with regard to painting. In 1792 Johann Georg Sulzer wrote in his *General Theory of the Fine Arts* that the designation "German school" is used by ignorant foreigners who do not perceive the diversity of styles and the lack of a singular unifying characteristic in early German painting which prohibits the use of the term "school." He felt that the first true painters of modern times who restored the arts are the Italians Leonardo, Michelangelo, Titian, Correggio and Raphael, in that order, and in this context he mentioned not a single German name. However, in his section on the history of the woodcut, Sulzer praised Altdorfer (as a Swiss artist) for "excellent, small woodcuts of most esteemed draftmanship and technique." No doubt he was referring to the series of *The Fall and Redemption of Man* (W. Gr. 24-65, ca. 1513).[19]

So completely forgotten was Altdorfer's name, so low the esteem of his art, that a description of the *Battle of Alexander* from 1799 omitted the artist's name altogether. Characteristically for the time, this catalogue entry of the Hofgarten Collection in Munich was written in French. Under Number 16 one reads:

> La Bataille entre Alexandre et Darius, on y voit fuir le dernier. Le nombre des combattants est très grand. Les Perses ainsi que les Macedoniens ont le même costume qui est celui des chevaliers allemand du temps du peintre. Peint sur bois.[20]

In view of the heroic neo-classical painting of the time Altdorfer's *Battle of Alexander* (Plate 4) must have seemed inferior and hopelessly antiquated to the eyes of the author of this catalogue. Only two years later Friedrich Schlegel was to see in this painting a model of the art of the future.

Around 1600 the chronicler Raselius had recognized and praised qualities in a painting by Altdorfer which went beyond the mere rendering of the subject. Two hundred years later the first philosopher-critic to discuss Altdorfer was fascinated by another of his paintings, again because he saw that much more than a story was told.

The German romantic poet and philosopher Friedrich Schlegel saw the *Battle of Alexander* (W.G. 50, 1529) in the Louvre where the picture was undergoing restoration.[21] He found it a revelation and published a pioneer essay of appreciation in his own journal.[22] In terms of its revolutionary impact and enthusiasm, this essay was to be as influential on the rediscovery and reevaluation of German fifteenth and sixteenth century painting as Goethe's essay on the Cathedral of Strassburg was for Gothic architecture.

In order to account for this apparently sudden recognition of Altdorfer, a summary of the concepts in art criticism and philosophy of art which anticipated Schlegel's interpretation of the *Battle of Alexander* is called for.

Treatises on art written between the sixteenth century and Lessing's *Laokoon*—he restricted each art within its proper limits of expression—nearly always draw on the affinities, the close relationship between painting and poetry. Erasmus spoke of the visual arts as "silent poetry."[23] Early nineteenth century philosophy of art perceived criteria of excellence and the purpose of art to be the same for both painting and literature; examples were used interchangeably. One could speak of a continuation of the doctrine *ut pictura poesis* because these critics, like those who had fashioned the doctrine, ". . . ranked painting with poetry as a serious interpreter of human life, and the humanistic critic who is deeply concerned with art as a repository of enduring values will always believe that human life is as supremely the painter's province as it is the poet's."[24]

To the old maxim *ut pictura poesis,* art criticism of the German Romantics added a second: *ut poesis pictura.*[25] A pertinent example can be found in August W. Schlegel's lecture series on literature and the fine arts (winter semester at the University of Berlin, 1801-02). For the first time, he presented to a large audience the Romantics' critical categories "classical" and "romantic" and emphasized the necessity for recognizing the Christian Middle Ages in Germany. He compares the spirit of Romantic drama to a painting whose description bears an uncanny resemblance to Altdorfer's *Battle of Alexander,* which his brother Friedrich discussed in great detail a year later. August said:

> One must imagine the romantic drama as a large painting which shows not only complex movements of various groups of people but also their surroundings. These surroundings do not merely represent the close vicinity, but reveal a significant view into the vast distance. All of this is bathed in a magic illumination which creates the overall mood. Such a painting will be far less self-contained than [classical] sculpture because this painting is a fragment, a segment cut from the optical stage of this world. By framing the foreground and, by directing the light toward the painting's center, and by other means, the artist will be able to focus the attention of the beholder. . . .[26]

Quite properly the painting is compared to a fragment with boundaries drawn willfully and temporarily, a work pointing beyond itself to the infinite universe.[27] The concept of infinity was the *leitmotiv* of Romantic aesthetic theory and art criticism. This concept is closely linked to a strong religious-didactic emphasis in Friedrich Schlegel's philosophy of art. Wilhelm Wackenroder perhaps stated most poignantly the logical interdependence between these two claims, namely that art should express the infinite and that it should also elevate to a moral and ethical consciousness. By suggesting infinity, art reveals God; thus art can and must, in turn, elevate the onlooker to a state of consciousness which induces cognition or prayer.[28] Romantic art criticism therefore had a "programmatic" aspect; expressed negatively, art should not be created for art's sake. Artistic activity is thought of as a religious act and enjoyment of art as prayer. The three central concepts in Romantic art criticism of around 1800 were thus: infinity or universality, moral or ethical consciousness, and redemptive mission.

A major consequence of the idea that each work of art is a mirror image of the universe, a product of the spirit, is a tolerance towards art from all epochs. In this vein, Wackenroder dared to declare that ". . . to the Creator, the Gothic temple is as pleasing as the Greek temple."[29] An understanding of a work of art in terms of its significance as a manifestation of the spirit of the universe could thus not be achieved by merely applying a set of neoclassical criteria and rules.

In the relative emphasis on all art traditions, the Romantics found the roots of renewal of their own national consciousness. Friedrich Schlegel and his friends related their philosophy of art to the German national movement.[30]

They did this, in part, as a reaction to that great incursion of French as the language of eighteenth century society. The decline of national self-consciousness had resulted in the decay of the German language. Not a single great writer between Luther and Lessing had used German. This circumstance is noteworthy in this context because a similar, if only temporary, emphasis on national consciousness in the arts can be observed in the early sixteenth century. Classical Latin had become the language of the educated and German had fallen into disuse. It was nearly a revolutionary act when Ulrich von Hutten (1488-1523) published in German for the *first* time in 1520, three years after having been crowned *poeta laureatus* by the Emperor Maximilian in Augsburg. Von Hutten used the German language as an instrument to obtain personal and national freedom from the Latin domination in all facets of culture, theology, and politics.[31] Von Hutten aimed to be understood by the people, as did Johannes Aventinus when he wrote his German version of his *History of Bavaria* (1526-1533).[32]

Johann Gottfried Herder (1744-1803) went even further to develop systematic objectives of historical inquiry and criticism. In his essay on the Middle Ages (1774) Herder gave art historical inquiry and art criticism crucial impulses by stating four *a priori* principles: (1) that each era stands on its own, has its own justification, and may not, can not be compared to others; (2) that after the collapse of the Roman Empire, new sources of strength became active in Northern Europe; (3) that all history is an attempt to establish order in opposition to chaos; (4) that art is a major "ordering" force, and that chaos is always contained in art but is also always overcome by art.[33] With these principles in mind, it became possible to approach any work of art from any era without prejudice.[34] Thus, Wackenroder could compare Dürer and Raphael without selecting one above the other as an *absolutum*. He warned against the establishment of absolutes in criticism.

But these objectives constituted only one aspect of Herder's influence on subsequent art criticism. Like Goethe, he was moved by the monumental architecture of the cathedrals. To both Herder and to Goethe, this monumentality symbolized a human greatness which could not be explained in terms of the rationalism of the Enlightenment. The reevaluation of the art of the Middle Ages, including northern painting of the fifteenth and sixteenth centuries, began with a rediscovery of the Gothic cathedral in conjunction with a search for the renewal of Christianity. The Romantics believed they had found in Gothic architecture what they themselves desired most, the roots of art in the unity of faith.[35]

Friedrich Schlegel's (1772-1829) description of A. Altdorfer's *Battle of Alexander* was part of a collection of essays entitled *Letters on Christian Art*. These are further descriptions of paintings by Flemish and German masters which Schlegel dared to put on the same level of excellence and quality as those by the celebrated Italians. In his fourth and last "letter" he declared the *Battle of Alexander at Issus* the masterpiece of German late medieval, chivalric art.[36]

Schlegel's essay relates to prior and subsequent Altdorfer criticism in three ways. It compares favorably to Joachim von Sandrart's philosophy on the role of art and what is characteristic in Altdorfer's art. It reflects Schlegel's own involvement in the Romantic movement of his time, as shown in the discernment of those criteria used in the interpretation of the *Battle of Alexander.* Finally, in the elucidation of critical criteria, it reflects Schlegel's ideas of what art should be. This latter point is what the essay is essentially about; it remains the only instance which presents Altdorfer's art as exemplary. Each of the three points will be taken up separately.

In his introductory notes to the "Academy" Sandrart spoke of his desire to arouse sensitivity in his reader, to counteract the reigning taste for crude sensationalism in literature which he deplored. Similarly, Schlegel's attraction to the *Battle of Alexander* was based, in part, on the fact that, despite its being a battle theme, the horrors of war did not constitute the theme nor the focal point of the painting. Both writers imply that art should be an *exempla virtutis* and should teach as well as delight; both were guided by the humanistic ideal of the function of art. Also, both acknowledge Altdorfer's originality of invention, the excellence of his craftsmanship. However, while Sandrart discussed form[37]—the "beautiful effects"—Schlegel's overriding concern was with the question of meaning in the work of art.

In order to discern specifically Romantic criteria in Schlegel's essay on the *Battle of Alexander* one may begin by analyzing the initial cause of his astonishment. Schlegel felt startled by this painting because it eluded classification in traditional, academic subject categories. He observed that landscape, historical painting, and the battle piece, usually carefully separated, were combined here to create something new and as yet indefinably more significant than the sum of the traditional categories. This statement signifies the Romantics' ". . . admission of the aesthetic legitimacy of the *genre mixte; . . .* of his [the Romantic's] revulsion by simplicity; the aesthetic antipathy to standardization. . . ."[38]

The *Battle of Alexander,* Schlegel felt, constituted a totally new category, the underlying conception of which had yet to be formulated. He compared the utter astonishment he experienced when he first saw the painting with that of someone who suddenly finds himself confronted with Shakespeare after a steady diet of Italian verse. Schlegel was quick to add, however, that this comparison with Shakespeare applied only to the richness and originality of Altdorfer's vision and not to its dominant mood, the spirit of chivalry. According to Schlegel, the spirit of chivalry was the painting's true meaning.

What does Schlegel mean by "spirit of chivalry"? In an 1875 English edition of Schlegel's *Letters on Christian Art,* the expression "spirit of chivalry" (*ritterlicher Geist*) was translated as "romantic."[39] Schlegel does not make such a simple equation. He uses the word "romantic" just once in this essay, in the last sentence where he recommends the study of Altdorfer's work to painters of these and of future times who wish to abandon Catholic imagery in order to produce a truly *romantic* painting. "This little Iliad of colors," he continues, "could teach the significance of the spirit of chivalry." Thus it may be seen that Schlegel did use the concepts "romantic" and "chivalric" in conjunction, but he did not substitute the one for the other. In this context Schlegel means by "romantic" an ideal futuristic art, the *ethical basis* of which was to be the spirit of chivalry.

Schlegel regarded the Middle Ages as paradigmatic for an ideal social organization, which combined political and religious authority with the integrity of the individual nation.[40] This is also why, in Schlegel's eyes, the medieval setting and manner of the painting is intrinsically better than the imitation of the historically correct classical setting. For one who was as prepossessed in favor of the Middle Ages as Schlegel, it is obvious that Altdorfer's meticulous rendition of the costumes, armor, and accoutrements of his own times should have great appeal.[41] This view was supported by Wilhelm Wackenroder in his *Effusions from the Heart of an Art-Loving Monk* (1797), which exerted great influence on his contemporaries, and particularly on the circle of the brothers Schlegel. In his *Memorial to Dürer* Wackenroder said: ". . . I think that every artist who lets the spirit of former centuries pass through his heart has to give it life from the spirit and breath of his age. . . ."[42]

Schlegel felt that costume should primarily serve to express the idea of the work of art and therefore be attributed secondary importance to historical realism. Similarly, the costume used in theatrical productions of the fifteenth and early sixteenth centuries had the function of symbolizing the idea of the play.

Contrary to numerous subsequent descriptions of the *Battle of Alexander,* Schlegel did not focus on its cosmic landscape. Rather, he felt pleased that the horrors of war were hardly visible and that Altdorfer's rendering of the vanquished Darius allowed the beholder to be deeply stirred by the noble feeling of sympathy, even empathy. Schlegel was above all interested in the manner in which the human drama was represented. Madame de Stael, who knew the brothers Schlegel and whose views were very much influenced by them, wrote poignantly of Friedrich Schlegel's equation of the Middle Ages with the spirit of chivalry:

> . . . it is to modern, what the heroic was to ancient times. Chivalry consisted in the defense of the weak, in the loyalty of valor, in contempt of deceit, in that Christian charity which endeavored to introduce humanity even in war; in short, in all those sentiments which substituted the reverence of honor for the ferocious spirit of arms.[43]

Like the brothers Schlegel, Madame de Stael felt that Romantic poetry is Christian, medieval, and chivalrous, and is associated with painting rather than sculpture.

The suppressed soul seeking its models and analogies in the Middle Ages, and later in India, was an exoticism Schlegel shared with many other Romantics. This emotional "medievalism" was coupled, however, with thorough historical research which led Schlegel to argue against the term "Dark Ages" and to give a favorable account of medieval civilizations which stressed the survival of antiquity and the beginnings of the Renaissance as early as the times of Charlemagne.[44]

In a context which stresses the medieval aspects of the painting, Schlegel's reference to "the little Iliad" seems at first disconcerting. Yet there had been a period when Schlegel discovered some of the romantic aspects of classical writing. Schlegel conceived of the structure of Homer's work as one of naturally evolving organic patterns in contrast to that of Dante, which was contrived, he felt, according to scholastic principles. The metaphor of "the little Iliad" is thus appropriate for a painting which displays the breadth of a novel (*Roman*).

Schlegel's romantic desire to see in a work of art the representation of a universal truth, one that is founded in Christian religion, led him to interpret the sun in the *Battle of Alexander* as a rising sun. In this context a rising sun, behind Alexander, would symbolize the victory of Light as the attribute of the risen Christ, that is, of renewed spiritual life; the moon near Darius would signify Darkness in the sense of spiritual darkness, that is, evil. Indeed, popular theological tradition portrayed Darius as *typus* in the prefiguration of Christ's crowning with thorns, whereas Alexander was interpreted as divine judge and prosecutor through divine right.[45] Such an interpretation transposes the meaning of the painting from a historical narrative to a metaphysical level.

In Altdorfer's time, the simultaneous appearance of the sun and the moon was seen as an omen. In his *History of the World* (1493) Hartman Schedel accompanied his account of the birth of Alexander the Great with a woodcut which shows the sun and the moon engaged in battle.[46] In popular theological texts and in illuminated manuscripts such as the *speculum humanae salvationis,* the sun assumes anthropomorphic characteristics and is always represented in conjunction with Christ.[47] The sun as a motif in battle scenes occurs for the first time in fifteenth century miniature painting. Here—without the simultaneous appearance of the moon—the sun indicates the hour of day (morning) or the topographical location (East). The *Battle of Alexander* originated in this iconographic tradition.[48]

It has been shown that the historian Aventinus, who wrote his *History of Bavaria* in Regensburg between 1527-1534, furnished Altdorfer with source material for the *Battle of Alexander.*[49] The victory of Alexander took place at the end of day, at sunset. Aventinus describes other historical battles as having taken place in the span of time between sunrise and sunset. But Aventinus' accounts are never entirely factual or objective, and the sun assumes anthropomorphic qualities. It "helps" the victorious party; its rays reflect so strongly on the metal armor that the enemy is deluded into thinking that the sky is aflame; the sun frightens the enemy.[50]

Similarly, in Altdorfer's painting may be observed a mutual penetration of the realms of objective, "scientific" narrative and the acknowledgment that all of creation and every human endeavor is part of and subject to a higher sacred order.[51] For if one looks at the motif of the sun in Altdorfer's entire oeuvre one finds that this motif is not only very prominent but that it represents a modified continuation of the tradition of the halos;[52] that the motif of the sun in Altdorfer's art signifies the supra-personal visual tradition in which he worked and which was his frame of reference.

It has been pointed out that Schlegel's interpretation of the sun in the *Battle of Alexander* as rising—that is, as a symbol of the victory of the Good— corresponded to the facet of Altdorfer's vision which relates the history of man to the promise of redemption (to God's order). In his search for meaning in the work of art Schlegel was not interested in the concrete aspects of the motifs.

Schlegel similarly interpreted another motif: the landscape, which he described as cosmic. Again Schlegel is only partially right. Altdorfer combined in this landscape both the specific and the general, the factual and the symbolic. But his point of departure was a conventional commission.

The *Battle of Alexander* was commissioned in 1528 by Duke William of Bavaria as part of a cycle depicting classical and Biblical history, and a number of artists contributed to it.[53] The humanistic spirit of the time thought it a matter of course that historical events worthy of depiction had to be those of classical antiquity. Furthermore, the story of Alexander enjoyed great popularity.[54] But in 1528 the story of Alexander's victory over Darius was particularly topical because the Turkish armies were standing at the gates of Vienna; they were therefore a threat to the Holy Roman Empire.

The theme of the historical battle piece was not new and therefore Altdorfer was working in an artistically established tradition.[55] Similar paintings depicted definite places and persons, and it has been shown that Altdorfer also meant the setting of the battle to be an identifiable location. The painting is based on a map of the Eastern Mediterranean, but with a reversal of the usual north-south direction.[56] Altdorfer painted this landscape from a northern vantage point looking southward. The high bird's eye vantage point which the artists assumed here certainly differs from his "pure" landscapes; the latter are mostly perceived from a very low vantage point and give an illusion of the artist's immersion in nature. The thesis that Altdorfer's landscape in the *Battle of Alexander* is entirely "dreamt" (as a recent monograph of the artist will have it)[57] cannot be supported nor sustained, especially in view of the numerous topographical drawings and paintings for which artists were commissioned in Altdorfer's time.[58]

There are yet other aspects of Altdorfer's rendering of the *Battle of Alexander* which correspond to established convention and are concerned with the factual: for example, the inscriptions on the flags indicating the strength of the troops, and the inscriptions of the names of the main protagonists of the battle; or, the architecture of the town, which has been identified with specific buildings in Verona, Padua, Venice, and Trient.[59]

But the way in which all of these elements fuse as particles of infinite space under a vast sky is Altdorfer's own, original contribution to the genre. It was this aspect of the painting which Schlegel described as "cosmic." What then was Altdorfer's perception of "cosmic"?

It is known that Altdorfer's painting of the *Battle of Alexander* was cut at the top, but the implication this bears on the novelty of his conception needs to be pointed out. Originally the emphatic direction of the composition was vertical, a format strongly minimizing the horizontal axis of the human action and reducing it to slightly less than one-third of the total space. Originally the "sky scape" would have had equal importance to the landscape. Its glowing celestial bodies were Altdorfer's transcriptions of the golden sacred spaces of the Middle Ages. The transitions between these three realms—battle, land-scape, and heavens—are fluid. The whole seems to be animated by the same life-giving force.

The philosophical-theological (*geistesgeschichtlicher*) background for Alt-dorfer's characteristic vision can be traced to the treatises of Nicholas of Cusa (1401-1464), as well as to those of Altdorfer's contemporaries, Paracelsus (1493-1541) and Cornelius Agrippa von Nettesheim (1486-1535).

Nicholas of Cusa thought that the revelation of God was immanent in all creatures since His essence pervaded all things.[60] This was a belief in the inseparable unity of nature and human action, and of nature and man. The mystical experience of nature in Northern Renaissance art meant that nature—the world and all its phenomena—was seen as a totality, as one being. There was an intense experience of space and of the simultaneity of all being in space. There was also a feeling for the structural unity of the manifestations of existence: the organic and the inorganic, rock and tree, man and animal, earth and sky, all of which spring from the same life-giving force.[61]

Paracelsus wrote:

> . . . God spins ultimate matter out of himself. This yields, by separation, the prime matter of the individual objects, a watery matrix, perpertually spewing nature, perpetually resolv-able back into ultimate matter. Human creativeness in art, alchemy, or pharmacology re-peats the primal act. . . .[62]

To Paracelsus, "Above" and "Below" are substantially the same: "Heaven is man and man is heaven, and all men together are one heaven . . . but microcosm and macrocosm are contained by membranes or partitions."[63] Artists such as Cranach, Altdorfer, his brother Erhard, and Wolf Huber pictured the play of forces in nature so that everything seems to be in motion.[64] This art reveals a *Weltanschauung* rooted in the concept of the *omnia animata,* a concept expressed by Cornelius Agrippa von Nettesheim in *De Occulta Philosophia* (1531); the manuscript circulated among German humanists as early as 1509/10. Here he expounded the doctrine of cosmic forces whose flux unifies and enlivens the universe.[65] No documents exist which would pertain to Altdorfer's intellectual life or "connections." Nevertheless, he may have been aware of Agrippa's ideas through his acquaintance with the humanist Joseph Grünpeck and with the Augustinian and Benedictine scholars in Regensburg.

Schlegel's description of the landscape in the *Battle of Alexander* as "cosmic," as a revelation of the "infinite" did correspond to Altdorfer's own intention.

It remains to elucidate those criteria of criticism in the essay on the *Battle of Alexander* which reflect Schlegel's concept of the purpose of art. In 1798 Friedrich Schlegel and his brother August, together with Ludwig Thieck and Novalis, founded the journal *Athenaeum*. Friedrich Schlegel's contributing essays to this journal formulated the basic conceptions of the German Romantic movement and established him as its head. Initially Schlegel's ideas on aesthetics were strongly influenced by Schiller's treatise *Über naive und sentimentale Dichtung* in which the antithetical terms *naiv* and *sentimental* are introduced. These Schlegel renamed classic and romantic. Schiller's "naive" artist (Schlegel's classic artist) *is*, in the sense of spontaneously accepting nature; Schiller's "sentimental" (Schlegel's romantic) artist *seeks* nature, being forever conscious that the world falls short of an ideal.[66] But there is a shift in emphasis here. Schlegel's "romantic" artist dominates nature through his personality, whereas Schiller's "sentimental" artist remains separate from nature while always seeking it.

Schlegel does not, however, consistently use his notion of romantic as a contrast to his notion of classical. In a frequently quoted passage of the 1798 edition of the *Athenaeum* (No. 116), Schlegel attempts to characterize the poetry of the future as "progressive, universal poetry."[67] In this context he uses the term "romantic" in the sense of "modern" or "interesting," but not in preference to those qualities. In his essay on the *Battle of Alexander* Schlegel uses the word "romantic" in this same "double" sense, both as "contrast to classic" as well as in the sense of "ideal art of the future."

Schlegel, addressing himself particularly to painters, urged young artists to study deeply the Romantic genre because only then could they learn the religious feeling, love, and devotion from which arose the inspiration of the old masters. He maintained that the Romantic has its roots in the Middle Ages, ". . . in that age of knights, of love and fairy tales, whence the thing and the word are derived. . . ."[68] In the conclusion of his remarks on the German school of painting Schlegel recommended the study of ". . . Shakespeare, and the best Italian and Spanish dramatists, those also of the old German poems which are most accessible, and next such modern productions as are dictated by the spirit of romance. . . ."[69] Schlegel had concluded his essay on the *Battle of Alexander* with a similar appeal to young painters.

The idea of the importance of the artist's expression of his individuality is developed by Schlegel to the point that ". . . it is the original and eternal thing in men . . . the cultivation and development of this individuality, as one's highest vocation, would be a divine egoism."[70] Hence Schlegel's recognition of and enthusiasm over Altdorfer's individualistic original vision of a traditional subject.

Schlegel insisted repeatedly that the true source of beauty and art is feeling, and that the true object of art should lead the mind upwards into a more exalted and spiritual world. He felt that *Das Schöne* is expanded consciousness and nobility of character; that in its widest sense it is the pleasant rendition of that which is good; and finally that it has three components: variety, unity, and universality.[71]

Therefore, it was the purpose of art, he felt, that it should reflect the element of Christian hope in order to elevate the spectator to a plane of spiritual beauty instead of leaving him in the maze of merely external representations.

> Beautiful is that which reminds us of nature, which inspires the feeling of *infinite* vitality. Nature is organic and therefore highest [most perfect] beauty is eternal and always renews itself (*vegetabilisch*) and the same is true of morality and of love.[72]

Thus the theme of infinity emerges as a central concept in Schlegel's philosophy of art: "A Work of art is complete when it is contained within sharp boundaries, but within these boundaries it must exceed all bounds and be inexhaustible . . . it must be true to itself, of even quality, and yet it must be sublime" (Fragment 297).[73] Or at another place Schlegel said: "Only he can be an artist who has a personal religion, an original concept of infinity" (Ideen 13).[74]

For Schlegel then, Altdorfer's painting of the *Battle of Alexander* suggested the vision of the infinite, the infinite as the definition of the Creator, just as Johannes Aventinus had written: "The whole world—all men—all religions agree that the only highest good who is without beginning and end, without goal or time, and who is called 'God' in German, has the power to do all things."[75]

Ultimately this is why Altdorfer's painting appealed to Schlegel with such immediacy. It afforded him that which the Romantic longed for and which art was to make possible: a vision and a moment of oneness with the infinite.

Nineteenth-Century Altdorfer Criticism: The Beginning of Art History as an Academic Discipline

Every generation has an innate sympathy with
some epoch of the past wherein it seems to find
itself foreshadowed.

—Bernard Berenson[1]

Once Friedrich Schlegel had brought the name of Albrecht Altdorfer to the attention of a large audience, it remained in art historical and art critical writing. The first echo of Schlegel's essay on the *Battle of Alexander* can be found in Johann Dominik Fiorillo's (1748-1821) *History of the Graphic Arts.*[2] While the beginnings of German art historical literature with Sandrart had taken its orientation from baroque tastes and preferences, the beginning of art history as an academic discipline under Fiorillo was guided by the spirit and the ideas of the Romantic movement. Moreover, Fiorillo was an influential educator of the so-called Romantic generation.[3] The study of art and its history ceased to be the exclusive concern of philosophers, poets, and painters and became a science studied by specialists. Trained as a painter in Prague, Bayreuth, Rome, and Bologna, Fiorillo became court painter in Braunschweig until his move to Göttingen in 1784. There he became academic instructor of drawing, curator of the University's collection of paintings and prints and holder of the first academic chair of art history. Initially the purpose of Fiorillo's teaching activity was to prepare young gentlemen for their so-called "artistic journey," but Fiorillo's scope of inquiry stretched from the beginning of German art to the history of art in Russia, from a discussion about the beginning of oil painting to a critical examination of the sources Vasari had used in his "Vitae."[4] A true child of the eighteenth century and its endeavors of encyclopedic completeness, Fiorillo was guided by an ambition to comprehend the total scope of his discipline.

In the introduction to his *History of the Graphic Arts* Fiorillo spells out the art historian's first and foremost obligation, namely the study of the purest sources. He sees his purpose in the preservation of national monuments of art in order to save them from destruction and oblivion, and all of this is to serve the love of truth. This was written at a time of political upheaval in the wake of the Napoleonic wars, when churches and monasteries were secularized and many were destroyed.[5] However, because of the scarcity of source material Fiorillo treated German art more superficially than Italian art. His treatment of fifteenth century art reflects his sympathy with the Romantics' taste for painting which antedates Raphael.

He simply copied Schlegel's descriptions of paintings of the school of Cologne as he also copied Schlegel's essay on the *Battle of Alexander*. But there is one significant omission. Fiorillo omitted Schlegel's programmatic appeal to his own generation and to future generations;[6] nor did he share Schlegel's mission to "activate" historical insight. His otherwise uncritical adoption of Schlegel's text probably means that Fiorillo used Schlegel as the best available source on Altdorfer's painting. As an "eyewitness account" Schlegel's essay constituted a primary source which needed no further critical validation.

Fiorillo then continues his entry on Altdorfer by enumerating three more paintings[7] which inspire him to remark on the "diligence" of the execution. Since Fiorillo understood Altdorfer to be a pupil of Dürer he measured his art solely against Durer's and found the result to be less perfect than the master's. Because of his activity as curator of the University's collection of prints, it is certain that Fiorillo knew drawings, engravings, and etchings by Altdorfer. In his capacity as connoisseur, Fiorillo made one significant contribution toward knowledge of Altdorfer's art: he attributed to Altdorfer the woodcut cycle *Fall and Redemption of Man,*[8] which was thought to have been Dürer's work. Fiorillo begins to perceive Altdorfer's characteristic vision and lifts him above the shadows of Dürer even if it is for the purpose of negative comparison. From now on Altdorfer's oeuvre appears in encyclopedias and handbooks of art not because the respective writers had actually seen it or had been "touched" by the work but because it is part of the sum-total which is being reconstructed. For example, when Nagler's *Künstler Lexikon*[9] appeared in 1830 it had copied all of Fiorillo's entries on Altdorfer and it referred readers who desired to know more to Schlegel's essay on the *Battle of Alexander*. But the cue that a change in the perception of Altdorfer had occurred lies perhaps in Nagler's choice of the *Leavetaking of Christ from his Mother* (W. G. 26, 1513/14) as the "best" of Altdorfer's paintings (formerly in the possession of the prince Abbot of the Benedictine monastery of St. Emmeram).

During the same time Hegel, in his lectures on aesthetics and particularly in passages on the religious domain of romantic art, had developed the idea that the love of Mary (the love of a mother (*Mutterliebe*) and of Christ as He *is* divine love), constitutes the perfect object of religious romantic imagination: ". . . maternal love, the picture as it were of the Spirit, enters romantic art in place of the Spirit itself, because only in the form of feeling is the Spirit made prehensible by art. . . ."[10] The following excerpts from Hegel's notion on the religious domain of romantic art read almost like an interpretation of Altdorfer's painting of the *Leavetaking of Christ from His Mother:*

> . . . what then comes into appearance in Christ is less the absorption of one person in another limited person than the Idea of love in its universality, the Absolute, the spirit of truth in the element and form of feeling.[11]

> Thirdly and lastly, the affirmative reconciliation of the spirit is displayed as feeling in Christ's Disciples and in the women and friends who follow him. These for the most part are characters who have experienced the austerity of the Idea of Christianity at the hand of their divine friend through the friendship, teaching, and preaching of Christ without going through the external and internal agony of conversion; they have perfected this Idea, mastered it and themselves, and they remain pensive and powerful in the same.[12]

These few examples have shown the change in the nature of art historical inquiry that accompanies the change from philosophers to art historians proper: from Schlegel's search for meaning in a work of art to a preoccupation with the accumulation of source material for an artist's biography and oeuvre; a change in emphasis from the metaphysical to the phenomenological; from the question of the essence of art to an inquiry directed at the knowledge of art as a historical science.

Franz Theodor Kugler's (1808-1858) historical orientation tended toward a universal art history.[13] Kugler, a poet, draftsman, etcher, but also the first secretary of art to be employed in the Prussian ministry of culture, strove to write a world history of art just as Alexander von Humboldt undertook to describe the geography of the whole world.[14] This goal of universality which both scholars shared was accompanied quite logically by another similarity. Alexander von Humboldt observed and emphasized an equality of worth of all the different people of different cultures he learned to know on his expeditions. Kugler in his turn attempted to comprehend extra-European and prehistoric art and therefore he felt it necessary to overcome the traditional categorizations of the visual arts into schools and national styles.

Kugler's *Handbook of the History of Art,* first published in 1842, was divided into four parts: (1) the art of early periods, (2) the history of classical art, (3) history of romantic (i.e., medieval) art, and (4) history of modern art (art after 1400). This fourth volume on the history of art after 1400 ("Modern") contains four pages on Albrecht Altdorfer in that part of the book which is called "The North." He is introduced as Dürer's most significant and most individualistic (*eigenthümlich*) pupil and follower. Identification of Altdorfer's art in this geographic manner evokes an emotional association contrasting it to "The South." Because Kugler understood and presented Altdorfer's art as exemplary of the northern "fantastic" art, a fuller discussion of the meaning of this concept is appropriate here.

He sought an explanation for the different appearance of Italian fifteenth and sixteenth century art with its realization of beauty which rests in the harmony of proportions and its idealized anthropocentrism, from the appearance of art in the North. Kugler does not simply want to "judge" northern art by Italian norms, as he believes in the autonomy of different manifestations of culture, e.g., art, and so Kugler sought for a non-partisan cause of cultural differences; he found this in the different geographical conditions. Thus Kugler concludes that the Italian form of beauty could not find its equivalent realization in the north because of an overpowering presence of opposing spiritual currents, particularly what Kugler calls the "element of the fantastic" which in turn originates in the particular—mostly hostile—character of northern nature. Because northern nature is forbidding and not pleasing man creates "fantastic" imagery through a process of repression. The preoccupation with the fantastic happens where man has to sublimate what nature negates. And yet, Kugler requires that "northern fantasy" exercise the "only true laws of Beauty by breaking the raw force of demonic powers in order to bear witness to an honorable, pure spirit directed toward the Highest."[15]

> . . . fantasy becomes a witness to the noble purified and uplifted spirit only when it has submitted itself to the true spirit of beauty alone, when the raw force of demonic powers is broken.

For Kugler, Beauty is the purpose of art. Beauty is defined as both temperance—the golden mean—and a manifestation of divine order. Therefore the "fantastic" may become destructive of Beauty ". . . when fantasy becomes more dominant than the sensitivity for the mean, when fantasy wanders into the infinite, then Beauty is endangered. . ." Kugler defines the fantastic as something unnatural, as a creation of man's mind to supplement barren or hostile nature. The fantastic, according to Kugler, is an element which prevents the flowering of "true art."[16] If fantasy is a dominant element in a work of art it allows and encourages subjectivity.

Kugler saw a first manifestation of the fantastic in the painted panels of the School of Cologne, in Memlinc, in Bosch, and particularly in German painting of the fifteenth century (Hegel's stage of Symbolic Art). At the beginning of the sixteenth century the element of fantasy in the form of a "liberation of the subjective" was encouraged because then art began to divide into different genres. Kugler understood and presented Altdorfer's art as the epitome of the fantastic element of his era. He called the effect of Altdorfer's rendering of nature "magical," the stuff dreams are made of. But because Kugler's definition of art centers on a concept of perfection which needs to keep the element of the fantastic in check, Altdorfer's art, by implication, remains second-rate. In at least half of his descriptions of Altdorfer paintings Kugler employed the adjective "fantastic," particularly in connection with the treatment of nature and light. Once more Altdorfer's art is introduced with a copy of Schlegel's essay on the *Battle of Alexander* minus Schlegel's metaphysical interpretation. In its place, Kugler interpreted the *Battle of Alexander* as a landscape by evoking a comparison with Patinir. Altdorfer's conception of landscape is judged superior to Patinir's in terms of "truth" and "grandeur." Kugler stressed the comparison-contrast with Patinir once more when discussing the *Landscape with Trees* (W. G. 67), praising Altdorfer's "truth of form, freshness of the vegetation and knowledge of nature." Another painting which Kugler praises for its landscape is *Madonna and Child in Glory* (W. G. 45).[17]

In general usage the term "fantastic" in German signifies the opposite of *real,* or *reality.* Fantastic may mean dreamlike but also "untrue." The term contains both positive and negative connotations. Kant defined fantasy as the power of imagination which produces also *"unwillkürliche Einbildungen."* Goethe, charging the word with negative values, thought that Dürer was handicapped by a "dreary fantasy bereft of form and boundaries" (*eine trübe, form- und bodenlose Phantasie. . .*).[18]

Schlegel had used Altdorfer's painting to illustrate his ideas on art. Kugler's criticism was based on comparisons which in turn received their direction from his notion of "northern" art. At the time Kugler wrote his *Handbook,* Gustav Friedrich Waagen (1794-1867), director of the imperial museum in Berlin,[19] compiled topographical surveys of art in Germany which became his *Kunstwerke und Künstler in Deutschland* (1843-45). Waagen—as well as Passavant—represented the school of the connoisseur. Waagen wrote enthusiastically about Altdorfer's *Finding of the Body of St. Florian* (Nürnberg, W. G. 35) which had never before been part of an Altdorfer discussion. Its concept Waagen calls *fantastic.* In order to place it stylistically and qualitatively he can only think of Rembrandt as a touchstone. One finds the same opinion one year later in Ralph von Rettburg's *Letters from Nürnberg* (1846) where he calls the *Finding of the Body of St. Florian* especially noteworthy because of its powerful conception (*Auffassung*) and the daring (*"dreiste"*) execution.[20] As a landscapist he is thought to have been ahead of his time.

Anton Springer (1824-1891) was by training a journalist, politician, and historian. In his *Letters on Art History* (1857) in contrast to Kugler and Rettberg, Altdorfer was considered to have been the least among Dürer's followers. Springer took up Kugler's concept of northern fantasy,[21] but he categorically denies northern painting the possibility of perfection, since northern fantasy hardly tends toward perfect form and the mean. The most adequate expressions of northern fantasy are in the media of engraving and woodcut, in which German art of the fifteenth and sixteenth centuries made its readily acknowleged important contribution.

After four pages devoted to Dürer and to Holbein the Younger, whom Springer praises as the heroes of German art, Altdorfer's work is described as ". . . historical paintings turned into colorful but childish puppet-theatre. He was the least able to . . . advance secular art towards recognition."[22] Not one specific work by Altdorfer is cited. In his *Handbook of the History of Art,*[23] Springer did not change his mind on Altdorfer's mediocrity as a painter, but praised the woodcut of the *Beautiful Mary* (W. Gr. 89; Plate 5). "He did not create anything as a painter that surpassed the richness of forms and mature beauty of the color-woodcut *Beautiful Mary;* his biblical paintings are popular . . . he stands out because of his poetic rendering of beautiful landscapes."[24]

Fifty years after Schlegel's essay had aroused interest in the *Battle of Alexander* the work was ignored by an art historian, Springer, who understood his main mission as ridding art history of philosophical interpretations.[25] Schlegel's essay could not be copied any more, nor adapted, by Springer whose heroes Dürer and Holbein also served as his touchstones. This is why he chose Altdorfer's woodcut of the *Beautiful Mary* as worthy of mention. It is the most tectonic of Altdorfer's compositions and one which most approximates the Italian "look." If Sandrart had favored the baroque quality of Altdorfer's prints, Springer's neoclassical orientation (environment) favored the Renaissance elements.

While Springer's judgment of Altdorfer was quite devastating in 1857, a novel published in that same year contains an interpretation of Altdorfer's painting *The Beautiful Mary of Regensburg* (W.G. 41) which implies highest praise.[26] The main protagonist, the architect Berthold, observes a pilgrimage to the miracle-working image of the *Beautiful Mary.* The author explains the magnetic power of the image: ". . . it is the first German image to combine the secret power of the sacred with the overt (*offenkundig*) power of beauty."[27] The author would have known Altdorfer's woodcut of the *Beautiful Mary,* a print of which was kept in the cabinet of prints of the imperial museums in Berlin, the same one which Springer had praised in his *Handbook.* The view of the role of art and aesthetics expressed in this novel are not guided by the largely normative aesthetics of Kugler and Springer, but by the thesis that a people finds its identity in its art. Art is the collective expression of the "soul" of the people or nation which produced it. If the art is true to itself, it at once serves and builds a nation. For the first time since Schlegel "German art" is as valid as any other. The architect Berthold rejects Italian illusionism, because "the beauty of a face can not be expressed alone by measuring mathematical relationships, but by the expression of an inner (moral) perfection."[28] This is why the image of the *Beautiful Mary* is celebrated, not because it approximates Italian Renaissance ideal form.

The most negative, even ridiculing, criticism of Altdorfer to have been written until this day appeared in Ernst Förster's *History of German Art* (1851-1860).[29] Ernst Förster (1800-1885) was a painter of historical subjects (*Historienmaler*), a lithographer, and a writer about art.[30] He had studied theology and philosophy; then he became a student of Wilhelm von Schadow and Peter Cornelius. He painted frescoes after sketches by Wilhelm von Kaulbach, he made drawings in Italy after pre-Raphaelite panel paintings and frescoes, and he helped to free Altichiero's and Jacopo Avanzo's frescoes in the Oratorio S. Giorgia in Padua from a layer of whitewash which had covered them. It is necessary to be aware of Förster's activities and interests as an artist in order to understand the reasons behind his wholesale rejection of Altdorfer. He wrote: "The *Battle of Alexander* and the *Story of Susanna* (W.G. 49) are travesties . . . the representation of the lead soldiers or knights including the hardly visible grasses and leaves is of a crazy and confusing diligence . . . there are neither Greeks nor Persians, neither heroes nor victims . . . he [Altdorfer] had a strange concept of historical subject matter." Förster thought that Altdorfer's "lack of ability in handling historical subjects" was symptomatic of Dürer's era. They were all "travesties which transposed events from the past with childlike, tasteless pleasure into the garb of the present, down to the smallest detail, erasing (in the process) every historical trace."[31] This is all Ernst Förster would say about Altdorfer. Altdorfer who had just been praised as "the Rembrandt of his school" and whose woodcut of the *Beautiful Mary* Anton Springer could not help but admire, failed in the eyes of someone whose understanding of historical truth was informed exclusively by historical paintings in the neoclassical manner and of pre-Raphaelite monumentality.

The period of the mid-nineteenth century—the time between Hegel's death (1831) and Nietzsche's *Birth of Tragedy* (1872)—has been characterized as an unphilosophical period in German intellectual history.[32] It was a time of specialists, a time of empiricism; generally the purpose of art was thought to be the imitation of nature, and increased realism was thought to support the notion of progress in art. Only the great personalities count, for they were thought to be responsible for "development." To trace the development of the artistic personality was the most important task of art historical writing. (Ernst Förster wrote biographies of Raphael, Peter Cornelius, and Johann Georg Müller.) Since Dürer was the great personality of his era, he and not Altdorfer was worthy of a biography. An outline of a first monograph on Altdorfer was not published until the first year of the new German Empire, 1872. The celebration of the 400th anniversary of Dürer's birth had passed; now Altdorfer was acknowledged as an artist whose vision was worthy of consideration only on the grounds of his artistic difference from Dürer.[33]

Especially he knew how to create through his composition and illumination a certain fantasy which sometimes seems slightly strange but which also often evokes a specific mood

. . . with this is combined the finest sensitivity for landscape as regards both the smallest detail as well as vast vistas. . . .

The *Battle of Alexander* is presented here, in Meyer's *Künstlerlexikon* (1872), as the most famous work of the artist. The next sentence contains the first sociopolitical explanation in the history of the reception of Altdorfer's work: ". . . Altdorfer employed all the power of his art in order to satisfy his high-ranking patron. . . ."[34] The author W. Engelmann feels that a comparison with a historical battle piece by Raphael such as the *Battle of Constantin and Maxentius* is futile because Altdorfer's concept of a battle piece is totally different. For the first time the painting is discussed in terms of its relation to its original context, namely the set of historical battle pieces commissioned by the same Duke, a comparison which emphasized Altdorfer's excellent solution of the commission. The symbolic meaning of the constellations of sun and moon are recognized once again and the effects of illumination through natural light are thought to be astonishing, not only in the *Battle of Alexander* but in Altdorfer's other paintings as well.

In 1877 a monograph sketch was published on Altdorfer as one of the German Little Masters.[35] This publication hardly adds to the discussion of Altdorfer, since it largely parallels the entry on Altdorfer in Meyer's *Künstlerlexikon*. It is noteworthy in this context only because it introduces a new qualifying category of Altdorfer's art. No longer is it "Northern," "fantastic," "childlike," or "childish." It is now placed in the category of *Dilettant,* a word which in German may function as a verb, adverb, or adjective, with repercussions well into the twentieth century. The author's premise, left unjustified, is that Altdorfer's major activity was that of a master-builder (architect). This explains why his work as a panel-painter, engraver, draftsman is that of a *dilettant*. The term was not to be understood negatively as it is in modern usage. Coined in Italy in the mid-seventeenth century, from the Latin *delectare,* it meant to have fun, to enjoy something. It was thus used by or for those who enjoyed the arts, either actively or passively. The difference therefore between an artist and a *dilettant* is that the latter is not a professional, has no intention to have a market, or to be competitive.[36] Thus in this connection it was said of Altdorfer, in the work cited earlier, that even in his famous *Battle of Alexander* "of course we do not encounter (here) an 'ideal' composition, although diligence of execution and fantastic effects are praiseworthy." Altdorfer's saving grace was that he was a "spirited man and therefore his art, even when it is not pleasant, is always interesting."[37]

Altdorfer's growing popularity is also to be seen in a wave of reproductions of his works at this time. For example, the color woodcut *The Beautiful Mary* was reproduced in the *Yearbook of the Royal Prussian Collections* (1886),[38] and *The Fall and Redemption of Man* appeared in facsimile reproduction in *Collector's Library of Old Masters* (1888).[39]

A major step was reached in Altdorfer's recognition in nineteenth century art history when Max J. Friedländer wrote the first monograph on him which had grown out of Friedländer's doctoral dissertation under Anton Springer in Leipzig (1891).[40] Friedländer succumbed to the same fixed view on a right way to do historical paintings held by Springer, his teacher, and Ernst Förster and Engelmann. Wrote he of Altdorfer: ". . . the childish attempt to replace the great through multiplicity could hardly succeed."[41] Friedländer expected a historical battle piece to demonstrate the pathos of a Greek tragedy, alongside which Altdorfer's version would surely be disappointing. Wrote Friedländer,

> . . . [Altdorfer] rendered the historical event as a faithful chronicler and not as a dramatic poet . . . the dramatic, the enthusiastic, forceful deeds, agony of suffering, powerful movement of men, achievement of the individual . . . none of these qualities determine the overall impression. On the contrary, the overall impression is determined through the mood set by the landscape, through color and light. . . .[42]

Friedländer's judgment did more justice to Altdorfer's artistic merit and intentions when the subject could be approached without being encumbered by set expectations of the tastes of his time. This was possible in the case of religious subjects, the *Virgin in Glory* (Munich) and the *Birth of Mary* (Munich). Here Friedländer called attention to Altdorfer's preoccupation with the representation of immeasurable, infinite space, and came to the conclusion that space as such is the artistic subject of much of Altdorfer's art. Schlegel had been intrigued by this in the *Battle of Alexander. Susanna's Bath* (Munich) which in 1872 was deemed unattractive because it used too many local colors, "hard" contours and "hard" light and multiplicity of forms (*Mannigfaltigkeit und Vielgliedrigkeit*), now is labeled "genuinely German" for those same qualities.[43] These stylistic characteristics had been called the "typical German approach" also in the discussion on the *Battle of Alexander.*

In his attempt to liberate Altdorfer's artistic merit from the shadow of Dürer, Friedländer spoke of Altdorfer's ability as an "inventor," a similar notion to Kugler's and Meyer's *"phantastisch,"* an ability in which Altdorfer surpassed Dürer. Friedländer attributed to Altdorfer qualities of "intuitive" and "unconscious" invention, differentiating these from "conscious" invention, an attribute of Dürer's art. Still, the unconscious or intuitive was deemed less valid; following Rettberg's *Letters,* the second half of the nineteenth century had likened these attributes to the "child-like," with both positive and negative meanings, but specifically denoting a northern and German characteristic. Franz von Reber labeled Altdorfer, without any embellishments, a "second rate talent."[44] Nevertheless, as editor of *Klassischer Bilderschatz* (Munich 1893, 12 volumes)[45] the same author published reproductions of the Berlin *Crucifixion,*[46] the Berlin *Rest on the Flight to Egypt,* the Nürnberg *Finding of the Body of St. Florian,* and the Nürnberg *Crucifixion.*

And 20 years after the unflattering words of Meyer's *Künstlerlexikon* about *Susanna's Bath* (Plate 6), von Reber praises it as an "extraordinary architectural piece" (1894, *Geschichte der Malerei*).[47] This cryptic comment, however, enlarged the view of Altdorfer as an inventor of landscapes and of fantasy; it coincides with Friedländer's observation that Altdorfer's main concern is the representation of space. Hildebrandt's book on Altdorfer, published in 1908, dealt exclusively with Altdorfer's relation to and handling of architecture and architectural motifs.[48] From then on "space" remains a constant point of discussion in Altdorfer criticism, even a synonym for his work, not in the sense of Schlegel's "infinite" space, but rather in the sense of concrete physical space.

The turn of the century produced the first monograph in the English language on Altdorfer, a popular booklet for the general public, the first of its kind on Altdorfer. Presented as Dürer's artistic antipode, Altdorfer's work is perceived to exude ". . . sweetness of fancy, homely pathos and romantic poetry of conception which Dürer himself fails to yield. . . ."[49] The tenor of this book is highly moralistic. So is its author's definition of art fashioned after the tenets of Ruskin and Morris: the sovereign command of the arts is to reveal beauty, because beauty exhilarates, refines, elevates mankind.[50] The interpretation of the *Battle of Alexander* for example reads like this:

> . . . this beauty, this stillness, this isolation is not the tragic crown of a great soul's effort —it is a romantic, dream-like charm unrestrained by reality. This heaven of romance is perhaps oftener visited by the man of the world and certainly of easier access than the high heaven of aspiration and fortitude.

One could imagine, according to this description, a picture of the *Dilemma of Hercules at the Crossroads*.

Hermann Voss's *The Origin of the Danube Style* (1907)[51] marks the point of demarcation ending nineteenth century Altdorfer reception. The needs of an earlier century, the turn of the eighteenth century, had led to rediscovery, followed by a period of searching for facts and taking stock. Now the lead question became: What was the context of Altdorfer's way of conceptualizing and what was the origin of his style? How and why did his characteristic vision evolve? Faced with the task of explaining a phenomenon, Voss sought an already known parallel to establish his point of comparison. Thus he compared German art of the turn of the fifteenth to the sixteenth century with the "Storm and Stress" literary movement of the late eighteenth century. Voss argued that Storm and Stress and early sixteenth century art were both characterized by a preference for the cruel, the strange, for the psychological moment, for subjectivity in the interpretation of a story or of a motif. The literary movement of the late eighteenth century and the art of the early sixteenth century share their roots in a revolt against the conventions of a preceding generation. Both are "carried by a rising middle class (*Bürgertum*). Both emphasized the artistic traditions of their respective native lands. Both honored the individualistic element in man and the idiosyncratic in nature. Voss spoke of the spiritual companionship (*Geistesgenossen*) of the master of the Danube School with the German Romantics, in particular Uhland, Eichendorff, Schwind, and Fohr.[52] Other writers share Voss's favorable comparison of art of the sixteenth and nineteenth centuries. Scheffler spoke of a parallel in the reaction to a sense of form, a predictable change in gestalt.[53] Applied to Altdorfer, this view of predictable reaction to an earlier epoch suggested that his early style corresponds to Storm and Stress; after 1506, Romanticism sets in. In like manner Romanticism had followed Storm and Stress in the late eighteenth and early nineteenth century. Thus Voss projected a historical regularity, immanent in the flow of events, upon earlier epochs. Benjamin has recently identified the essential attributes of this concept of a new school of poetry as a "reaction" to its predecessor, a new style as superseding an older one as "contemplative historicism."[54]

The result of systematic application of the foregoing historicist idea to the interpretation of Altdorfer's work was that certain works no longer fitted the scheme. The *St. Sebastian Altarpiece* in St. Florian (usually referred to as the *St. Florian Altarpiece*), at that time dated 1518, did not conform to Voss's preconceived notion of "Romantic" painting. "The cruelty in the caricatures of the protagonists. . . without refined taste"[55] looked to Voss like the overly anxious work of a student.[56] For these reasons he doubted that the work could be rightfully attributed to Altdorfer.

Voss's view of the Romantic movement of the turn of the eighteenth to the nineteenth century perceived an element of crisis, of conflicting aims. The dominant role of nature in Altdorfer's art and in that of the Danube School in general reminded Voss of Rousseau's dictum "back to nature" as it produced utopian dreams. This was bound to result in a conflict between a new idealism and the aspirations of a middle class. Similarly, the exalted love of nature of the Danube School artists is interpreted by Voss to be pathological.[57] This perception guides Voss's interpretation of the *Battle of Alexander*. To Voss the *Battle of Alexander* represents the culmination of Altdorfer's main artistic concern, the portrayal of infinite space filled with incredibly rich detail. While Friedländer had merely spoken of space shown through movement, Voss felt that Altdorfer's characteristic achievement consisted of the illusion of space through the dissolution of solid mass into an infinite number of particles resulting in an "unhealthy crisis," a dichotomy of the realistic and the fantastic.[58]

Voss saw an early anticipation of this utopian longing for nature—artistically not yet perfectly realized—in Altdorfer's *Rest on the Flight to Egypt*, whereas the *Battle of Alexander* constitutes the ultimate representation of any imaginable utopia. Thus to Voss, Altdorfer is a representative of that generation which launched visions of the new religious-communistic utopias. This image of Altdorfer modified Voss' interpretations of Altdorfer's work. For example, the woodcut of a monk praying before the Virgin (B. 49) is proof of Altdorfer's "deep religiosity which borders on mysticism." Not once does Voss consult the then known facts and circumstances of Altdorfer's life in order to substantiate an interpretation.

At the basis of Voss' understanding of the origins of Altdorfer's art and style is once again the notion of *dilettantism*. Thirty years earlier, Robert Dohme[59] had spoken of *Dilettantism* in the case of Altdorfer, a concept which allowed the comprehension and appreciation of an unorthodox, unacademic manner of drawing and painting. Through such an allusion Voss eliminated any point of comparison with Dürer and other "trained-artist" contemporaries. Altdorfer's talent has been pronounced noncompetitive; it is put on a pedestal all by itself: "Altdorfer never received a regular solid training in a craft. . . ."[60] This resounded the view of Lichtwark, an important contemporary of Voss, that folk art is essentially an autonomous art of dilettants.[61] Voss possibly used the term for Altdorfer in that same sense— tied to folk culture (popular)—when he established analogies of style and expressive content between folksongs of the early sixteenth century and the style of the Danube School of painting.[62] Voss characterized the style of the Danube School as rooted in the popular religious-social movements and the culture of its time, disregarding all the while Altdorfer's courtly commissions from Emperor Maximilian and the Duke of Bavaria. Voss strengthened his point of view by comparing Altdorfer with an already known entity, Venetian painting, especially the painting of Giorgione, where Voss found a similar conception of man's intimate relation to nature. Voss considered that a true historical understanding of the style of the Danube School is possible only when the general cultural conditions and contemporaneous movements in painting and poetry are considered.[63] Only in Venice did he find a phenomenon comparable to that of the Danube School. Giorgione's early paintings signify the same turning point as Altdorfer's early paintings. Both reveal the same relationship of man to nature: the scales of landscape and of the human figure hold an even balance. The similarity of Giorgione's *Moses* (Uffizi) and certain drapery motifs in Altdorfer is so close that it can be explained only by supposing a direct contact between the two artists through Giorgione's knowledge of Altdorfer prints or drawings.[64]

Voss was not the first or the only one to notice the parallel between motifs and metaphors in folk songs and in the work of the Danube School of painting. Rochus Baron von Liliencron had collected popular German folk songs, five of which dealt exclusively with the expulsion of the Jews from Regensburg and with the ensuing cult of the Beautiful Mary. Ludwig

Uhland (1787-1852) had noted that the most beautiful folk songs of the early sixteenth century combine in perfect harmony thought and sentiment with images from nature. Johannes Janssen had emphasized this idea when he noted that popular poetry of early sixteenth century ballads and hymns were pervaded by a love of nature which was believed to be at the root of life.[65] Different kinds of natural illumination and the forms and movements of plants express a particular mood or sentiment. Songs invoked the trees and flowers, birds and beasts, sun and moon and stars to take part in man's joys and in his sorrow, and sometimes nature-imagery directly mirrors emotions of sorrow in a song about the Passion: ". . . all leaves and all grasses are stirring—now bend, you tree; now bend, you branches, now bend, you leaves and green grasses. . . ."[66]

Part II

Altdorfer Criticism
in the Twentieth Century

Image Makers

In the twentieth century Altdorfer reception and criticism becomes so concentrated and diversified that the chronological approach to analysis only confuses the issues. Since this research investigates interpretations of Altdorfer's work rather than problems in the scholarship pertaining to his artistic sources, attributions and dating, a topical approach to Altdorfer's reception in the twentieth century is more feasible. Accordingly, subsequent chapters will discuss the uses made of Altdorfer's work for ideological purposes, most importantly in the Third Reich (1933-45); the interpretations of Altdorfer's art in terms of his spiritual and intellectual orientation; and the creative reception of Altdorfer by modern artists, particularly Oskar Kokoschka. In this way the varied impact which Altdorfer's work had on criticism and on art becomes discernible.

This introduction will survey that portion of twentieth century reception of Altdorfer which does not pursue a singular point of view and therefore is difficult to integrate with the themes developed in the ensuing three chapters.

In 1923 four monographs on Altdorfer were published at once in Germany's and Austria's culturally leading cities: Berlin, Leipzig, Munich, and Vienna.[1] This multiple focus on Altdorfer was unprecedented; it represented the first of several waves of receptivity for his art. Of these four, Hans Tietze's book on Altdorfer stands out because of its very "cleverness."[2] It was written for the series "German Masters" (*Deutsche Meister*). Tietze measured Altdorfer's achievement against his definition of a master: a "true master's" art embodies and therefore expresses an ethical whole which in the process of reception becomes the glorified, ideal self-image of the nation.[3] Also, a "true master" is an originator. While this definition holds true for Dürer it casts Altdorfer as a "mere amateur."[4] But Tietze's subsequent discussion dwells on Altdorfer's originality in the representation of infinite space, an observation which Friedländer had elaborated already a generation earlier. Tietze declares that Altdorfer's artistic goal was the concretization of the notion of infinite space, the recognized contribution of northern art since Wölfflin had drawn distinctions between Italian and German concepts of form. Tietze concedes that Altdorfer's "devotion to infinite space"[5] and particularly to the representation of "spatial eternity" constitute a contribution to the language of northern art. Thus Tietze is justified in expanding his initial definition of master in his conclusion: the qualification "master" is also earned by artists such as Altdorfer who have contributed to their respective cultural-national language.

After a decade of economic and political turmoil in Germany the next wave of Altdorfer reception commemorated in 1938 the quadricentennial of his death, by an exhibition in Munich. Most of the related literary reaction to Altdorfer's art, such as Otto Benesch's monograph, will be dealt with in the following chapters. But Ludwig Baldass's book on Altdorfer, which acknowledges indebtedness to the Munich exhibition, deserves discussion here. His approach to Altdorfer differs from Tietze's in that he traces the "inner logic" of Altdorfer's artistic development. For him the crucial aspect of Altdorfer's creativity is his stylistic versatility in response to the particular challenge each new work—each commission—presented to him, a characteristic which Winzinger also found to be dominant.[6]

Baldass presents Altdorfer's artistic evolution in terms of period concepts borrowed from literary criticism. The "young romantic" moves through periods of storm and stress of increasing intensities until the storm subsides.[7] The last decade of his activity is described by a sudden switch to art historical concepts of style, namely in terms of degrees of mannerism.

A chapter devoted to Altdorfer's secular art contains Baldass' view of his significance within the framework of European art history. In contrast to Dürer, Altdorfer's art conveys an inherently secular tenor. If religious subjects predominate in his oeuvre it is because of economic expediency, because these were in demand at the time. Altdorfer's actual contribution must be seen as one of the most important harbingers of seventeenth century secular painting. Themes from the religious, mythological, and secular domains are treated with equal emphasis on the human element.[8] Baldass calls Altdorfer's secular interpretation of sacred stories fundamentally humanistic. For example, the Berlin *Crucifixion* depicts an episode not accounted for in the New Testament, and the painting of *Lot and His Daughters* depicts a human situation of insatiability without shame.[9]

In his conclusion Baldass ranks Altdorfer as "not really great" but as occupying a special position in German sixteenth century art: its "most charming phenomenon."[10]

Eberhard Ruhmer takes issue with this latter judgment in the first comprehensive Altdorfer study after World War II, a full decade after Baldass' Altdorfer book of 1941. Certainly illustrations chosen for dustcovers are symptomatic of the author's and the publisher's reception of the artist. Ruhmer's Altdorfer monograph displays a flaming-red sunset framed by lush dark green vegetation and steep mountain cliffs in the shadows of dusk; branches hang heavy with growth, leaves sparkle with the reflection of the last rays of sun. This glowing piece of nature drama is a detail from the *Gethsemane* panel of the St. Sebastian altarpiece in St. Florian, a landscape imparting an air of ominous foreboding. Like Tietze's monograph this one was also written for a specific series, "old art in new perspective." The intention is to free Altdorfer's image from that of a romantic painter of idylls, an image Friedländer had already warned against.[11] Ruhmer takes the extreme opposite point of view when he writes that Altdorfer "cultivates the genre of the criminal."[12] The Altdorfer phenomenon is explained in terms of a polarity between dynamism and demonicism discernible throughout Altdorfer's oeuvre, and between the intellectual and the practical, as apparent in the major role architectural motifs assume in his work.[13] Like Baldass before him, Ruhmer emphasizes Altdorfer's subjective re-creation of any source or model he may have employed. But unlike Baldass, Ruhmer gives Altdorfer the status of pioneer because in his art Germany had found its own Renaissance style.[14] However, when the author proceeds to describe Altdorfer's characteristic landscape and his use of architectural motifs as "giorgionesque" and "bramantesque" he contradicts himself. By using comparisons derived from Italian art Ruhmer indirectly acknowledges Italian art as his touchstone and with that the artistic primacy of Italy. He is above all fascinated with Altdorfer's graphic style, calling his line "portentously driven," as if motivated and moved by some ulterior *Kunstwollen*. Certainly this observation ascertains a mystical element in the creative process.

Franz Winzinger's study of Altdorfer has now spanned nearly half a century. He too received the initial inspiration for his lifelong pursuit of Altdorfer through participation in the organization of the 1938 Munich exhibition. Winzinger expanded Altdorfer's oeuvre by new attributions, thereby establishing Altdorfer as the principal artist of the Danube School, particularly through the uncontested attribution of the miniatures of Maximilian's *Triumphal Procession* to Altdorfer and his workshop in Regensburg. Winzinger further suggests influential patrons of fine arts such as the administrator of Regensburg's diocese John III who had commissioned the wall decorations of the public bath in the episcopal residence. However, Winzinger concludes that what is left of Altdorfer's work today must not be thought of as representative.[15] Within the context of sixteenth-century German art Winzinger asserts Altdorfer's stature as equal to Grunewald's, Dürer's and Holbein's.[16] Of his three major volumes on Altdorfer's drawings (1952), graphic art (1963), and paintings (1975), the first and the last book state explicitly Winzinger's view of Altdorfer's foremost artistic qualities. Like Ruhmer, Winzinger sees in Altdorfer's graphic style, in his line, more than a mere record of visual experience, but rather a conveyance of a magical world in which the artist feels himself to be the *centrum naturae.*[17] Both authors also agree that the essence of Altdorfer's art consists in a pervasively dynamic quality which is present in the later precious style of the *Battle of Alexander,* for example.

Winzinger carefully delineates the boundaries between Altdorfer's vision and that of his fellow artists in Germany. Considering that Altdorfer was thoroughly acquainted with Dürer's work and that both artists collaborated closely on Maximilian's projects such as the *Prayer Book* illustrations and the designs for the *Triumphal Arch,* Altdorfer's artistic independence appears all the more pronounced. Winzinger suggests that the art of Dürer and the art of Altdorfer represent two very different, even antithetical, modes of perceiving nature. He criticizes Burckhardt for identifying the origin of modern European individualism too narrowly with the Italian Renaissance concept of man, thus overlooking the equally significant concept of the infinite developed initially by Nicolas of Cues in the fifteenth century. The individual's experience of the notion of the infinite is the precondition for the development of landscape, of *Raum an sich* (space in itself), as an independent theme in the visual arts. This experience of infinite space is the most important contribution of German thought to modern intellectual consciousness and must be valued alongside the Italian humanist concept of a well-ordered finite cosmos.[18]

Altdorfer's polarity to Dürer is manifest in several domains of artistic expression. It extends to the representation of the nude. While Dürer searches for the perfect image of man, Altdorfer always shows man as a part of the totality of nature. In their use of color, Dürer and Altdorfer must also be understood as antipodes. In Dürer's painting color plays a secondary role whereas Altdorfer gives color primary consideration. For example, Altdorfer achieved the illusion of spatial continuity and spatial depth in his *Battle of Alexander* through color.[19] Winzinger sees a further consequential difference in the religious visions of the two artists: Dürer's as profoundly Christian, Altdorfer's as expressive of devotion to nature, of pantheistic piety.[20] If any one painting represents these qualities it is the *Two Sts. John* extolled by Winzinger as "an instructive expression of the German spirit which rarely revealed itself with such purity in a work of art,"[21] and the *Battle of Alexander* which constitutes the pinnacle of Altdorfer's creativity, resulting from on overwhelming personal experience of nature like Petrarca's mountain-top experience. When Winzinger calls this painting "miraculous" and Altdorfer a "painter by the grace of God" he expresses, like Ruhmer, a notion of creativity which is dependent upon divine intervention.[22]

Meanwhile, in the United States the scholarly and the popular reception of Altdorfer have taken on visible proportions during the last decade. The 1977 second edition of H. W. Janson's widely used text on the history of art reproduces Altdorfer's *Battle of Alexander* as a full-page color plate, the first of eight to illustrate the section on the Baroque in Italy and Germany, whereas the first edition of the same book contained only a small black and white photograph of the same painting. In addition the same textbook singled out Altdorfer from his German contemporary artists: the time chart places the *Battle of Alexander* between Correggio's *Assumption* and Parmigianino's *Madonna with Long Neck*.[23] Discussion of Chinese landscape painting in the same book suggests that within the history of Western painting only Altdorfer together with Leonardo, Breughel and Ruisdael would have understood the Chinese attitude toward landscape painting.[24]

The 1969 exhibition at Yale University featuring *Prints and Drawings of the Danube School* presented Altdorfer as its central artist and the authors' interpretation of his stylistic characteristics converge with Winzinger's in all points.[25] Charles Talbot, one of the organizers, was able to show in a subsequent study probable sources of Altdorfer's expressive graphic style never before considered. These are the woodcut landscapes executed by Michael Wolgemut and his shop for Hartman Schedel's *Nuremberg Chronicle* and Erhard Reuwich's woodcuts for Bernhard von Breydenbach's *Journey to the Holy Land* (Mainz, 1486). Altdorfer's early pen drawings of landscapes (W. Z. 28 and W. Z. 29) reflect a close artistic kinship to these woodcuts both in the compositional devices and in the graphic means they employed. Altdorfer must have recognized the expressive potential in these early woodcut landscapes. In his search for a mode of representation adequate for his dynamic view of nature he borrowed from them and at the same time transferred from the woodcut style to his own drawing style.[26]

In 1974 an American dissertation attempted a contextual explanation of Altdorfer's art by adopting Dvořák's method to write *Kunstgeschichte* as *Geistesgeschichte,* but the author found little more than the truism that an artist's work tends to reflect, even to illustrate, the cultural and political trends of his time and place.[27]

Tietze, Ruhmer, and Winzinger all emphasize that Altdorfer's art is particularly expressive of a so-called German artistic temperament and vision. For Tietze and Winzinger this consists in the preoccupation with the representation of infinite space and its impact on the development of landscape and space as themes in art. For Ruhmer this Germanness finds expression in Altdorfer's dynamic line, his sense of animation and movement. Baldass, on the other hand, emphasizes the humanistic aspect of Altdorfer's art, of particular fascination to Kokoschka and to Picasso. The emergence of these themes in the twentieth century reception of Altdorfer will be treated in the following chapters.

Altdorfer and Ideologies

Kenneth Burke, the contemporary literary critic, has equated ideology with "illusion, mystification, discussion of human relations in terms like absolute consciousness, honor, loyalty, justice, freedom, substance, essence of man, in short, that 'inversion' whereby material history is derived from 'spirit' (in contrast with the method of dialectical materialism whereby the changing nature of consciousness would be derived from changes in material conditions)."[1] This does not mean that ideologies are unreal; they make very strong, if passing, empirical claims about the condition and direction of society. It is the purpose of criticism, like some sciences of culture and society, to understand ideologies—what they are, how they work, what gives rise to them—and through criticism to force them to come to terms with reality. This is the best guarantee against ideological extremism.[2] Altdorfer plays an important role in several German nationalist ideologies.

But the national-socialist era was not the first to use art, past and present, to buttress the national consciousness of the people, and to strengthen the myth of the nation's glorious past in order to legitimize the aims of the present, usually during a crisis of political instability. Altdorfer himself was involved in the creation of art for this purpose, both at the national level in his *Ehrenpforte* (triumphal arch) (W. Gr. 66-75) and for his *Triumphzug* (triumphal procession) for Maximilian, as well as his numerous official commissions to help propagate the cult of the Beautiful Mary in Regensburg.

We had observed that Friedrich Schlegel's interpretation of the *Battle of Alexander* had concluded with an appeal to national art. During these same years Max von Schenkendorf composed a poem to celebrate the collection of old German paintings which the brothers Sulpiz and Melchior Boisseré had assembled in Cologne during the chaotic, destructive years of the Napoleonic wars, occupations, and ensuing secularization. This collection included at least one painting by Altdorfer.

A beautiful old hall beckons, two brothers have built it,
there, in the *purest beam of light,* I beheld my *Fatherland.*

It was in those dark times a gracious, quiet *place of pilgrimage*
where the *glory of the fathers* sought refuge in a secure port.

The host of martyrs and saints, many of God's faithful and valorous heros,
the tender women mild and serene who are *aglow* for the Savior;

Many an image of the *purest* of maids as she envisioned God's angel,
sometimes she mourns her son, sometimes as the wise men kneel before her;

That which *pious* diligence and *chaste* art had nurtured in the *old German world,*
here it had been saved and displayed according to God's council and grace.

Many a *faithful* heart came to see the beloved paintings,
blessed be the deep sorrow which then ensued in him.

O fiery love of fatherland and of the bygone days of heros,
you, bitter pleasure and the hand of God have saved us from the yoke.

Now we behold you, and you encourage us joyfully, you pictures,
however, a true man does not yet desire any repose.

First, you must walk through our free lands (guided) by the hand of an artist,
never again shall one see heathen images on any German wall.

You dearest *saints* come to the fore and bless us, we emplore you,
and you gracious *maidens*, adorn the house, and you, *knights,*
protect the *Empire.*

You, hall of pictures, continue to stand for a long time hence,
you, brothers, exercise your duty so that the beam of the pious past
will *set aflame* many a breast.[3]

The poem is symptomatic of a dogmatic interpretation of art that is couched in
a terminology of religious emotionalism mixed with national militancy. The
picture gallery has become a sacred space. The spectator is aroused by an
emotional fire—he "glows," is "aflame"—to the point of self-sacrifice, not
for his religious conviction, but for his country. The implicit color symbolism
of the poem is that of white and red: the colors of moral purity and sacrifice. A
century later, in 1916, as Germany was embroiled in World War I, the same
poem appeared as the preface to a biography on the Boisseré brothers. The
Third Reich was to use very similar language when talking about art.

Before dealing with ideological art manipulations of the Third Reich, the
scholarly treatment of a German (national) concept of artistic form by Heinrich
Wölfflin must be examined. In a lecture on German Renaissance architecture in
1914, the first year of World War I, Wölfflin explained that "the topic is
conditioned by the times which demand something German."[4] His concluding
remarks in a book on his basic ideas about art, published one year later in 1915,
concluded with a discussion of "national characteristics" in art:

From the beginning we have made reference to the way in which the modes of vision are refracted by nationality. There is a definite type of Italian or German imagination which asserts itself . . . to set up a scheme of a national type of imagination is a necessary aid to the historian. Germanic imagination . . . reacts more strongly to painterly stimuli than the southern. Not the line but the web of lines. Not the established single form but the movement of form. . . .

They plough up the depths, they seek the stream of movement working upward from below. . . .

Here there is also room for the flash of inspiration, for the apparently willful, the indirectly applied rule. The presentment strives to pass beyond the law-bound toward the unbound. . . .

Thought seeks the unity, the all-filling, where system is abolished and the independence of the parts is submerged in the whole . . . and just in that fact lie the conditions of northern landscape painting. We do not see tree and hill and cloud for themselves, but everything is absorbed in the breath of the one great scene.[5]

A seminal essay on the subject of national art characteristics, written in 1922, and another written in 1928 for the quadricentennial of Dürer's death, formed the core of his *Italy and the German Concept of Form* (*Italien und das deutsche Formgefühl*)[6] in which he analyzed not only the question of national characteristics in art, but also the historic roots of the issue, in particular the early sixteenth century. The general premises of art as the physiognomy of a national mode of seeing were laid out in a 1936 essay for the international congress of art historians in Zurich.

There is no work of art which is not also conditioned by the factors of place and time . . . . As long as one understands art as the process of finding *gestalt* for that which previously had not had *gestalt* . . . form as changing expression of a changing content must be allowed to claim the name art.

. . . One may speak of the national form as a tangible most powerful source. . . . What is true for architecture obviously is also true for sculpture and painting. They have their roots in the most profound recesses of the national character and the national world view. However, the highest values of art are not synonymous with the merely-national. It is the distinguished quality of all great art that it addresses the realm of the universally human.[7]

Here a distinction was made between the determinants in an art's national characteristics and the ultimate values of art, which must be more than just national. At the height of National Socialist ideological activity in 1940 Wölfflin would defend his premises about art by saying that art is determined by race and time, as well as national character.[8]

In his 1931 *Italien und das duetsche Formgefühl* Wolfflin was interested in establishing the Italian concept of form and the extent to which it could be adopted by the North.[9] The notion of the *"deutsche Formgefühl,"* an emotional, unrational feeling, not correctly translated by "concept," suggests a strong contrast to the Italian concept of form. Wölfflin cites four works by Altdorfer as the purest illustrations of this German national vision—imagination, as he preferred to call it. "Certain works by Altdorfer are freer than any produced before his time . . . in Altdorfer's paintings we find things which surpass all that was customary, yet, evidently, such formlessness became psychologically possible only on the basis of a greater awareness of form."[10] One work by Altdorfer which had previously received little or no attention in criticism, and is featured repeatedly by Wölfflin in four chapters, is the *Birth of the Virgin* (see Plate 2), and each time it exemplifies another aspect of German national style. In the chapter on "Form and Contour," for example, Wölfflin discussed the *Birth of the Virgin* for its perfect characterization of the difference between German and Italian conception of space as follows:

> . . . space is undefined and in motion. An immense garland of angels twines around the piers and cuts across the divisions between nave and aisles. It is a horizontal movement, no Gothic upward élan. . . . In Altdorfer's interior, the nave and aisles flow into one another and . . . a rotating whirling movement throws the entire space into turmoil. The church's ground plan remains intentionally unclear . . . the boundaries of space are kept inconspicuous . . . he intended the interior to be a modern one, but the spatial conception is no different from that expressed in late Gothic architecture . . . spatial content is not contained within distinct limits.[11]

In the chapter "Regularity and Order" Wölfflin writes about the *Birth of the Virgin:*

> Altdorfer dared an extreme loosening of the tectonic structure, although the church interior, where the scene takes place, could have offered the imagination sufficient material for a regulated order. . . . However, even rectangularity as a principle of pictorial order, was allowed to become effective only to a limited degree, and a tectonic impression was undermined from the start by the oblique view of the stage.[12]

The same painting serves to illustrate the opposite of classical relief conception in the chapter on "The Relief Conception":

> . . . the principle of the classic relief character is disregarded . . . it cannot be considered a composition in the relief style, everything has been done . . . to avoid any suggestion of the concept of the picture plane.[13]

The chapter on "Clarity and the Subject in Art" features the *Birth of the Virgin* to prove the thesis that:

> . . . in German painting—most of all, of course, in the works of the painterly painters—the colors have much more contact with one another, and overpassing the objects, achieve a self-sufficient effect. The red in Altdorfer's *Birth of the Virgin* constantly clings, it is true, to Joseph's robe . . . but the overall impression is still a free play of color that has no counterpart in Italian art.[14]
>
> Altdorfer presented the church interior of the *Birth of the Virgin* in such a way that the actual architectural system cannot be figured out from the painting . . . correct drawing would produce a less vivid effect.[15]

Yet the *Birth of the Virgin* remains a *Schulbeispiel,* while to Wölfflin as well, the *Battle of Alexander* constitutes Altdorfer's ultimate achievement. In the chapter on "Grandeur and Simplicity," Wölfflin spoke of the *Battle of Alexander* as the:

> . . . most singular example of the German pictorial conception . . . with its combination of the infinitely great in its space that stretches far into the distance and the innumerable small, yet fully executed figures in the foreground. The limitless expanse surpasses anything to be seen in Italian landscapes, but equally un-Italian is the juxtaposition of a near view and a distant view.[16]

Altdorfer's *Birth of the Virgin* provided another art historian with "the classic witness of the German concept of the picture." In an essay on "The German Concept of the Picture Form of the Late Gothic and the Renaissance," (1952) Otto Pächt wrote of the painting's classic German concept of the picture, as follows:

> There is on the one hand the view from the dark aisle—which now functions as a lying-in room—into the bright nave and choir. The circling (rotating) playful flight of the angels allows once more the experience of the whole interior space and one senses this space differently now than during the first merely passive glance. Altdorfer's picture allows the realization just what the conquest of the planar organization, the discovery of the picture-depth meant to the German painter: the opening-up of the third dimension is understood as an invitation to enter into the interior of the picture space and to wander through the hollow space in *all* directions, not just in one. . . . To stand in front and be inside, to watch and to partake, the combination of these two states of being continues to be the demand which German painters make on themselves and on their public. This basic attitude and its tendency to unite two contradictory, even mutually exclusive approaches poses a genuine artistic problem. The solution could only be fully realized where, as in the case of Altdorfer, the character of the representation assumes openly and without hesitation that of a fiction, dream-vision and a fairy tale.[17]

The reawakened consciousness of a German national style, which Wölfflin had initiated in 1914, fostered the courage to pursue the question of German art's effect upon foreign art. Thus Theodor Hetzer, in 1929, strongly advocated a kinship of style and artistic intention between Tintoretto and Altdorfer. He suggested that Tintoretto must have known at least Altdorfer's prints.[18] In 1936 the author of a book entitled *Magic and Love of Nature (Magie und Naturgefühl)*[19] which deals with the art of Grünewald, Cranach, Baldung Grien and Altdorfer, dedicated her work to the "battle to win recognition of German art and literature abroad." On the dustcover of the same book, hope is expressed in awakening an "echo for the *eternal values* of German art." The proximity of military and religious realms is noteworthy. Another indication of a heightened emotionalism which transferred religious missionary zeal to that of cultural politics is the author's justification of using Latin typesetting in her book instead of Gothic letters (normally *de rigueur* in Nazi Germany) so as "to better reach her foreign readers."[20] The end justifies the means also when characterizing the work of individual artists. The author claims that "Germany's eternal artistic heritage consists of an underlying dichotomy: on the one hand a striving for self-expression, predominated by demonically charged reality, incomprehensible magic, wild sensuality, and a dream of infinity."[21] Samples of Altdorfer's art are selected and described to fit these categories. Yet the ideology of the superman (*Herrenmensch*) which Closs sought to serve, did not tolerate individualistic self-expression as the content of art. Therefore she was careful to distinguish twentieth century Expressionism which she feels is negative from expressionism in early sixteenth century German art. In the sixteenth century the striving for expression did not lose itself in a "foggy dream world" but was held in check by a "will to form." The other part of the dichotomy—which the author believes is equally inherent in the German soul—is a striving for classical balance. This Dürer accomplished, not because of alien influences but rather due to the German's own inward hope of achieving self-control.[22] Thus, in the light of this dichotomy, Closs views the *Battle of Alexander* as "a nostalgic display of Romanticism of the waning Middle Ages," but basically as a painting about sensually-experienced visions. Altdorfer is seen as a painter of fairy tales, an inventor of a genre of landscape painting that understands nature in its mysterious infinity to be a mirror of one's own thoughts and reflections. By employing this nineteenth century Romantic concept and its genre of the *Stimmungslandschaft*[23] to describe Altdorfer's contribution the author clearly implies that she perceives nineteenth century Romanticism to be a continuation of a sixteenth century Romantic period. As a consequence she regards the painting *Waldstrasse* (Munich, W. G. 46) as the climax of Altdorfer's achievement. It allows the loss of self in "unlimited longing for movement, for the call of the open and the silence of nature where man can dream his dreams."[24] Therefore Altdorfer emerges in this book as the antithesis to Dürer whose art is summarized as the embodiment of German striving for heroic self-control.

If the purpose of the foregoing book was to disseminate the notion of the greatness or uniqueness of the German artistic heritage of which Altdorfer was seen as a crucial element, then Hans Watzlik's biographical novel *The Master of Regensburg*[25] could be used even more successfully to popularize the artists of the nation's past. This novel was one of at least 40 biographies on painters and sculptors of the early sixteenth century published in Germany between 1930 and 1941, popularizing them as heroes in the ideology of the Third Reich.[26] Set in Gothic script, Watzlik's 1939 Altdorfer novel emphasized the same leading ideas as those in Hanna Preibsch-Closs's *Magic and Love of Nature* (1936) discussed above: (1) The duality of the soul which Altdorfer struggles to resolve is the propelling force of the creative process.[27] The painting of landscape brings ultimate resolution to the struggle, in that soul and landscape merge.

("... Seele und Lanschaft werden in dieser Welt des Schauens eins ... in dieser Einheit hat alles Sinn und Sendung. Und ihr höchster Sinn aber ist die *kämpferische Wandlung.*")[28] The adjective "kämpferisch" (struggling) adds the Nazi ideological color, in view of the novel's underlying caricature of the Jews. (2) Altdorfer's art is truly German in that it originates from the woods (forests) and the love of nature. Watzlik has Altdorfer say at one point:

> I am a child of the forest, therefore I paint the forest. You Southerners do not love your forests, you destroy them. But my forebears walked through the *sacred wilderness*. Just like our great streams Danube, Nab and Regen hurl out from the forests so the German man breaks out from the forest, and this green image remains his eternally.[29]

In connection with landscape etchings, Watzlik's Altdorfer is described: "... and he knew that despite his dream-born work he was intimately rooted in that land which now lay beneath him under the cover of dusk, in the land of the Danube, in Germany."[30] And as Altdorfer's *Battle of Alexander* is presented to the Emperor Charles V, Aventinus tells him: "Majesty, it is a German work." And to Altdorfer: "Your work transcends the capriciousness of the moment, it will remain in the eternal property of the nation, and it will be said in Germany: what a spirit has dwelt among us."[31] And when upon contemplating the painting of *Susanna's Bath,* Aventinus exclaims: "... but your painting is spontaneous and nimble in spite of its Bavarian nature and it is colorful as a pearl. Germany shall build a pyramid and write on its golden spike: Albrecht Altdorfer beholds the beauty of the country!"[32] Thus, (3) Nature and forest are sacred. Altdorfer's mother knew the secret healing powers of plants when she was a child. She cast a spell on Altdorfer's eyes near a spring in the woods.[33] Thus the mother is the mediator between the supernatural, the sacred and the natural, the ordinary. Through his mother Altdorfer's vision has become sensitive, attuned to nature, it has received supernatural divine powers. While the father transmitted only the craft, the mystery of the creative power and process is explained through the mother's extraordinary faculties in her relationship with nature. In this manner the Third Reich mystified the woman. Under the theme of "Mother and Child," images of Mary became acceptable art objects for the Third Reich. An exhibit in Vienna in 1939 illustrates this; Austria is compared to a "fertile woman" beside male Germany.[34]

All of this makes Altdorfer a hero of the nation. He has struggled to overcome weakness; his vision transcends the fallacies of time; he forges ahead into something new. It suggests a culminating idea in Watzlik's novel that reflected National Socialist ideology: (4) National heroes (like Altdorfer) partake of the divine. Altdorfer is placed in the ranks of genius artists whose works were created through the intervention of divine powers. The creative process lies beyond human rationale; the creation of a work of art becomes "the incarnation of a higher spirit."[35] Completion of the *Battle of Alexander* is possible only through divine intervention.

Then before him rested the consecrated work in which the far distances of the earth and the remoteness of the universe embraced each other, and everything was a congealed, grand, wild dream, perfect, unfathomable, wonderfully structured and yet incomprehensible. That which had struggled in his soul so painfully, now it lay blissfully before him on the panel, separated and strange. Is this his work which was painted with the vision of an air-born eagle? Man, earth, sea, sun, the fiery-whirling sky, which finally escapes . . . icyly . . . into the airless nothing, all, all below him! Through the crevaces of the clouds the shuddering gaze moves into the infinite. From the remoteness of his childhood the man heard a word resounding: You shall see what no one has seen before you!

Anna felt that Altdorfer had no reverence for the limits which are set for men. . . .

Aventinus deeply moved looked at the Battle from whence emanated the wild breath of world-history. "This is unwieldy but still it is created with wise controlled power and with a spirit which only you possess," he shouted, "you are German. Because what you do you do with all your might." He folded his hands, "and God saw that it was good. . . ."

". . . Altdorfer, how magnificently does the German soul reveal itself in your work! How it penetrates down to the deepest foundations! And you have forgotten nothing: it is the history of the earth, it is the history of humanity and it is the movement of the Universe!"[36]

Pantheism—"the face of God is nature"—which in this novel is Altdorfer's motivating moral force is also the Third Reich's alternative to the Church. Through the voice of Aventinus the author comments on his own contemporary intellectual and political situation, ". . . we are uncovering a hidden heritage. Science and art will be taken from the hands of the shaven-headed (priests), the superstitious dreams of monks will be replaced by a strong searching Spirit, and Germany will become proud and confident of itself."[37] Thus nature is God, and the Third Reich replaces the Church. Altdorfer's religious stance in the sixteenth century is neatly avoided.[38]

The Altdorfer novel appeared on the market just when a large public had had the first opportunity ever to see almost the entirety of Altdorfer's extant oeuvre exhibited in one place. In 1938 the first Altdorfer retrospective ever to be held was staged in Munich in the Neue Staatsgalerie. It was entitled "Albrecht Altdorfer and his circle" (*A. A. und sein Kreis*) as the show featured Altdorfer as the major inspirational source of the painting of the Danube School. A deeply red circular plaque suspended on golden ropes from the gable of the Neue Staatsgalerie announced the exhibit to which more than 8,000 visitors came on one Sunday morning.[39]

Munich had been the scene of two other related, highly politicized, art events of major import to the decade just a few months earlier in 1937. Within steps from each other, the House of German Art (*Haus der Deutschen Kunst*) had been dedicated personally by Hitler, who prophesied the ultimate victory of ethnic art (*völkische Kunst*), while the exhibit derogatorily labeled by the regime "Degenerate Art" was on view nearby. This show featured works by artists, despised by official ideology, who had translated Altdorfer's heritage into a modern idiom.[40] They will be discussed in Chapter 7.

The ostensible art historical reason for the 1938 Altdorfer retrospective was the 400th anniversary of the artist's death. The occasion was, however, exploited by its organizers as well as by the press to justify the annexation of Austria to the Reich which had taken place earlier in the year through a political coup.[41] The exhibit's explicit goal was neither to provide aesthetic pleasure, nor to alert the viewer to a heightened knowledge of self, nor to reconstruct a historical epoch through its art, but, what was far more important symbolically, to "prove the spiritual and cultural unity of the traditional Bavarian eastern provinces—from the river Lech to the Leitha. The erection of the unified empire (*Reich*) sanctifies this exhibit. If ever an exhibit of old German art was spiritually justified, even necessary, it is this one."[42]

The introduction to the catalogue of the exhibit characterized Altdorfer as a Bavarian folk hero, literally the "embodiment of Bavarian popular culture (*Verkörperung bajuwarischen Volkstums*).[43] Altdorfer's style, his "line," was compared with that unique phenomenon of Bavarian folk music, the yodler (*"lustige Jodler"*).[44] Nouns and adjectives with military connotations betray the ideological direction of the exhibit; "striking force" (*Schlagkraft*). "full of blood" (*blutvoll*); descriptive terms such as "elemental" (*elementar*), "primordial" (*ursprünglich*), and "racy" (*urwüchsig*), emphasizing the organic, quasi-mystical relationship of the artist to nature, the same emphasis which dominated Watzlik's Altdorfer novel and Priebsch-Closs's book.[45] This view was emphasized as well in the opening ceremonies. According to a newspaper report:

> Just how much the deeper ethnic voices were present in the goals of the organizers became apparent on the occasion of the solemn opening of the exhibit, when the choir of Regensburg's *Domspatzen* sang the old German tune from those (Altdorfer's) days: 'Rise in God's name, you beloved German nation!'[46]

An artist whose popular image was that of a painter of fairy tales and idylls, a "dreamer," was now literally "built up" to appeal to the militant defenders of this new empire. The director of the exhibit singled out the military as the only group of people whom he addressed in particular. He called their attention to the miniatures for Emperor Maximilian's Triumphal Procession: ". . . they (the military) will enjoy Emperor Maximilian's artillery, especially in Munich, the city which knows how to stage parades!'"[47]

National-socialist ideology provided even more openly the guidelines for an exhibit of "Old German art in the lands of the Danube" (*Altdeutsche Kunst im Donauland*) organized in Vienna in 1939. As a matter of fact, this exhibit understands itself as a "thank you" for having been "brought home" to the Empire. "Thank you" for what happened in 1938. Altdorfer's art was centrally featured in this exhibit. The first sentence of the preface set the unilateral direction: the traditional arts have to serve in the building of the national socialist state. ". . . the authoritarian state . . . which embraces and penetrates all things with one singular, total impulse can neither allow the monasteries nor anyone else a special position. The German artistic heritage is the spiritual and cultural property of the nation. . . ."[48] Therefore the show's goal was to appeal to a general public. "The show is *not* addressed to the intellect but it is to arouse perception and love for our glorious artistic past. . . ."[49] So here as well Altdorfer's art and that of his time is shown with the purpose to perpetuate the myth of a past worth emulating. It is a highly selective picture of the past which the organizers constructed:

> The intention was not to reconstruct an epoch but to show that art which appears vital and exemplary to us today, to show those aspects of the historical arts which concern us today: first, that which is beautiful and strong; second, that which has greatness and strength of character; third, that which portrays joy of living and affirmation of life. . . . These considerations guided the selection of the objects exhibited here.[50]

The number of crucifixions, passion scenes, lamentations, scenes of martyrdom were purposefully kept at a minimum in order to focus on the "positive side of life." The organizers of the exhibit tried very hard to find a rooting in the past that negates and even rejects the Church as the force behind that art in order to confirm the present ideology.

The major result of the exhibit was thought to consist not only in establishing the fact that the lands of the Danube were the most prolific area of art in all of Germany between 1300-1600, but that culturally as well this area had always been intimately connected with the German Whole, that this area has always been especially hospitable, and "fertile in receiving talents from neighboring tribes." These thoughts are repeated at least twice in both preface and introduction in the catalogue to the exhibition. Until the advent of national socialist ideology in art criticism and in the reception of art the *Battle of Alexander* was thought to be the climax of Altdorfer's work, his masterpiece. Now the focus has changed to the St. Florian altarpiece (W. G. 24).[51] Otto Benesch's announcement of the Munich retrospective pronounced the St. Florian altarpiece the culmination of Altdorfer's entire artistic output in an effort to deliberately disprove the traditional view of Altdorfer as the gentle dreamer.[52] The same goal was pursued by Ernst Buchner's introduction to the retrospective.

The St. Florian altarpiece was described as containing qualities better suited to the image of an artist hero—artist-ancestor—of the New Reich.

> . . . radiant display of colors, a conception of greatness and boldness of soul, power of expression which Altdorfer has never surpassed. All the impetuosity, all the expressive exaggerations, all the exuberance of his early works return, but now all this is valiantly controlled and combined into a striking force which confirms the master's equality with the greatest of his contemporaries.[53]

The language, once more, is saturated with words connoting a militant code of ethics. Not one word is said about the religious content of this polyptych. Instead the reviewer acclaimed the artist's command of the expressive range of natural light—from sunset to sunrise and the cool even light of morning—and the vivid narrative peopled with characters from all walks of life; all of this permitting a rather direct appeal to a general public.

The *Battle of Alexander,* on the other hand, is thought to be liminal (*Grenzfall*) of that which is possible in art and as such it may not be considered the culmination of Altdorfer's achievement. Benesch preferred to place the *Battle of Alexander* together with *Susanna's Bath* into the category of those precious, glittering *objets d'art* for princely collections (*Kunstkammerstücke*).[54] Behind the ideological front scholars working during the national socialist era carried out solid, groundbreaking research on problems of Old German painting. Thus the Munich retrospective featured a new Altdorfer attribution, the 1519 painting of the *Beautiful Mary* (Regensburg, St. Johannes).[55] This was the first and the last time until 1977 that this painting was on public view outside the sanctuary of the church. Immediately after the Munich exhibition the Bishop of Regensburg declared the image sacred and forbade its display in a secular context.[56] The exhibition catalogue, however, did not feature this new discovery in any special way, nor did the reaction to the exhibit acknowledge this new addition to the Altdorfer-oeuvre. The religious content was too explicit to warrant an admiration which the official ideology could approve of—it clearly was not one of those Madonna and Child representations which portrayed the *"urdeutsches Mutter-und Kind Motiv."*[57]

Of the varied reactions to the Munich exhibit,[58] and direct art critical developments drawing influence from it, Wilhelm Pinder's essay on "Romanticism of German art around 1500" deserves mention.[59] Admitting inspiration from the 1938 Altdorfer retrospective, Pinder forwards the thesis that the main characteristic of Romantic art is a "blurring of boundaries" (*Grenzverwischung*). He asserts that only Germany produced true Romanticism (*"Nur Deutschland hat es zur yollen Romantik gebracht"*).[60] This came to fruition at two different periods in history. Germany's visual Romanticism took place around 1500, while that of literature, music, and philosophy reached a climax around 1800.[61] The purest examples in visual images of blurring of boundaries (*Grenzverwischung,* or *Synaesthesie*) can be found in Altdorfer's *Wilder Mann* (W.G. 6) where forms of nature and man flow into one another; the *Birth of the Virgin,* the *Nativity* in Berlin, and the *Nativity* in Bremen, where there is an "unnatural" illumination of the night; the *Rest on the Flight to Egypt,* where there is a vascillation between the sacred story and the realities of child's play; *St. George in a Landscape* and the drawing of *Christ in the Garden of Gethsemane,* where the author finds the mergence of the figure into landscape.[62] The St. Florian altarpiece is described as the "greatest miracle" of the master, surpassed only by his *Battle of Alexander*. This achievement resulted, according to Pinder, from Altdorfer having "seen the face of the sun," thereby ascribing to the artist superhuman powers.[63] Pinder did not describe or analyze the painting, instead he juxtaposed it with excerpts from Goethe's *Faust II* and from the conclusion to Jean-Paul's novel *Flegeljahre*. Both texts are to demonstrate Pinder's thesis of *Synaesthesie* as the leading charcteristic of romantic artists, as well as that found in the *Battle of Alexander* 300 years earlier.[64] The Magdalena in the Berlin *Crucifixion* is interpreted by Pinder as a precursor of C. D. Friedrich's motif of the lone figure, "*Rückenfigur,*" in the landscape which serves to "blur the boundary" between the I and the image.

After the outbreak of World War II no documented reference was made to Altdorfer. Indeed, most journals in art history and other publication endeavors came to a halt. All major museums, libraries, cathedrals, had begun by 1940 to safeguard collections and statuary.

The first exhibition after World War II including Altdorfer was organized by the Austrian cultural organization (*Österreichische Kulturvereinigung*) in Linz, featuring the art of the Danube School in Upper Austria.[65] Nine years and one World War following the Vienna exhibition of 1939, in a city occupied by Allied troops, the Austrian Minister of Education wrote in the fore-word to the catalogue that ". . . the exhibition is a gratifying sign of the rein-forcement of the cultural self-confidence of our Austrian homeland . . . may the population . . . gain assurance of the cultural worth (value) of its homeland." Another official stresses the same point: ". . . an important contribution toward the increase of knowledge about the art of our homeland . . . above all the discovery and the loving rendition of landscape in its peculiar-ity. . . ."[66]

Another contributor to the introduction makes the claim that it was ulti-mately the landscape of Upper Austria which inspired the style of the Danube School in Altdorfer and his co-workers. The exhibition was intended to demon-strate one of the "most significant periods of *Austria's* history of art and there-by it will prove the *eternally inexhaustible strength of the native soil.*"[67] The language here has not really changed since 1938, only the political units to which it is addressed, and the holocaust has subdued it a little. In 1947, as well, a commonality was noted between the first quarter of the sixteenth century and the writer's epoch. But now it was the element of crisis which precipitated the Reformation and the Peasant uprisings which was recognized and compared to the contemporary twentieth century uprooting of man's religious, spiritual and physical foundations, whereas in 1938 this same past was "handled" as a model and a source of strength. The religious motivation, content, and intensity of most of the art of the Danube School, short of being denied by the Nazi era, was now not only recognized, but explained in terms of the hopelessness (*Ausweglosigkeit*) of earthly life.[68]

In Germany, Altdorfer's reappearance within an ideological framework did not occur until the polarization of the country into Eastern and Western camps. How was Altdorfer perceived in the East, under the guiding doctrine of Marxism-Leninism? Certainly not as a hero who had sided with the peasants as had Dürer, Cranach, Jörg Ratgeb, Tilman Reimenschneider, the Petrarca Master, and Grunewald. However, in the lavishly illustrated *History of the Early Bourgeois Revolution* (*Frühbürgerliche Revolution*) by Adolf Laube, Max Steinmetz, and Günter Vogler (1974), Altdorfer's work is nevertheless represented three times.[69] A brief chapter on the new concepts of the world and of man in the arts reproduces Altdorfer's etching of a small fir tree as well as a landscape with ruins of a castle, drawn 1525,[70] as representative of the discovery of landscape as a genre.[71] Altdorfer's Nürnberg *Crucifixion* of 1526 (W. G. 48) is also reproduced, done the year the peasants had been defeated a week before Easter and had also suffered terrible punishment at the hands of the feudal lords.[72] Suggests the book's text, ". . . the numerous representations of the Passion theme permitted the understanding of the Lord's suffering as the suffering of the people under feudal rule."[73] In the context of the book's prevailing ideology the painting illustrates social criticism in the guise of realistic portrayals of man. Altdorfer's Nürnberg *Crucifixion* depicts the moment just after Christ's death; the deposition is about to happen, and he is quite alone. Three "Roman" soldiers surround the cross and mock him, carrying halberts of the type used in the peasants' wars.[74] The grief of the men and women over the unjust suffering of Christ is explained to evoke a parallel to the victims of the Peasant War and the sorrow of the simple people whose cause was lost.[75]

While the German Democratic Republic put art, including Altdorfer, into the service of realizing the revolutionary goals set into motion for the first time by peasants during Altdorfer's lifetime, in the Federal Republic of Germany Altdorfer is used to serve the ideology of a "value-free" science and teach the educational implications of democracy.

In the early 1970s the *Battle of Alexander* was used in a sixth grade art education class as a point of departure for the study of the theme "Fighting and Killing" (*Kämpfen und Töten*).[76] The implications of this theme are utterly disregarded. The theme is treated by the teacher as a strictly formal problem. An initially unaesthetic event may be changed into an aesthetic experience through manipulation of form and organization. But this use of Altdorfer's painting as illustration of the theme "Fighting and Killing" as merely a formal aesthetic problem, cannot be labeled other than amoral, an example of the ideology of a so-called value-free science. Indirectly, students are imbued with a favorable attitude toward killing, a serious misinterpretation of the artist's intention.[77]

The use of Altdorfer's art in the realization of the goals of democracy, within the educational context of the Federal Republic of Germany, affords a less distorted interpretation. According to the statutes of the West German government, democracy is defined as the emancipation of the individual.[78] In art this means that the "myth of the original," the idea of a work of art of timeless value, creates a barrier between the viewer and an enlightened perception of the work. Furthermore, the viewer needs to be aware of the fact that

> . . . the work of art is a visualization of human consciousness and a document of specific socio-historic relationships and conditions; he needs to be aware that the function of art changes and with that the significance of individual objects. Works of art have meaning only in so far as they continue to produce effects in present thought and perception and that they are not the exclusive right of a certain class in society. Only when this is understood can the viewer relate to the work of art as an emancipated person.[79]

To demonstrate these points a group of young art educators and art historians researched and staged the exhibit "Altdorfer's Battle of Alexander— A Didactic Exhibition" in Munich in 1974, the year of the 150th anniversary of the Munich Art Association (Münchener Kunstverein).[80] The information leaflet for the exhibition explained its intention: (1) to investigate to what extent form expresses content; (2) to investigate the factors which influence perception (of a work of art) such as: the museum situation, the proliferation through mass media, interpretations of the work in art-literature, etc.; (3) which expressive means and which historical conditions combined to make possible the specific kind of representation of war in the *Battle of Alexander;* (4) to investigate the extent to which the crisis situation of the sixteenth century is reflected in the *Battle of Alexander* and which concept of history is expressed in the painting.

This was an art exhibition without an original work of art. Instead, Altdorfer's *Battle of Alexander* was featured as a photographic blow-up dissected into large squares to each of which were addressed specific questions relating to content. In addition there were all kinds of communications media: a video camera established the connection to the Pinakothek, allowing the observance of visitors in front of the original Altdorfer painting; there was a slide-show, hundreds of reproductions, graphs, pointers, illustrative materials, and finally, as examples of "active reception," the only "originals" of the exhibition: drawings by pupils based on studying the various aspects of the *Battle of Alexander.*

The aim is total education through rational analysis. In fact, such a process de-mythologizes the work of art, and as such, it is the reversal of the national-socialist approach to art.

The limit of this approach is that the unique aesthetic qualities of the painting are explained away, that Altdorfer's specific achievement has not been accounted for. The experiment of this unorthodox exhibition created a didactic model which may be applied to any reasonably complex work of art. The concepts for the didactic exhibition had grown out of work towards an alternative method to traditional art-education at the German high school level. Its propagators sought to revise art curricula along the lines of an interdisciplinary emphasis, to avoid the limitations of the style historical (*stilgeschichtlich*) approach. The goal was to permeate all subjects with political as well as aesthetic query (*Fragestellung*). Confronted with the painting of the *Battle of Alexander* the student should learn to approach it from the point of view of the various disciplines such as art history, history, German literature, Latin, Greek and religion. Furthermore the student should then learn to relate the knowledge gained to the following larger questions: he should be able to understand the work of art as concretized history and address to it questions which relate to his own interests; he should recognize that the interpretation of historical works of art may serve as a means to self-reflection, but that an interpretation also offers the possibility to *correct* the merely verbally transferred picture of history; he should recognize that the principles of class distinction between the privileged and the less privileged often are transferred symbolically from the realm of economics to that of *Kultur*, and that this phenomenon explains the elitist character of some museums.[81] The implementation of this level of awareness toward traditional (*"tradierte"*) works of art is hoped to preserve democracy as it endeavors to teach students not a utopian but a rational-political way of life.

The Quest to Identify Altdorfer's Intellectual and Spiritual Position

Das müsste gar eine schlechte Kunst sein, die
sich auf einmal fassen liesse, deren Letztes von
demjenigen gleich geschaut werden könnte, der
zuerst hereintritt.

—Goethe

Parallel to the persons who sought to put Altdorfer's art to the service of nationalistic or racialistic ideology, serious scholarship continued on the nature of Altdorfer's fifteenth and sixteenth century intellectual and spiritual influences. This chapter explores studies of Altdorfer's probable ties with, and influences from, major figures such as Paracelsus, Conrad Celtis, and movements such as the New Devotion (*devotio moderna*), sixteenth century northern Humanism and the Italian Renaissance.

Unlike Wölfflin, who asked *how* Altdorfer has been distinctive from other artists, Otto Benesch a generation later, asked *why* Altdorfer had been different. Benesch constructed his monograph (Vienna, 1939) on Altdorfer[1] around the assumption of a spiritual kinship and analogy between the painter and the physician-philosopher Theophrastes von Hohenheim, better known by his pseudonym Paracelsus (1439-1541). Paracelsus' worldview is thought to have found its most convincing visual correspondence in Altdorfer's paintings.

The Romantic movement of the early nineteenth century had generated renewed interest in Paracelsus, emphasizing the mystical aspects of his thought, culminating in Arthur Schnitzler's dramatic poem *Paracelsus* (1920).[2] Interpretation of Paracelsus in the second quarter of the twentieth century focused on the objective cognition inherent in his writing. Now a parallel is seen between Paracelsus' understanding of physical and spiritual man in his interdependence with the forces of nature, rather than as nature's end-in-itself. It is also seen in the renewed search, after an epoch of atomistic materialism stimulated by the electromagnetic theory of light, to understand all phenomena—all matter—in the context of a holistic theory (*Ganzheitslehre*). Central to Paracelsus' philosophy is the implication of the alchemist's command "*solve et coagula*" (dissolve and coagulate).[3] He thought that the primal act of creation, the emergence of nature, which is life, takes place through the separation of prime matter out of ultimate matter and perpetually resolving back into ultimate matter. This contains an idea, important for this context, of continuous movement, that is decay and generation. Human creativeness in art thus also repeated this primal act of separation and new synthesis. Artists were referred to, in Paracelsus' work, as alchemists.[4]

In his writing Paracelsus often used metaphorical comparisons from the activities of both painters and sculptors. Some passages contain beginnings of a symbolic theory of color. For example, when writing on the imagination:

> . . . as the sun physically affects work, and more, thus does the imagination. It gives the fire, and all tools, as does the sun. It wouldn't be necessary to have instruments [the sun] work through that which it lights . . . as does the imagination, the latter paints on its base, draws without anyone seeing its brush, its scalpel or paints.[5]

Benesch literally framed his book with such quotes from Paracelsus, but he also juxtaposed specific paintings with texts from his work. Paracelsus is the key which Benesch now hands over to the reader to do the unlocking of Altdorfer. The key should fit well because it was fashioned by the same times and places as that which it is commanded to unlock. At the beginning Benesch placed a Paracelsus paragraph on color:

> Then there are also the elemental particles, so that no perfect colors can be mentioned by name. What comes from them has its clearly understood or named colors. The elements do not possess perfect colors, rather the manner of painting. Thus not one but many colors grow from them. Therefore [the elemental bodies] comprise many colors.[6]

Color is seen as elemental force, as a natural principle (*Naturgewalt*), realized in and characterized by Altdorfer's art, according to Benesch.

The *Martyrdom of St. Catharine* (Vienna) is interpreted as an example of Paracelsus' cosmic-pantheistic thought, a slurring of optical phenomena and an all-penetrating animation of the imagery, an animism.[7] The Berlin diptychon of *Sts. Francis and Jerome* is compared with a passage on plants which deals with the transmutation of the elements; man becomes plantlike and plants become humanlike.

> This growth is like humans, because it has its skin, which is the shell; has its head and hair, which are the roots; its face and markings, its senses; has its sensitivity in its stems so that its injury follows in its death. . . .[8]

In describing the *Satyr Family* (Berlin) and the *Nativity* (Bremen) Benesch uses Paracelsian terminology in speaking of a pictorial microcosm

(*Bildmikrokosmos*), as well as a pandemonicism (Pandämonium), of "earth spirits" and "magic light."[9] The *Rest on the Flight to Egypt* is interpreted to illustrate the "genesis of a new cosmos" in which no distinction between living and dead matter is possible; the symbol of becoming and decay, the winged egg of the phoenix, crowns the image.[10]

The true content of the *Two Sts. John* (Regensburg; compare Plate 1) is, according to Benesch, a "painted cosmology," an illustration of Paracelsus' doctrine of the analogy between the macrocosm (nature) and the microcosm (man). The two saints are integrated with the wilderness into a piece of earth which pulsates with life, and yet, true to Paracelsus' belief in the divine origins of life, the whole is crowned with the vision of the apocalyptic Madonna, Mother of God.[11] Paracelsus is quoted again in order to underscore the purer, stronger coloration characteristic of Altdorfer's mature art, for example in the panels of the St. Florian legend, tending toward the simple, basic elements (*einfache Grundelemente*).

> To speak further of colors / I say / that all true / full colors are no more than six: Black, white, yellow, red, green and blue . . . Thus one can also understand closely related colors and color mixtures, as all painters testify / that it is possible from these six colors to derive over thirty colors / not one being like another.[12]

Benesch had compared the painting of the *Two Sts. John* with the Song of Songs of the Bible and claimed that it was Altdorfer's Song of Songs of Man becoming one with nature. When it came to the description of the *Battle of Alexander* Benesch offered a culmination of superlatives which takes the painting out of the realm of the humanly possible: it is an "overwhelming apotheosis," a "paracelsian chiromancy of the terrestrial globe."[13] Here again macrocosm and microcosm fuse, and the marvel lies in the fact that this "hundred voiced fugue" does not become inarticulate.

Continuity within the diversity of Altdorfer's art is seen in his ability to give painterly expression to the interpretation of the visible world. His being possessed a closeness to life, a directness which turned all perception of reality to an interpretation of the life-forces revealed in this reality. This is the meaning of Paracelsus' theory of chiromancy; a theory of the interpretation of expression.

> And you should know and recognize / that there are many chiromancies / not only those possessed by humans now / as we are prone to judge them by / and which you meet, both good and bad. Rather there are still other chiromancies: of medicinal plants / of tree leaves / of wood / of landscape / of the streets and rivers.[14]

These explorations by Benesch into the spiritual analogy between Paracelsus and Altdorfer were expanded and tested on the northern art of Paracelsus' time in general. G. F. Hartlaub, for example, followed Benesch's lead to seek substantiation of specific, although unconscious, correspondences between Paracelsus and artists of the time on the basis of morphological, stylistic, thematic, and iconographic similarities.[15] Of the painters and sculptors of the time analyzed, including Cranach, Hans Baldung Grien, Adam Krafft's *Sakramentshaus* in St. Lorenz (Nürnberg), the altar of Seven Pains by Douvermann in Kalkar, the Breisach High Altar of Master HL, Grünewald, Hans Witten, and others, Altdorfer's art is seen as the closest approximation and visual expression of this Paracelsian spirit, reflected in its "magical pandynamism."

The painting of the *Two Sts. John* reflects both Paracelsian organization and style as well as Paracelsian themes, according to Hartlaub. The organizational style of Paracelsus had been described by Benesch in terms of its alchemical or magical transformation, as if the whole cosmos were contained in a retort: ". . . out of the sea rises steam, which turns to smoke, and then crystallizes into mountains and snowfields, which in turn again transform into moving galleys of clouds, cliffs, and crystal formations, out of which there emerge cities; ships emerge as mineral formations from the water. . . ."[16] The Paracelsian subject of the painting is the appearance of the evangelist and the baptist as prophets and diviners, but especially as physicians and alchemists. The painter is seen to have emphasized their close relationship to nature by immersing them in a lush summer landscape and by surrounding them with plants, three of which are prominently portrayed because of their formidable healing and destructive powers: *sage* (Salvia pratensis L.), *henbane* (Hyoscyamus niger L.), and *mullein* (Verbascum Thrapsus L.).

Another writer, Lottlisla Behling, follows Benesch in attributing Altdorfer's artistic work to the Paracelsian connection. With regard to these three plants, she notes that Paracelsus had defended knowledge and use of medicinal plants for healing: ". . . all pastures, moors, mountains, and hills are pharmacies (*Apotheken*), God himself is the physician."[17] Of the plant sage the following is stated:

> The forest sage is called "Ambrosia of the Gods," because, as the legend tells us, the Gods became immortal when they ate it . . . and it is prescribed for the treatment of the lame and the epileptic. The toad is drawn to the roots and leaves of sage, but repelled if the sage is planted with rue.[18]

In Altdorfer's painting this plant is placed nearest the Evangelist John who had spoken of Christ as the Living Bread, the true physician, and thus the plant becomes, in this context, a symbol of salvation through Christ. It is depicted so as to check the hallucinatory faculty of the Evangelist. The central position is given to the henbane, which contrasts visually and symbolically with the lamb right behind it. This herb may be used to induce sleep, but it is also a poison which destroys the mind, according to Albertus Magnus.[19] Practitioners of black magic required the use of henbane to evoke the demons, according to the same source. The mullein (king's candle) next to John the Baptist was actually used as a candle, but also as a medicine for treatment of gout. In Upper Austria, on the feast day of John the Baptist, this plant is burned in the stable to protect the animals against evil; in Homer one reads that it was the plant Mercury gave Odysseus as a protection against the witchcraft of Circe.[20]

The theme of plant protection and invigoration occurs in yet other paintings by Altdorfer, and these also are explained with reference to Paracelsus. In *Susanna's Bath* the nettle (Urtica dioeca L.) is depicted behind the mullein, as if to juxtapose plants that are regarded as essentially evil and essentially good. Here and in other uses the combination of evil and good becomes dynamic, suggesting renewal and transformation from the former to the latter. This theme is central in Altdorfer's *Rest on the Flight to Egypt.* Instead of associating it with plants, however, visual prominence is given to another symbol of renewal, the mercurial fountain of life and the winged egg. Here again Paracelsus was held to be the inspiring source of imagery and idea for Altdorfer. Paracelsus, it was noted, held the firm conviction that the fountain, the origin of all knowledge, is God; from Him all things derive, and artists must be aware of this origin.[21]

Some writers base their claim of Altdorfer's dependence on Paracelsus on Altdorfer's "handwriting" and "style." This influence is suggested both in coffee table editions like Chastel and Klein's *World of Humanism*[22] and in scholarly works such as Gradmann's essay on the significance of the fantastic.[23] In the latter, Altdorfer's style can be seen most clearly in his drawings, where the Paracelsian philosophy is visualized in terms of emerging form and dissolving form (*Formwerdung und Formauflösung*).[24] The analysis of the drawing *The Dead Pyramus* (Berlin, W. Z. 27; Plate 7) exemplifies how a rhythmic structure of Altdorfer's drawing style generates a multiplicity of phenomena and at the same time the highlighted patterns negate all substance and emphasize the transitory. The theme of the drawing itself is that of fluid transition, transformation, metamorphosis of matter—a principle of combustion—as the dead soldier's gestalt merges with earth and vegetation surrounding him.[25] This exemplifies in its very form the Paracelsian idea that decomposition is the beginning of all birth. If one speaks of Paracelsus' belief in animism, magic, and pantheism in connection with Altdorfer's art one ought to go the next logical step and consider the probability of a spiritual commonality between the science of alchemy and Altdorfer's artistic procedures and visions. Paracelsus thought of the visual arts as a kind of alchemy; in turn he called alchemy an "art." To him "art" meant the creative changing of the raw and the formless into form, and with that, into the realm of the spiritual; a liberation and purification of qualities and possibilities inherent in matter. The concept of the artist's activity is that his work lies hidden in nature and in his materials and needs only to be "recovered." Thus the creative process is understood as a continuation of the generative processes in nature.[26]

The medium of the etching is perhaps most closely related to the spiritual attitude of the alchemist. The technique was developed within the boundaries of knowledge and the specific consciousness of alchemy according to Alexander Friedrich's book on process and form of etching and engraving.[27] The primary process in etching is that of disintegration, destruction of the copper plate through the action of the acid; only then is the emergence of new form possible. Etching demands of the artist mastery and application of elemental functions; he needs to let the etching happen, the control being in the artist's intimate knowledge of the elements and forces in nature. This is not a passive process; rather the acknowledgment of other powers.[28] Altdorfer's landscape etchings (W. Gr. 175-183) may be seen to illustrate this process.

Benesch, who in the late 1930s was the first to call attention to Paracelsus in order to circumscribe the intellectual-spiritual provenance of Altdorfer's particular style and content, did so at a time when one did not ask Gretchen's question to Faust: "Und wie hältst Du's mit der Religion?" But a generation later Alfred Stange did ask that question of the Danube School painters and with that of Altdorfer as well. He saw his art as the reflection of the New Devotion, the *devotio moderna* whose foremost teachers and practitioners had been Thomas of Kempen (1379-1471) through his *Imitation of Christ* and Nicolas Cusanus (1401-1461). Since the New Devotion had its roots in mysticism it allowed for subjective inward perception and taught the sanctification of daily life without the renunciation of the world. Alfred Stange characterized this influence with the following quotation from Thomas of Kempen:

> One should not think too highly of oneself, or vaunt oneself because of one's art or science; rather, one should acknowledge one's ignorance. One should not be proud of good works; wherever one goes, repose will only be found in humble obedience. He who works out of love, will accomplish much; true love unites with God. One cannot always live on the higher levels of contemplation, one must also carry lowly things and the weight of mortal life. Nature, the Holy Writ, and all of creation should be studied by man so as to draw utility from them, but not more than this, since one should live in spiritual moderation.[29]

According to Stange, Altdorfer takes his orientation not from the concept of the *uomo universale* of Humanism, but he allows his figures to proclaim the spirit of *devotio moderna*. His men are at peace with themselves, not because of the fulfillment of their natural characters, but because they rest in God. In Him their earthly and daily life healed. These figures are earthy, and customary persons; Altdorfer's *Holy Family with St. John* (Vienna) illustrates this theme.[30] In Stange's portrayal, Altdorfer was above all a religious man, a religious artist.[31] In the woodcut of a *Young Priest Praying before a Virgin and*

Child Enthroned (W. Gr. 87) the young clergyman is not the conventional donor portrait, rather he impersonates Altdorfer's personal creed, expressed also in the many works devoted to the mariological theme, including those which he executed in connection with the cult of the Beautiful Mary, culminating in the Munich *Madonna in Glory.*

The adjective which Stange uses to characterize the emotional level of the *devotio moderna* is "quiet"; their best was given by the Danube School painters in 'quiet' pictures."[32] Quiet empathy, a quiet sorrow, feelings of compassion rather than pain, suffering grief, these were the emotions they depicted. This is exemplified in the crucifixion scenes in Nürnberg and in Berlin; or the *Leavetaking of Christ from his Mother* or the *Separation of the Apostles* (Berlin). Stange suggested that this same disposition, which has its roots in the *devotio moderna,* also is characteristic of contemporary mythology-based literary themes such as "Marcus Curtius," "Horatius Cocles" or "Pyramus and Thisbe," themes which could be interpreted to illustrate the Christian notions of sacrifice and love. Finally the piety of *devotio moderna* is captured and again expressed in Altdorfer's few portraits: the *Portrait of a Canon* (private coll., 1520), that of *A Woman* (Castagnola) and the donor portrait of the St. Florian altarpiece. In all of these, the expression of the eyes is "quiet" and kind, of "mysterious solemn inwardness."[33] Stange understood the particuliar religiosity of the New Devotion to be the major undercurrent for Altdorfer's art, but not exclusively so. He relies on the analogy with Paracelsus' philosophy, as Benesch had done, to explain the new relationship to nature and its major role as subject and theme in Altdorfer's art. He quotes Paracelsus' metaphor of man's plantlike organism, and he quotes numerous passages on color, some of which he feels read like descriptions of paintings by Altdorfer.[34]

The kinship between Altdorfer and Paracelsus also rests, Stange thinks, on their mutual faith and love of fellowman as the primary reason for their work. This is where he links Paracelsus to the main theme of *devotio moderna.*

Stange's description of the *Battle of Alexander* is written to fit the Paracelsian scheme: micro- and macrocosm have become in this picture a universal symphony of colors and forms flowing together against one another into a thousand contradictory yet intertwined variations and nuances. The beauty of the painting, however, rests on the elevation of an earthly slaughter ground to a cosmic event. It is a cosmically played out battle of painterly movements, a painterly and musically based monumentality.[35]

Stange and others have claimed that the New Devotion was also a widespread popular movement, not only an exclusive speculative theology. Its ideas were disseminated through sermons, mostly propagated by the Augustinian monks.[36] The idea of the sanctification of everyday life and activity generated a widespread lay piety through popular sermons and art commissioned by those monasteries on the Danube which were centers of the *devotio moderna* move-ment.[37] Thus, because of the popular, homely emphasis of *devotio moderna* piety, Altdorfer and the other Danube style painters were most sure, most con-vincing, when painting their own people, as for example the Mary Magdalen of the Berlin *Crucifixion,* the women of the Susanna painting (Munich), and above all the folk surrounding the *Miraculous Fountain* of the St. Florian cycle (private collection).

Almost all scholars agree that the art of the Danube School is related in a special way to the people. In contrast to Stange, Franz Lipp pointed out that during the years 1490 to 1525 the religiosity of the people was not directed by the spirit of *devotio moderna* but by the belief in salvation through "works."[38] The statistics of votive offerings and donations to monasteries and churches during this period are staggering. Lipp argues that this attitude toward sanctifying work (*"Werkheiligkeit"*) was more widespread than *devotio moderna,* in fact that *devotio antiqua sive rustica* stood in *contrast* to *devotio moderna.* The former was the religious vehicle of the people. The latter with its postulate of sanctification of daily life without negation of the world, combined with a new attitude toward nature, could only be realized through Humanism and the Reformation. Therefore it was shared only by the intellectual and artistic elite. Artists such as Cranach, Dürer, Altdorfer, and Huber had been devotees of this new religiosity and *Lebensgefühl.* Thus the New Devotion may be seen as existing in a tense relationship with the traditional materially-oriented piety. Lipp argues that from this tension between artists and the people grew a convergence between artist and people, a new awareness, on the part of the artist, of the people.[39]

The prime example for Altdorfer's alleged acknowledgment of his people-hood (*Volkstum*) is his panel of the *Miraculous Fountain in St. Florian,* hailed by Stange as the earliest precipitator of Dutch genre painting, a painting depicting, in Stange's terminology, a "happening" with journalistic flair for the factual. The dress exactly replicates the commoner's garb of the day and indicates the social class to which each person belongs. Topographically as well as ethnographically the work is also an exact rendering of the common man's belief in the healing powers of the spring next to the church dedicated to John the Baptist and St. Florian in the town of St. Florian. The painting documents the people as carriers of the faith and religious zeal as expression of the soul of the people.[40]

Another controversial issue in the scholarly study of formative impulses on Altdorfer's art is the impact Italian art and thought may have had. Rasmo's inquiry into the possibility of an Altdorfer journey to Italy is representative of this aspect of Altdorfer scholarship. Rasmo's goal is to investigate the pre-con-ditions and the development of Altdorfer and the Danube School from the Italian point of view. He is basically in agreement with Benesch, Stange, and others that the new element is not the discovery of landscape *per se* but rather the special new experience of landscape viewed as the cosmic reflector (*Schallspiegel*) of the human soul. The roots of this attitude may be found in St. Francis of Assisi's *Cantico delle Creature.*[41]

Rasmo is convinced that during the years of his training (sometime between 1496 and 1505) Altdorfer journeyed to Venice where he became acquainted with the work of Giovanni Bellini.[42] Bellini had transformed Mantegna's Renaissance ideas into a lyrical, inner mode of vision which discloses the essence of form through atmosphere.[43]

> This atmosphere which imbues all colors with tonal luminosity; the predominantly contemplative harmony between man and nature; the bestowing of soul to landscape, giving it a living, many mooded, tension-filled presence; these are the fundamental insights which Altdorfer owes to Venetian painting.[44]

Altdorfer's *Satyr Family* is thought to owe its inception to one of the popular small-scale capricci such as Bellini's *Allegory*. Altdorfer's *Christ in the Garden of Gethsemane* is indebted to Bellini's *Mount of Olives* (London, National Gallery). The *St. George* of 1510 is thought to be dependent on Bellini's *Martyrdom of St. Peter* (London, National Gallery). Likewise, the *Virgin between St. Joseph and John Evangelist* (Vienna) and the *Beautiful Mary* (Regensburg) are thought to be derived from Bellini prototypes.[45] The *Nativity* in Bremen is linked to Leonardo's *Adoration of the Kings* in the Uffizi, and the *Birth of Mary* (in Munich) is believed unthinkable without Altdorfer's knowledge of Bramante's work.[46] Altdorfer's late style as well, Rasmo claims, owes essential stimuli to Italian art: for example, the dependence of Altdorfer's frescoes of the Bishop's palace in Regensburg upon Longhi's architecture and Dossi's and Romanino's frescoes in the Castello of Trient. The reclining nude in Altdorfer's *Lot and his Daughters* is allegedly inspired by Titian's ideal of female beauty, his Venus. In terms of traceable Venetian influence Altdorfer's painting of the *Martyrdom of St. Florian* (Uffizi) is acclaimed by Rasmo as one of Altdorfer's finest achievements. Venice had taught the balance of man and nature; Altdorfer added the elemental dimension of the tragic, a mystical duality which was absent in Italy. This line of argument then left nothing at all to say about Altdorfer's *Battle of Alexander,* the author's implication being that it is one of Altdorfer's most "German" works.

Carl Linfert's interpretation of Altdorfer's art focuses more on themes which were widespread in European art of the time. In a 1938 essay, "The Unveiling of Landcape," he notes that at the turn of the sixteenth century landscape and nature in German art had very special significance. Linfert's title "the unveiling" suggests sexual overtones; in German, landscape and nature carry a feminine gender. Nature "beckons, yet remains wondrous, mysterious, strange."[47] It possesses at times a "sexual appetite."[48] At the turn of the sixteenth century, during the transition from the medieval order which had been determined by the transcendental, there was an overwhelming desire to discover nature. Altdorfer is seen as the artist whose work best illuminates this transition from one world-view to another. Altdorfer's pictorial image is that of nature having "caught fire from within." The transcendental dimension is not completely lost in the process, but it now seems to spring from nature whereas formerly nature had needed to be illuminated from the heavens above.

Because nature to Altdorfer was not a segment, but a projection of geological formations, believes Linfert, he created the image of "eruption" (*Ausbruch*) such as the explosive crater in the drawing of the *Deathly Leap of Marcus Curtius* and the sun-crater in the *Battle of Alexander.*

> . . . The heavens swirl in flames, on the one hand, and dissolve into ethereal, airless ice on the other; in both is the illusion conveyed that the sky, like the smoking earth, is seen from above. That which is to be seen of the earth encircles this unreliable crater of sky like a rim of rubble and brush. No longer does the sky provide a vault for the earth, or bounds it quietly as a distant backdrop. No restful point exists from which one might enter this picture. However, emerging from out of the sun crater the eye comes to rest as on a shore. It is more a map than a picture; but a map of events rather than of places.
> . . . The sky is a sea in which paths cannot be fixed, neither for God nor for Man. Below, in the shadows, humans fight their battles. Dominating here is a precise and sober grasp of power relations and the use of domination. However things may have been only a moment before [in the battle scene], there is none of the catastrophic puzzle which characterizes the heavens. The battle is an event carefully depicted just like any other quieter scene such as that portrayed in the camp of the distant town. But here begins Altdorfer's real uniqueness—even in those remote "idylls" there still is to be found that sparkling, glowing light emitted by the whirling eruption in the clouds.[49]

Nature, in this view, and seen "cosmically," conveys a sense of fright and the incomprehensible threat of the elements. This is observed by Linfert in Altdorfer's three Nativity scenes in Bremen, Berlin, and Vienna. The night is not dissolved, although the sun enters in a swirling crater of light, an uncanny gassy ball. The images of eruption and peacefulness simultaneously present in these nativities are not seen to contradict each other; all scenes contain both the fiery as well as the petrified, lapidary "element." The *Adoration* (Frankfurt) for example and other "quiet" images seem to represent the remainder of that first eruptive vision; it is the fiery glow of the ruins from which emanates light; they represent both natural destruction and unobtrusive protection. Ruins, once dams against the course of time, testify to the course of nature.[50]

In this view of nature, it is the purpose of architecture to gain control of this daring disclosure of nature. In some paintings, such as *Susanna's Bath* (see Plate 6) the buildings are not ruins, but palaces based on Italian Renaissance prototypes. Nevertheless, in these latter, the "fine many-layered many-faceted form of the Medieval north is preserved."[51] Although the details appear to be functional, the building is in fact almost impossible to enter. It is a symbol, a sign which contrasts with that which is merely an illusionistic image tied to the picture space with linear relationships, obeying laws of perspective. Landscape is treated sometimes in a similarly ambiguous way Linfert feels. The *Separation of the Apostles* (Berlin) is a painting about the beginning of the new discovery of nature.[52] Roads lead into several directions, but the treacherousness of their paths prevails ominously. To emphasize this visually the natural perspective is frequently interrupted. Nature is the new miracle continually being sought by man. That which seems mutually contradictory in much of Altdorfer's art comes together to form the prevailing image of it:

> The crater cools into a refuge, but the protective place does not completely protect from all danger. That which appears to be a crater, is not only a fountain of fire, it is also beautiful sea, beckoning light and glistening storm; out of the hard rock earth emerge strongly stated extremes: fire and forest. Each has in Altdorfer's work the form of rays, that strangely pulling line, as if rays of light and growth were of the same nature. Men intertwine with these rays of light and of growth in a manner which is singular to German art, and this perception of nature cannot be interpreted as an idyll. The harshness of the minute multiplicity and endlessness, is the more significant.[53]

Linfert believes that Altdorfer's perception of nature is fascinated with nature's double origin: eruption (the same as Paracelsus' principle of combustion) and decay. In Altdorfer's art nature appears as if he had discovered her for the very first time: everything is laid bare and recorded with equal minutia. The eye is chased to a thousand places as it follows the volcanic fire which seems to be immanent in each of Altdorfer's pictures. All is composed of flickering elements which do not tolerate fixed form but which contain all forms and produce and release them desultorily.[54]

Linfert's essay does not mention Paracelsus, but the emphasis is similar to that of Benesch, perhaps even closer to Paracelsus, who had believed in the theory that decay is the beginning of all birth, and that the combustible principle, sulfur, is more important in the process of creation than elementary fire.[55] Linfert's argument was directed against those, such as Pinder and Hamann, who interpreted Altdorfer as a "Romantic" portraying "idylls."

The influence of humanism, and particularly Konrad Celtis, leader of the *sodalitas danubiensis,* upon Altdorfer and the vision of early sixteenth century artists, was studied by Karl Öttinger[56] and shrouded in a Freudian view of history. He interprets the historical process, and its reflection in art, as the vying for dominance between the male and the female principle. This leads him to development of a theory of sacred art, with the claim that ". . . as the forest belongs to the man, the hunter, so the garden belongs to the woman. The bower is her symbol, the holiness of growth is female."[57] Öttinger argues that the cathedral of the thirteenth century was expressive of a balance between the male and the female principle and he cites the example of the Crowning of the

Virgin above the West portal in Reims cathedral. The period around 1400 appears to have undergone, at least within the framework of Christian religion, a matriarchal phase. But Öttinger sees in what he calls "the extremely feminine ideal of the celestial garden" the beginning of decline: "The sentimental sensibility of mariolatry now dominates also the male protagonists."[58]

During this same period, around 1490, it was Konrad Celtis who "tore open the garden, broke out of the garden and discovered the forest, the stream and the open landscape." Enthused by Tacitus' *Germania* Celtis praised the life of the forebears which was close to nature and especially their worship in the open grove. These and related thoughts of Celtis, Öttinger believes, inspired a new perception of nature and a new vision in German painters around 1500,[59] which also led to a new conception of the image of the Virgin: she leaves the loggia (*Laube*) and the garden and enters the vastness of the open landscape and the forest. The theme of the *Rest on the Flight to Egypt* provided a welcome excuse for this change to happen, such as Altdorfer's version of 1511. Now the masculine element asserts itself again because forest and open landscape are expressive of and belong rather to the male principle.[60] This process Altdorfer rendered in visual terms in his *Susanna*; the Christian interpretation of the Susanna theme sees her as a prototype of Mary, symbolizing Marian virtues, but at the same time the unbounded forest encroaches upon the garden. Altdorfer depicted other religious themes similarly, as in the *St. George* (Plate 8) and the *Separation of the Apostles* where the dominant limitless forest and landscape seem to cast the traditional themes in a new light and seem to call for a new interpretation of the traditional themes. This transition from the garden to the dominance of the forest in sacred art of the early sixteenth century is reflected also in the then popular theme of wild men and witches, examples of which may be found particularly in Altdorfer's early engravings and drawings.

Another motif first introduced by Celtis and used by Altdorfer is the Italian derived garland, the "humanist's symbol of dignity, honour and victory,"[61] though in Altdorfer's work it has a far less central importance than the forest and the open countryside.

A more recent study attempted to portray Altdorfer as a humanist in the context of his imperial city.[62] In the first part of the essay the author traced Altdorfer's career in terms of the social role he played in Regensburg, such as the office of judicial supervision of the craftsmen, of ombudsman, of city councillor, of diplomatic emissary guided by the hope for peace and justice. If humanism is defined as a balance between life and work, then one may argue that humanism determined all aspects of Altdorfer's life. The author sought to substantiate this thesis by pointing out that according to the inventory of Altdorfer's estate his large garden had been used for agricultural purposes, and this in turn may be interpreted as putting into practice what Celtis had inspired: the revival of horticulture as it had been practiced in the Augustan period of ancient Rome. Altdorfer's intimate relationship to nature may be traced to the influence of the Viennese humanist and his circle and so may Altdorfer's penchant for cosmological speculation. Both of these traits are illustrated by Altdorfer in what needs to be considered his most genuinely autobiographical statement, his Ex Voto painting commonly referred to as the *Rest on the Flight to Egypt*. The author claims that the *Bukolika* translation of the Strassburg physician and humanist Adelphus Mülig, who cites Ovid and Ficino as his sources provides the key to the iconography of the puzzling fountain configuration and possibly its source.[63] Accordingly, the male figure which crowns the fountain is Saturn as he reigns over the Golden Age, e.g., Christian Paradise; the small boy on Saturn's right side is Eros while opposite Eros Saturn holds the cosmic egg (*Weltenei*), alchemically speaking, the *prima materia*. In this humanistic context the Virgin then must be interpreted as the personification of the New Justice of the Golden Age, as the *fons justitiae* of Christian doctrine. This explains her high-style dress and her throne-like chair, the prerogative of a judge. The ruins of man's world in the background are the remnants of the Iron Age which is now superseded by the Golden Age.[64] This fusion of Christian religion with the moralistic interpretation of the literary tradition of Classical antiquity indeed qualifies Altdorfer to be called a humanist.

The Cranach scholar Dieter Koepplin used the intrinsic method of iconographic inquiry and style analysis in order to establish the particular quality of Altdorfer's vision. Guided and inspired by Roth's and Schöne's studies on the history of light in painting[65] Koepplin investigated the motif of the constellation of the sun as a leitmotiv in Altdorfer's work.[66] He argued that Altdorfer's use of the sun-motif derived from the suprapersonal pictorial tradition of the halo, and that therefore it retains the quality of a sacred presence. Altdorfer employed the motif in his paintings, woodcuts, and engravings when he intended to give gestalt to the representation of a religious experience (*Erlebnis*). This presupposes a simultaneous and equally strong experience of darkness, an experience which was fostered and encouraged by the humanistic fascination with magic, demons, and animalistic "blind" passion. Koepplin refers to Altdorfer's engraving of St. Christopher (1515-20, W. Gr. 124) as the most poignant example of the completely new, unprecedented interpretation with which Altdorfer depicts the sun and which reflects a philosophical reorientation. Because Altdorfer bends the rays of the sun it assumes consequently a different reality. The perspective foreshortening of the dome of rays suggests the immanence of the sun's movement, which introduces unrest and therefore anxiety in the beholder. A contributing factor to this newly introduced unrest and anxiety is the tension between St. Christopher in the foreground and the sun which is at once the least corporeal and the most active form in the picture.[67] Furthermore, because the sun behind St.

Christopher is still surrounded by night it evokes associations with a monumental star and with those foreboding astrological speculations which constituted such a major preoccupation in Altdorfer's time.[68] On the other hand, the symbolic meaning of the sun within the context of the St. Christopher legend is primarily Christian. It refers to the Coming of Christ to one still blind, but ready to accept faith. Thus the meaning of the sun as Altdorfer interprets it in the St. Christopher engraving vascillates between a promise of salvation and an ominous power of fate.

Koepplin feels that this ambivalence is characteristic of the art of Altdorfer and the Danube School in general. One need only look at the numerous images which depict a coexistence of both dying as well as profusely growing nature, the frequent motif of the dead, leafless branch in the midst of sprouting vegetation, or the medicinal as well as poisonous plants on the painting of the *Two Sts. John.* This vision which unifies the complementarity of opposites (*ganzheitliche Doppelwertigkeit*) contributes to the "mythical" character of this art. Saran's iconographic analysis and Linfert's literary interpretation of Altdorfer's art had pointed out this same characteristic.

The Eye of Darius: Altdorfer Interpretations in Kokoschka and Other Modern Artists

Denn der aller edelst Sinn des Menschen ist das
Gesicht. Darum ein jedlich Ding, das wir sehen,
ist uns glaublicher und beständiger weder das wir
hören.

—Dürer[1]

An artist's creative use of a fellow artist's work may also be regarded as a form of criticism, most certainly as one kind of *Rezeption*. Here a distinction needs to be made between a spiritless or simple transferral of motifs as in the case of the Nürnberg artists Hans Lautensack (ca. 1520-1554/5) and Augustin Hirschvogel (1503-1553)[2] and those whose contact with Altdorfer's work showed their own creative endeavors. Oskar Kokoschka (1886-1980) represents the epitome of critical and creative Altdorfer *Rezeption* in his paintings as well as in his writings.

The earliest such instance of creative Altdorfer-*Rezeption* by an artist may be seen in some of the work of Adam Elsheimer (1578-1610). His teacher Philipp Uffenbach introduced him to the tradition of old German painting. Then his artistic pilgrimage, which ended in Rome, took him to Munich and Venice, both places which may have afforded him increased knowledge of Altdorfer's art. Elsheimer shared Altdorfer's love of nature and of landscape; his work shows a similar preference for the small format on which he achieved the illusion of vast space. Both artists employ light to model form, and more importantly, to function as the visible emanation of the spiritual. Elsheimer's painting of the *Holy Family with Angels* (ca. 1598-1600, Berlin) in particular contains not only Altdorfer's characteristic oblique arrangement of figural groups but also an almost literal repetition of the figure of Joseph as it appears in his *Rest on the Flight to Egypt*. The iconographic type of the holy family with angels may be traced to Altdorfer as precursor as well. But perhaps it is to Venice that both paintings owe their material and spiritual kinship.[3]

Another painting which is particularly reminiscent of Altdorfer is Elsheimer's *Three Maries at the Tomb of Christ* (Bonn, ca. 1603-05).[4] Each scholar of Elsheimer has remarked on a kinship with Altdorfer,[5] and at least two Altdorfer scholars call on Elsheimer's name in order to elucidate, for example, the quality of the late Berlin *Landscape with Allegory* as anticipating Elsheimer's "quietly-solemn joining of figure and landscape," and the central motif in the *Separation of the Apostles* is also thought to anticipate Elsheimer.[6] Elsheimer indeed seems to have continued aspects of Altdorfer's late style. He was active when taste of the Baroque had not yet obliterated the perception of the forward-looking trends of the immediate artistic past.

If it is impossible through documentary evidence to establish proof of an artistic fertilization between Altdorfer and Elsheimer, whose life barely touched the periphery of Altdorfer, then one may ask if such a link may be established more readily with artists who trained or were active in Regensburg. The eighteenth century yields only two such names, and their work may be only superficially linked with Altdorfer's because their main subject is landscape illuminated with the muted tones of dusk or moonlight. The first, Christoph Ludwig Agricola (1667-1719), worked in the tradition of the French heroic landscape of Poussin and Lorrain.[7] If Altdorfer's spirit had touched him at all it is manifest in the *absence* of heroic pathos in his landscapes. The second, Peter von Bemmel, was born in Nürnberg and died in Regensburg (1685-1754).[8] He specialized in landscape paintings and etchings, a series of which he printed in Regensburg in 1716.

In the nineteenth century the work of Caspar David Friedrich (1774-1840) appears to have a material and spiritual kinship with Altdorfer, but close examination and comparison of similar themes only illustrates the conceptual difference between the two artists. Certain aspects of Altdorfer's treatment of landscape may be cited as the earliest prototypes for C. D. Friedrich's work. The representation of nature and landscape is shown not only as the *locus amoenus* but also as a metaphor of destructive elemental forces. It is specifically the motif of the cross in a special relationship with the landscape which recurs in Friedrich's work and which may be traced to Altdorfer, particularly to the Berlin *Crucifixion*.[9] Von Einem made the poignant observation that the historical episode which actually is represented here for the first time is the moment *between* crucifixion and deposition. The silhouette of the three crosses against the agitated evening sky and the quiet contained figure of Mary Magdalene with its back to the viewer convey the *mood* of the painting. The cross of the Tetschener Altarpiece (Dresden, 1807/8) is not the historically objective cross of Golgotha but a symbol of faith. The evergreen of the firs is symbolic of the hope of redemption. Instead of the historically objective basis of religious painting of the early sixteenth century, C. D. Friedrich's work represents the symbolic or conceptual essence of a "solitary confession."[10]

W. Pinder, in his essay on Romanticism in German art around 1500, suggests that the "Friedrich" of that time was named "Altdorfer."[11] He also established a comparison with Philipp Otto Runge's (1777-1810) *Rest on the Flight to Egypt* (1805/6). Pinder suggests that both Friedrich and Runge strive in their work to transfer to nature the emotions of the human soul, to create what he calls the *"beseelte Landschaft."* But their form is dominantly tectonic and linear, and there is no hint of a transfer of human emotion into the representation of nature to the degree achieved by Altdorfer.

A fuller and more effective use of Altdorfer's vision is represented in the work of surrealist artist Max Ernst (born 1891), whose own testimony acknowledges Altdorfer's impact on him. In 1941 at the age of fifty, Ernst was asked to recollect poets and painters from whom he had drawn inspiration. Next to Grünewald, Lukas Cranach, Nikolas Manuel Deutsch he listed Albrecht Altdorfer.[12] In some of his paintings Altdorfer appears in surrealist guise. A recurrent theme—perhaps the most important—is that of the forest in conjunction with glowing celestial bodies, double rings, and circles, which may be interpreted as sun or moon or both, creating images of cosmic resonance and order. Both motifs, the forest and the sun, are dominant in Altdorfer. The organic, biomorphic quality of Altdorfer's style is also present, as a predominant characteristic, in Ernst's art, even though he arrives at it by means of a very different technique, the frottage. This consists of rubbing to capture the pre-existing organic structure of something like wood, which is the unifying principle that determines emergent structure or vision. In his childhood Ernst's fantasy was captivated by the forest. He experienced it as protection, as fountain of life, but also as ambivalent, suggesting freedom of open space as well as hostility and the threat of potential danger in its dense vegetation. Between the years 1926-44 and again in the 1960s, Ernst created numerous paintings of the forest, such as *La Foresta Imbalsamata* (1933) and *The Last Forest* (1960-69, Plate 9), or the series called "The Horde" which may be linked to the "Wild Man" theme in Altdorfer's early works. This ever-present ambivalence between good and evil, between the security of the known and the insecurity of the unknown, is characteristic too of Altdorfer's treatment of the forest, the best example being the *St. George* (Munich) of 1510. Altdorfer's sun is primarily the symbol of religious order; Ernst's sun is the symbol of the spirit of the painter who masters the evocations of his memory and his visions.

Georg Grosz (1893-1959), painter of the New Objectivity school in Germany, also drew inspiration from Altdorfer. This was discussed by him in a satirical article published in 1931, the last year of the Weimar Republic.[13] The article was entitled ". . . among other things, a word for German tradition," and was for the most part a stinging social criticism that has surprising relevancy 40 years later. Materialism has corrupted men and has caused the loss of religion and ideals of human rights of freedom and dignity, he argued. The artists are alienated from the people, and find their escape in abstraction. Like Kokoschka later, Grosz attacks nonrepresentational art, asserting that the artist's task in such faithless and materialist times as these is to show men their "hidden devil's grimace."[14] This may be accomplished not by an orientation along the current French schools but by the recollection and continuation of (*Anknüpfung*) their own native tradition: ". . . look at them, Multscher, Bosch, Breughel and Malesskircher, Huber and Altdorfer, they did not know the standardization-and-keep-smiling concept."[15] In his discussion of this tradition, he put "German" in quotation marks to distinguish it from the painters of a so-called German tradition who pulled the wool over people's eyes with their cute, sentimental, and pathetic rendering of life. He predicted an epoch similar to the waning Middle Ages, full of terror. In contrast to his own time, he believed that the Middle Ages had been fruitful to the artist, who had been able to face the upheavals. The National Socialists used the slogan "German tradition" as a halo to strengthen their political goals. Grosz called for a continuation with the tradition of the aforementioned artists because he felt they had artistically drawn from their own soil, and that they were critical artists.[16]

These opinions had grown directly from Grosz's experience. The world economic crisis of 1929 had shattered all illusion of stability. Grosz himself had been tried for blasphemy because of his 1927 drawing *Christ with Gasmask*. He was exploring new avenues toward pure painting, eliminating drawing as the artist's primal act.[17] Traces of direct inspiration from Altdorfer cannot be found in his work of the late twenties. The *Kunstblatt* article precedes his emigration for the United States, at this time, only a few days before the Nazis take power and burn his books.[18] In the United States he must redefine himself as an artist in his own right. "I have no illusions left. One has to survive. That's all . . . the field for me is the field of my art."[19] From 1933 on, his work begins to reflect a different transformation of reality, including nature studies, some with a decisive painterly treatment. "Nature is rejuvenating like spring water," wrote Grosz.[20] As in Altdorfer, C. D. Friedrich and Max Ernst's rendering of nature, a painting such as Grosz's *Central Park at Night* (1933)[21] or his pen and ink drawing *Hansel and Gretel* (1934)[22] portrays nature as being ominous. His pen and ink drawing *Rocks and Ferns at Bornholm* (1935)[23] attests to his discovery of the pantheistic feeling manifest in plant and nature studies by Dürer, Altdorfer, and Huber. *Rocks and Moon* (1936)[24] receives its compelling aura from the crater-like opening around the celestial body of light, light which flickers and dances as in Altdorfer's *Bremen Nativity*. Grosz's pen and ink drawing *No Let Up* (1936)[25] appears like an atheistic inversion of the St. Christopher motif so popular in the early sixteenth century and so frequent in

Altdorfer's graphic work. The shore to be reached had disappeared, the sun is black, without power; there is no other transcending, more powerful light than a man-made candle. Finally, *Apocalyptic Landscape* (1937)[26] is reminiscent of the apocalyptic "fire in the flood" of Altdorfer's painting of *Lot and His Daughters*. This painting appears the same year Grosz's work is included in the Degenerate Art Exhibition in Munich.

Otto Dix, another artist of the New Objectivity school, drew inspiration from Altdorfer and fellow sixteenth century German masters. Dix (1891-1969) was banned from his professorship at the Dresden Academy in 1933, the year of the spiritual collapse of Germany. Not only was he forbidden to exhibit his works, 260 of them were confiscated, sold or destroyed.[27] During the following years of banishment within his own country he escaped into the exploration of landscape. It is Dix's landscape painting of this period which has suggested comparisons with Altdorfer (Plate 10).[28] He discovered in nature the same demonic qualities which he had once depicted in his images of men and women, and which are present in Hans Baldung Grien and Altdorfer. His techniques were similar to those of the early German masters, with sharply constrasted light and dark tones. Some similar motifs were chosen. A Christophorus series, in six variations, allegorical and political in nature rather than Christian, was done during the 1938-44 resistance period.[29] The symbolic interpretation of the Christophorous motif is that of a man carrying the personification of *Logos* (spirit) through the dangers of the times and thus preserving it, a most timely theme for the years 1933-45. Other motifs from the Old German tradition appear in his work, such as *Melancholy, Vanitas, Witch, Seven Deadly Sins, Triumph of Death, Temptation of St. Anthony*. A 1939 painting *Lot and His Daughters* depicts the flaming background of war-torn German cities.[30] His abbreviated signature, the abstracted, schematized initial of his name, is a tribute to his self-conscious continuation of the Old German tradition:

> . . . in protest against aestheticizing painterly finery, Dix wanted to paint in an unpaint-erly way, objectively, critically, unsentimentally, with horror of all the pathos around him. He found this in the old German masters . . . so he used their themes, titles, schemes of composition, their techniques.[31]

Altdorfer had not only captured the imagination of German artists during their personally and politically trying times of the twenties and thirties. During one week of November, 1953, Pablo Picasso copied and designed lithographs after black and white reproductions in Otto Benesch's Altdorfer monograph which Daniel Henry Kahnweiler had lent him. "I made some Altdorfers for you," he told Kahnweiler. He had indeed signed some in Gothic letters "Albrecht Altdorfer." Picasso's attention focused particularly on one Altdorfer painting which had never till then received special attention in the body of criticism on his work: the *Finding of the Body of St. Sebastian,* one panel in the St. Florian altarpiece. Within this panel Picasso focused on one motif, the very young, ornately dressed, gentlewoman on the right, kneeling in a most devout manner. Her most compelling presence resides in the gesture of her hands. This woman and her gesture Picasso tries to recapture, as well as the transformation into a graphic pattern of the rich, varied tones and textures of her dress (Plates 11 and 12).

The only other German master Picasso had copied was Lukas Cranach, as early as 1942.[33] Such "copies" are always reinterpretations, a new discovery with the visual means of our time of the seemingly closed visual world of the original. Art may thus overcome time and space. Picasso's choice of works thus reworked was autobiographical, bearing witness to his love, at a particular moment, of a theme or image, in this case Altdorfer's young woman. Kahnweiler reports Picasso to have said of the drawing:

> How good that is, Altdorfer. It's all there, a small leaf on the ground, a cracked brick— not one like the other. All the details are integrated. Beautiful. Later, all that was lost. Maybe that is progress, but that is a different subject. . . . one should copy these things as used to be done. But I know well, one will not be able to understand.[34]

Picasso has said at various times that for him the creative process counts more than the finished result, the historically completed work. Thus he sees in the works of the old masters not so much the historical works of the distant past but "contemporary figures and images, a landscape, a face, a jug, so many opportunities for the artistic reaction."[35] Picasso's work, more than almost any other artist, reflects these influences from other artists. But more than in any other artist, it is also clear that he translates this artistic "vocabulary" into his own terms.

Of all contemporary artists to have been influenced by the work of Altdorfer, however, none is more noteworthy than Oskar Kokoschka. He shared with Max Ernst, George Grosz, and Otto Dix the wrath of Nazi censorship, and like them was shunned and had his work banned. Kokoschka's Altdorfer criticism has become better known than their's through his extensive writing, in particular his essay on Altdorfer's *Battle of Alexander* entitled "The Eye of Darius."[36] His commentaries on Altdorfer occur along with statements on other artists such as Franz Anton Maulbertsch, Dürer, Michelangelo, Titian, and Rembrandt. However, it has not been recognized that there is a strong affinity between Kokoschka's literary appreciation of Altdorfer and his own painting, particularly his 1953 historical battlepiece composed as a triptych, the *Thermopylae*. The painting and the essay originated at the same time (1953/54) and showed an identical generic makeup. Both represent Kokoschka's attempt to interpret the world in terms of tragic conflict, and his all-pervasive deep humanitarian concern for survivors of conflict.[37]

Kokoschka's earliest written reflections on Altdorfer date from 1947 in connection with an exhibition of Old German paintings which had been organized in Schaffhausen.[38] Kokoschka had made a first trip to the Continent after World War II, after his years of exile in Prague and London. He wrote:

> With Altdorfer the evening finally closes over a world which had great sympathy for the carriers of a tradition dealing with the sacred. We have a picture such as the *Finding of the Body of St. Florian,* in which the sunset scene finds a man of the Danube region returning home from his field, tired from his day's work. He is stopped at the road and asked to carry on his wagon the deceased St. Florian. Who would have the gall to leave a poor dead man overnight to become victim of the ravens and wolves? St. Florian is a human like the rest of us.[39]

Altdorfer is seen as standing on the threshold between the "whole" world of the Middle Ages and the "tragic" world of the Renaissance. The breakdown of the world order around 1500 is seen in the isolation of the self, in the flight from reality which leaves little but skepticism.[40] Dürer and his contemporaries reflect a deep melancholic premonition regarding the human world. Kokoschka sees this attitude expressed precisely in Altdorfer's *Madonna in Glory* in the contrast between the brilliant luminosity of the heavens and the grey pallor enveloping the earth despite the grandiose scenery of mountains and palaces. In commenting on a comparable Altdorfer work, *Birth of the Virgin,* Kokoschka says it is

> . . . a complicated, diverse architecture, using the methods of the Renaissance perspective, one which threatens to overwhelm all the mysteries of the life of Mary. However in his joy at the new discovery the artist appears to be as innocent as a child. In a remarkable insight he introduces a huge arc of hovering angels into the geometric space, where they announce in all the more exceptional and believable effectiveness, from heaven on high, the glory of eternity, something that lies beyond the possibilities of the measured and calculated framework in which they are found. Aren't these the same angels that sing in the High Mass of Altdorfer's latter-day compatriot, Anton Bruckner?[41]

What excites Kokoschka here is the fact that the central perspective is *not* carried through consistently, for had it been done, it would have brought the mystery of belief down to a rational and materialistic level. He views Renaissance perspective construction of space negatively because it leads to a purely technological orientation. He favors the free perspective, found also in his own work, "which is used by naive artists, children, and all civilizations which do not share this technological orientation." This essay of 1947 is an attempt then in Kokoschka's words to trace in works of art the change of worldview which is time-bound even though each generation believes its thought to be the only possible reality.

At the age of 80 Kokoschka wrote his autobiography, not in terms of dates but of "what he had seen." In the concluding chapter entitled "The Inner Eye" he declared that only when the artist possesses inner vision can his art be expressive of true humanity.[42] Rembrandt was the central figure in this essay, in which the history of art since the Baroque was described as the process of "visual art having had more and more to do with theoretical principles and logic, and less and less to do with the vision of life."[43] The central problem of art for several centuries, he noted, has been that of finding a solution to the gradual fading of the "inner light." To preserve it there were experiments with, for example, twofold sources of light, candle flames, and moonlight, as in the work of Altdorfer and Caravaggio, or in El Greco.[44] Altdorfer, cited as the first example of artists who struggled to retain and to express the "inner light" of spiritual content is seen by Kokoschka to stand at the threshold between the medieval and the modern world. This is the interpretation Altdorfer received in Kokoschka's 1947 essay on Old German painting.[45] The central importance of Altdorfer as someone who retained this inner light is conveyed by an analogy Kokoschka draws between himself and the Romans:

> I am more like the Romans, saving the household gods from a burning house . . . I am unwilling to forget my own spiritual ancestors! I have not made a break with the past, for without it there can be no future.[46]

His essay "The Eye of Darius" takes up a fuller discussion of his concern with inner vision.[47] Darius is victim of Alexander in Altdorfer's *Battle of Alexander,* but to Kokoschka the painting is the very household god which provides continuity within history's changes. Survival of the human spirit depends on art such as this. "The expression of true humanity is given to art alone."[48] The basis of the essay was a cathartic personal experience, as in so much of Kokoschka's art and writing. He was on one of his first journeys to the continent after the war. Finding himself in a desolate, war-destroyed Munich, he sought solace in the museum before the *Battle of Alexander.* Contemplation of this painting gave him the courage and will to continue.[49]

As in previous and subsequent essays, Kokoschka begins this one with a critique of modern times. He feels that Marxist thinking, the mechanistic interpretation of natural law, and Christian transcendentalism—or Bosch's chiliasm—are simplistic eschatologies, based upon linear and therefore utopian movements from evil to paradise; illusions rather than reality. He finds a comparable focus upon illusion in that modern art which is influenced by the Freudian notion of the unconscious self, thus emprisoning the self-determination of free creativity. The resulting automation, a sort of mechanistic vision, is akin in its illusion to the one-point—"peepshow"—perspective of Renaissance art. Kokoschka's leading question becomes that of where one may search for the nature of reality in view of the threat illusionistic utopian fallacies such as "progress" or "enlightenment" pose to spiritual freedom.

He finds the answer illustrated in Altdorfer's *Battle of Alexander* and also in Aristotle's notion of aesthetic harmony,[50] further in the major principles of

Baroque art, namely movement, and finally in the contrapuntal structure of Beethoven's Fugue in B major op. 133 of 1825, one of Beethoven's last works.[51] Aristotle thought nature to be dynamic and purposive. As art emulates nature, art must be defined as patterned energy. "The physical elements are not atoms nor definite kinds of substance, but *tensions between* contraries."[52] If nature was for Aristotle primarily a vital process working its way out into and up through natural products, that is the developing and producing, coming into being and passing away of objects according to a plan, art was a doing and shaping, a *movement* set up in some medium by the soul and hand of the artist. Nature and art, according to Aristotle, are the two main initiating forces in the world.[53]

When Kokoschka writes that there "lies a harmony" over the painting of the *Battle of Alexander* he does not mean the Renaissance idea of harmony but rather that of Aristotle who thought that "it may perhaps be that nature has a liking for contraries and evolves harmony out of them and not out of similarities . . . the arts apparently imitate nature in this respect. . . ."[54]

Similarly, Kokoschka's philosophical posture is Aristotelian when he advocates—adamantly—the necessity of approaching the question of reality with two standards of values simultaneously, thinking and seeing. Aristotle had grouped the activity of the imitative artist (the painter) and that of the philosopher together, claiming that universals are the concern of both.[55] Only the simultaneous act of seeing and thinking allows the perception of reality in terms of antinomies, tensions, and the harmonious. Reconciliation of separate motifs is achieved only by art which is based on this perception of reality. This is what Kokoschka means when he calls the *Battle of Alexander* "a work of absolute painting," absolute in the sense that it brings together opposites and tensions; but it also means the breaking of tensions, and the catastrophic mood that accompanies it. Altdorfer does this in visual terms; hence Kokoschka calls the *Battle of Alexander* a product of "absolute visual experience." This definition of reality and of "absolute" is based on the principle of struggle of opposite and separate entities, which therefore involves the principles of movement and time. The sun moves like a meteor across the skies; land and water ebb and flow into each other; Alexander's momentary victory is countered by Darius' confrontation with his own reality; the passive endurance of the women is countered by the active involvement of the men; the two armies are pitted against each other; the tablet of empty figures relating history is counter-poised to history acted out in terms of human individuals below; the tablet is suspended in the eternal sky; and so on. These are the separate motifs as they struggle toward reconciliation in the flow of time.

To illuminate this thesis Kokoschka compared the "absolute painting" to what to him is the best "absolute music," the "crown of European music," Beethoven's fugue. The fugue, sharing the same underlying structure with the absolute visual experience, the painting, contains an antinomy in which resides the pivotal force of its power or conviction: the "obstinately maintained beats, such that the shortest most elementary sounds in music reveal eternity itself." This musical notation is like the "monumental miniature," the "colored speck in the middle distance of Altdorfer's cosmic picture," the face of Darius which bears expression in the midst of the faceless armies of thousands of men (Plate 13). Alexander's profile shows less "face," less expression. Darius is complex, not so Alexander.

The values of the Baroque—its art defining an art of movement—had had a formative and lasting influence on Kokoschka's art, especially the paintings and frescos of Anton Maulbertsch.[56] He once said that his professional diseases are movement and expression.[57] It is the characteristic quality of Baroque art, movement, which he notes first in the *Battle of Alexander*. He also remains the only critic to have begun his description of the painting with the memorial table suspended in the skies high above the human drama and to interpret it in terms of its function as a Baroque *memento mori*, i.e. *vanitas*. If all that remains of man's victories in history are empty names and numbers, then what is man? Then his victories are but vanities.[58]

Kokoschka interpreted the *Battle of Alexander* in terms of the Aristotelian definition of tragedy and its crucial moment of catharsis. To Aristotle tragedy is properly the representation of an action involving a reversal of fortune brought about by some error on the part of the protagonist—"a transformation of the action into its opposite"—this "tragic flaw" or "error of judgment of frailty" on the part of a noble character is not one of vice or depravity. Hence the inward resignation with which he willingly accepts the outward penalty of physical suffering for his deeds renders him heroic, or "renowned." By this elimination of customary social determinants, human acts take on "free" choice for which the *actor* can and must assume unambiguous responsibility. Concepts of "error" and "wrong" thus assume unambiguous meaning, and ethics becomes possible. Aristotle's tragic "catharsis" follows a moment of "recognition in which a character comes to understand the true meaning of his dilemma and his relation to his fellow-men and the world."[59]

Kokoschka had written an article entitled with the query "Non-objective art?" two years before the "Eye of Darius." It becomes clear why the figure of Darius is so important for him, to the point that he identifies with it.

> The one unchangeable thing in a world of change is still today the human gift of extending the boundaries of the human spirit ever wider, and of adding depth to man's knowledge of himself. And here lies the vocation of the creative artist, which is to guard his insight into the purposes of human activity and into the purposes of his art. . . . All life is a risk, but that is no reason for panic. In the normal course of things it ends in death. . . . But to anyone who is clear about the risks of life and learns to confront them with open eyes, the inscrutable, humanized in art form, becomes comprehensible and thus loses its terror.[60]

Almost contemporaneous with Kokoschka's inception of the essay on the *Battle of Alexander* he worked on his historical triptych *Thermopylae* (Plate 14).[61] Technically this painting would be part of the tradition of historical battle pieces, a late link in the chain to which the *Battle of Alexander* also belongs. And yet, like the latter, and like Picasso's *Guernica,* this historical painting expands on the genre, it is more than the re-telling of a historical event. It interprets the historical event in terms of the historical situation of the artist's own time, the salvation of the Western world not then, but in the idiom of the present day. Kokoschka's choice of the format of the triptych suggests that he claims a supra-historical meaning for the painting, a decision comparable to Max Beckmann's similar use of the triptych-format for paintings which make statements about the human condition.

> The central motif is the struggle of the Greeks against the Persians (480 B.C.) as described by Herodotus in the seventh Book of his History. Led by Leonidas, a small number of the defenders occupied the narrow pass of Thermopylae and held it against the vastly superior numbers of the army of Xerxes until they were betrayed, outflanked and completely destroyed. The left panel shows in a peaceful spring landscape the house of Leonidas and the hero taking leave of his wife.
>
> The central panel shows the seer, Megistias, who had prophesied the downfall of the Greeks. The principal figure, a warrior standing upright, symbolizes the European man. As a Greek sentinel, he holds his hand before his mouth to signify silence, a gesture which in this case, however, is a sign of thoughtfully silent irresoluteness. Between him and Megistias is the Traitor, Ephialtes, depicted as a mis-shapen fool. In the background appears a god-like youth. On the right half of the central panel Kokoschka depicts the battle itself. The theme of the right panel is the breaking in of barbarism into Western antique culture. Athens is laid in ruins by the Persian soldiery, and while these are exercising a reign of terror, Freedom, represented by a female figure in chains, takes flight. But Freedom will return when Themistocles has overcome the Persian fleet at Salamis, shown in the background of the picture.[62]

Kokoscha himself explained his interpretation of Herodotus' account in an essay which was written as a tribute to his friend the conductor Walter Furtwängler who had died shortly after Kokoschka had completed the *Thermopylae* triptych.[63] He felt that what Herodotus really wanted to illustrate with his account of the battles between the Persians and the Greeks was not a mere accounting of 50 years of victories and defeats, but rather the contrast between Hellenism and Barbarism. Xerxes had had the body of Leonidas crucified and mutilated even after Leonidas had already died on the battlefield. Xerxes did this in anger because he could not understand the secret of Leonidas' strength of soul, love of freedom and justice. Herodotus' definition of a barbarian is that he is faceless, without a sense of history. Therefore he is without a sense of time. On the basis of this definition of barbarianism, Kokoschka draws parallels to his own times, specifically to that mirror of life, art:

Does not our contemporary art, as well as our cultivation of forms, that unfold in real life, show a tendency to hack up and break apart and deform—the cynical price of the Occident over its self-destruction . . . Our soul sees its own image in the art that chooses to negate that which, as Humanitas, has thus far been valid. This art shows the picture of our spiritual condition.

This differentiation of Humanitas and Barbarism is repeatedly carried out in that battle-field which the Occident calls Culture. Thanks to the particular character of Greek art, whose meaning was not just aesthetic, but also ethical, we find in the image of the victor and the defeated a reflection of ourselves.[64]

In Kokoschka's late period, since the 1950s, it is allegory which occupies the central position among his thematic material. "His allegories do not depict the episode as an end in itself; his attitude is rather one of taking counsel with the symbolic meaning of the historical or mythological theme with a view to its interpretation in the idiom of the present day."[65] Just like Altdorfer's *Battle of Alexander* so Kokoschka's *Thermopylae* contains many levels of comprehension. Both are records of a historical scene, both may be understood as a warning or a message of hope—or both. Furthermore, as Werner Hofmann has pointed out, Kokoschka's protagonists and scenes are composed in such a way as to allow allusions to themes in the story of Christ's Passion:

The youth favored by the gods rises from the grave; in the man loath to draw the sword the true captain is perceived. Mary and John appear in the left hand field. Even the bloody turmoil of the battlefield is lifted to another plane as the terror of the Apocalypse breaks through.[66]

Thermopylae is Kokoschka's *Battle of Alexander*. Not the decision through force of arms but the spiritual decision is important for humanity. This idea guided both his interpretation of Altdorfer as well as of Herodotus' account of the battle at Thermopylae.

In Altdorfer's painting Kokoschka had noticed as the most intense red the billowing cloths suspending the chiffres of victories. Kokoschka's triptych contains as its most brilliant accent a cloud of sharp red like a battle fanfare, above the central figure of the Hesitant One whose spear stabs this provocative cloud right in the middle.

Both paintings are of equivalent luminosity: the luminosity of the triptych is one of the most striking aspects of the painting. Bathed in light the figures lose corporeality and the whole takes on the character of the visionary. Likewise, reflections of the prominent heavenly bodies of light are an integral and vital force of Altdorfer's *Battle of Alexander* where light serves to transpose the event from the material to the spiritual plane.

Conclusion

There is no naiveté greater than supposing that
ira et studium are incompatible with 'objectivity.'

—José Ortega y Gasset[1]

The question which initiated this research addressed the problem of the uneven
profile of the history of Altdorfer's fame and of the divergencies within the
body of primary and secondary criticism which has grown around his work.
The method chosen to first establish and then to explore the reasons for the
particular course which Altdorfer criticism took was that of *Rezeptionsgeschichte* because its dialectic viewpoint allows to objectify the subjective element in
criticism.

In his essay "In Search of Goethe from Within," in itself a model of
critical *Rezeption,* Ortega y Gasset concluded that objectivity in knowledge can
be obtained only from that precondition which studies history with passion and
enthusiasm: *ira et studium. Rezeptionsgeschichte* is a supremely historical
discipline in its attention to the process of passion and enthusiasm, of ideation
within a given tradition of criticism. This survey of the body of criticism of
Altdorfer's work has yielded a historic profile of such "touchstones" for his art
which an oeuvre catalogue cannot yield; it adds an ever expanding dimension
to the knowledge of the ouevre.

Such a cumulative recognition of Altdorfer's characteristics reveals clearly
the distinction between criticism which discerns only a *sensus litteralis* and that
which also discerns a *sensus spiritualis* of his work. The former refers to that
reception of Altdorfer's art whose knowledge of the artist serves ulterior
motives or whose critics are too deeply immersed in their own *zeitgeist* to
perceive the "other" and do not distinguish between their own categories of
perception, thought, and action and the determinants of the historic work
before them. Examples of such errant reception are the application of a concept
such as dilettantism in a sense which postdates Altdorfer's era and therefore

does not enhance the understanding of his art; or the construction of a unilateral, exclusive dependence upon one particular formative source such as Rasmo's Italian connection and Stange's religious bias; or the use of Altdorfer's art to teach concepts which are alien to his intention such as Sliwka's value-less materialism; or Voss' and Pinder's classification of Altdorfer's art within their fatalistic view of historic periodicity. But these biases also illuminate certain facets of Altdorfer's art and may be seen as links in the construction of the total picture. The most extreme example of errant reception, however, is that which used the *sensus litteralis* of the work of art to serve political ideologies with absolutist claims such as the Third Reich.

On the other hand, that reception which employs a dialectic attitude toward the historic process, which perceives the qualitative differences between itself and the other which it "receives" will even over a period of centuries reveal a commonality of thought about the essential constituents of Altdorfer's art. The comprehension of the qualitative difference between the I and the thou of the work of art is to comprehend, at least to search for, its *sensus spiritualis*. Herein lies the potential of objectivity of *Rezeptionsgeschichte*. A comparison between Schlegel's and Kokoschka's interpretations of Altdorfer's *Battle of Alexander* will serve as an example of such commonality over time.

For both Schlegel and Kokoschka the encounter with the painting was cataclysmal. It is described respectively as "miraculous" and as "absolute." Both felt moved to direct their thoughts and their action to the future. Both writers argued against prevailing tastes, Schlegel against the domination of French and Italian art and Kokoschka against the gaining influence of nonrepresentative and abstract art because he thought it was unethical. Schlegel saw the focal point of the painting to reside in the figures of Alexander and Darius. He noted particularly the aura of tragedy which surrounds Darius and he was moved by it. Kokoschka focused on Darius to the point of self-identification and to the exclusion of Alexander. In this instance Kokoschka seems to follow Ortega y Gasset's appeal:

> There is but one way to save a classic: to give up revering it and use it for our own salva-
> tion—that is, to lay aside its classicism, to bring it close to us, to make it contemporary, to
> set its pulse going again with an injection of blood from our own veins, whose ingredients
> are *our* passions . . . and *our* problems.[2]

It should also be noted that this difference in emphasis with regards to the protagonists in the *Battle of Alexander* may in part be ascribed to the factor that Schlegel was 30 years old when he went to see Altdorfer's painting in the Louvre, whereas Kokoschka was 70 years old when he returned to Altdorfer's painting, his age as well as his personal fate having deepened his sense of the tragic.

Schlegel had recommended strongly to young painters the study of masterpieces of the past and so did Kokoschka with equal emphasis. However, while Schlegel had accompanied this recommendation with a strong German-national emphasis, Kokoschka who understood himself as a European never thought in terms of "national" art or "national" style. That was a concept totally incongruous with his humanism and humanitarianism. The devastation of two world wars which Kokoschka had experienced rendered the notion of nationalism not only treacherous but obsolete. Furthermore, Kokoschka's actual as well as spiritual and cultural home, Vienna, had never been the capital city of a nation state. As a centre of an empire which extended from Mexico to the Coast of India, Vienna was "the ideal soil for the development of a common intellectual civilization."[3] But it was because of the uprooting of war and foreign domination that both Schlegel and Kokoschka had turned to the art of their German past and to Altdorfer to reestablish continuity and identity.

Schlegel had written that the painting's "true meaning" was expressed by its "spirit of chivalry," a turn of phrase by which he meant essentially "ethical." Equally, Kokoschka's concept of the purpose of art was that it be above all humanistic, e.g., ethical, and he found this emphatically verified in Altdorfer's *Battle of Alexander* and particularly in the figure of Darius.

Both Schlegel and Kokoschka recalled the Greek epic in their interpretations of this painting. Schlegel compared it to Homer's *Iliad,* while Kokoschka painted his triptych *Thermopylae,* inspired by the *Battle of Alexander,* with epic dimensions. While both critics were above all concerned with meaning in the *Battle of Alexander* Kokoschka avoided the metaphysical interpretation which Schlegel had developed. Herein lies the only basic difference between their respective reception of Altdorfer's work, a difference which resulted from the changed world view of Kokoschka's era: belief in a progressive perfectability of mind and soul could no longer be sustained.

In the testing of a former critic's interpretation such as Schlegel's it is not only acceptable but even necessary to bring to the fore all that is known of the artist and his motives. Not only are the valid views of past critics substantiated and the errant ones debunked, but a newly informed criticism reflecting latest scholarship is established. Through this method it had become apparent, for example, that Schlegel's interpretation of the *Battle of Alexander* as cosmic and supra-historical corresponded to Altdorfer's—and his commissioner's—own intention.

The quest for Altdorfer's intellectual and spiritual position has shown twentieth century scholarly reception of Altdorfer to be concerned with the reconstruction of a historic context which would support the discernment of major themes and leitmotivs of Altdorfer's art. These efforts may be described as the search for the key to his world view. They employ style analysis only as a means toward the discovery of Altdorfer's artistic significance—position—in the context of the art of his time. As divergent as these approaches—receptions—of Altdorfer are, they constitute cumulatively complementary, not contradictory views of Altdorfer's art. Thus the work of Benesch, who had suggested in the tradition of Max Dvořák the validity of explaining phenomena in the visual arts in terms of the prevailing philosophy of the time—Altdorfer's affinity to the cosmogenic ideas of Paracelsus—was supported by the research of Hartlaub, Behling, and the Altdorfer reception of Linfert and Kenneth Clark.[4] The iconographic analysis of Harbison, Saran, and Koepplin all agreed that Altdorfer used his raw material in an individualistic, innovative fashion, that the morphology of his style and his vision emphasize the coexistence of elements of eruptive generation and decay, that nature and man are seen in terms of dynamic complementary oppositions corresponding to Nicolaus Cusanus' definition of God as the *coincidentia oppositorum*. This is what is meant when Altdorfer's art is termed "ambivalent."

A number of critics reveal self-consciously their own stance and develop general criteria for style change on the basis of Altdorfer's work. For these theorists his art is received as a touchstone to validate their theories of change. Cases in point are Wölfflin who saw Altdorfer's art as the absolute embodiment of "northern" vision as opposed to Italian art; or Panofsky in whose treatise on "Perspective as Symbolic Form" Altdorfer is cited as the originator of the "absolute oblique space,"[5] thereby placing him on the threshold of the modern era; or Ottinger in whose theory of the changing aspects of sacred art at the beginning of the sixteenth century Altdorfer's art furnishes support for the argument. Here as well Altdorfer was seen as ushering in a new era.

The aspect of novelty in Altdorfer's work was consistently a central observation in its reception as Altdorfer's derivation from traditional norms is not restricted to the *Battle of Alexander* or the *Birth of the Virgin*. Raselius admired the fusion of subject categories and the dominance of nature in the painting of the *Two Sts. John;* Sandrart acknowledged Altdorfer's power of imagination, originality of conception in his drawings and prints; Schlegel felt that the *Battle of Alexander* could not be placed in any existing category; and Waagen's and Rettberg's exclamation that Altdorfer was the "Rembrandt of his school" expressed the same surprise at the unsuspected novelty of the treatment of illumination in the *Finding of the Body of St. Florian.*

The history of the reception of Altdorfer's work must take into account that this reception was for the most part based only on partial knowledge and limited accessibility of his art until scholarship had expanded the range of Altdorfer's artistic activity between 1891 and 1966.[6] For example, would Schlegel have responded to the St. Florian altarpiece or to the painting of *Lot and His Daughters*, and if so, what would his reaction have been? But after the 1950s the *Battle of Alexander* continues to arouse *ira et studium*. Kokoschka and Wolfgang Kehr are cases in point, so is the current research of Friedrich

Piel, a student of Sedlmayr, who has attempted a structuralist analysis of the *Battle of Alexander*[7] and the recipient of the 1977 Petrarca prize in literature, the Bavarian Herbert Achternbusch in his novel entitled *Die Alexanderschlacht*.[8]

The reception of Altdorfer's work by artists and the resulting artistic affinities also have established touchstones of Altdorfer characteristics which have parallels in the scholarly reception of Altdorfer. In the case of Max Ernst's forest paintings it is the rendering of the ambivalence between the positive and the destructive forces in nature and the depiction of the constellations as a supra-human, ordering principle, a subordination of nature to metaphysical principles.

For George Grosz and Otto Dix, Altdorfer represented a kindred spirit, a model of encouragement to stay true to their art in the face of a political regime which suffocated artistic freedom. When this latter was denied them, Grosz and Dix escaped into the study of nature and found in Altdorfer a teacher with whose vision of nature they felt a kinship.

Picasso's reception of Altdorfer reveals a quality in Altdorfer which is generally neglected in Altdorfer criticism: Picasso is not only moved by Altdorfer's ability to translate reality in terms of patterns and textures but also by Altdorfer's sensitive rendering of human interaction and emotion through a gesture expressive of both nobility and humility in the kneeling woman of the *Finding of the Body of St. Sebastian*.

Kokoschka's artistic kinship with Altdorfer consists in the employment of a free perspective, a high vantage point in the rendering of landscape, in the fusion of all phenomena through the same dynamic, short line or stroke which conveys an organic relationship between all matter, and the subordination of his artistic mission to a humanistic world view.

It has been established then how an "Old German" artist lives on in his works' critics and in other artists who draw inspiration from him. To have found converging lines of understanding and to have identified errant critiques demonstrates the objectivity possible in a study of relative judgment and brings this first *Rezeptionsgeschichte* of Altdorfer to this day.

This thesis has shown that the method of *Rezeptionsgeschichte* is particularly valid in assessing the work of artists whose reception appears on the surface to be inconsistent and contradictory. As applied to the reception of Altdorfer's work the method of *Rezeptionsgeschichte* has disclosed the authentic intrinsic values of Altdorfer's art on the basis of Walter Benjamin's definition of authenticity as not only consisting of the substantive duration of the work of art but as consisting also of the history which it has experienced.

Notes

Introduction

1. Lionello Venturi, *History of Art Criticism,* 1964, p. 9.

2. Kurt Martin, *Die Alexanderschlacht,* 1969, contains color reproductions of details of Altdorfer's *Battle of Alexander* and reprints of both Schlegel's and Kokoschka's essays on the painting, but without comparative or analytic commentary.

3. Ulrich Klein, "Rezeption," *Handlexikon der Literaturwissenschaft,* 1976, pp. 409-12.

4. Wilhelm Heinse, *Ardinghello und die glückseligen Inseln,* 1975 (first edition 1787), edited by Max L. Baeumer.

5. Klein, p. 409.

6. Ibid., p. 411.

7. Walter Benjamin, *Das Kunstwerk im Zeitalter seiner technischen Reproduzierbarkeit,* 1977, p. 71.

8. Originally published in a French translation in *Zeitschrift für Sozialforschung,* Jg. 5, 1936.

9. Benjamin, 1977, p. 18.

10. For a synopsis of Benjamin's "The Work of Art in the Era of Mechanical Reproduction" see Martin Jay, *The Dialectical Imagination, a History of the Frankfurt School and the Institute of Social Research, 1923-1950,* 1973, pp. 197-211; see especially pp. 209-10.

11. Jay, p. 210.

12. Benjamin, 1977, pp. 67-107; first published in *Zeitschrift für Sozialforschung,* Jg. 6, 1937.

13. Ibid., p. 71.

14. Ibid., p. 69.

15. Martin Warnke, *Das Kunstwerk zwischen Wissenschaft und Weltanschauung,* 1970. The book is the published version of a symposium organized on the same topic at the occasion of the 12th Congress of German art historians in Cologne.

16. Wolfgang Kehr, *Projekt einer didaktischen Ausstellung zu Altdorfers "Alexander-schlacht,"* 1973.

17. Klein, p. 412.

18. Ibid.

19. These writers and artists are discussed elsewhere in the study.

20. Harry Levin, *Contexts of Criticism,* 1957, p. 33.

21. Ibid., p. 35.

Chapter 1

1. Franz Winzinger, *Albrecht Altdorfer, Die Gemälde,* 1975, document No. 32, p. 149.

2. Walter Boll, "Albrecht Altdorfers Nachlass," 1938-39, pp. 91-92, states that the name Alt-dorfer does not appear in the archives of Amberg; Regensburg may well have been Altdorf-er's birthplace. The names of his siblings Aurelia and Erhard were those of highly vene-rated local saints in Regensburg and the name Albrecht also points to Regensburg as name-sake of Albertus Magnus, Bishop of Regensburg 1260-62, and the most eminent German scientist of the Middle Ages.

3. The assumption of 1488 as Altdorfer's birthdate, rather than the traditionally suggested 1480, would also explain why the earliest dated works from 1504 and 1506 appear artistically immature.

4. See Dürer's letter from Venice, October, 1506, reprinted in Wolfgang Stechow, *Northern Renaissance Art, 1400-1600,* 1966.

5. Carl Theodor Gemeiner, *Regensburgische Chronik,* 1803, p. 140.

6. Christian Gottlieb Gumpelzhaimer, *Regensburgs Geschichte, Sagen und Merkwürdigkeiten,* Vol. II, 1837, p. 585.

7. Gemeiner, pp. 194, 444, 458; see also Gumpelzhaimer, p. 585 and Leonhard Widmann, *Regensburger Chronik,* p. 39, the year 1521.

8. Gumpelzhaimer, p. 624. This practice was discontinued as late as 1808.

9. Gemeiner, p. 144. In 1505 a priest was freed from jail by his wealthy father for the sum of 600 Gulden, the equivalent of the price of four fine houses. See Widmann, p. 271.

10. Von Hutten, Ulrich. *Deutsche Schrifften.* Heinz Mettke, ed., 1972, pp. XII-XIII; see also F. Winzinger, *Albrecht Altdorfer: Die Zeichnungen,* 1952, Plate 4, *"Räuberischer Überfall,"* drawing, ca. 1506-08.

11. Gemeiner, pp. 493-94.

12. Hajo Holborn, *A History of Modern Germany,* Vol. I, 1959, p. 38.

13. By the year 1500 the printer Anton Koberger in Nürnberg had issued 150 volumes of Schedel's *Pictorial World History* for an international market. The view of Regensburg appears ' on folio XCVIII.

14. Heinz Otto Burger, *Renaissance, Humanismus und Reformation,* 1969, p. 321. Konrad Celtis' inspiration for this book probably came from Ficino's *Theologica Platonica* and Boiardo's *Amorum libri.* See Burger, p. 315.

15. Gumpelzhaimer, p. 33.

16. Gemeiner, p. 158; Gumpelzhaimer, p. 722.

17. William S. Heckscher, "Petits Perceptions," *The Journal of Medieval and Renaissance Studies,* vol. 4, no. 1, Spring 1974, p. 119, calls attention to the applause awarded artistic intention rather than to artistic achievement in Renaissance and Baroque art.

18. Guido Hable, *Geschichte Regensburgs,* 1970, p. 130.

19. Friedrich Paulsen, *German Education, Past and Present,* 1912, p. 28.

20. Grünpeck was allotted a yearly salary of 40 florins. An additional 10 florins were added to the first payment. The same stipend was given Holbein's wife by the city of Basle in 1526. In 1516 the city of Regensburg paid Grünpeck 8 florins for a "Judicum" or "Practica," the same sum which was given to Altdorfer for the painting for the Chapel of the Beautiful Mary. Gumpelzhaimer, p. 598; Hable, p. 130.

21. Altdorfer bought his first house in 1513, a property adjoining the Augustinian monastery. Winzinger, 1952, p. 54 ff.

22. Maximilian presented Stabius with a house in Regensburg. Boll, p. 93.

23. Paulsen, p. 28; see also Theobald Ziegler, *Geschichte der Pädagogik,* 1909, p. 35.

24. Boll, p. 92.

25. Johannes Janssen, *History of the German People,* Vol. I, 1896, p. 211.

26. Max J. Friedländer, *Albrecht Altdorfer,* 1891, p. 31; Winzinger, 1952, p. 17. Ludwig Baldass was not convinced by the Furtmayr connection; see his *Albrecht Altdorfer,* 1941, p. 23. Van der Osten assumed that Altdorfer's father was an illuminator; however, the municipal archives of Regensburg distinguished clearly between "painter" and "illuminator," and Ulrich Altdorfer was entered in 1478 as "*maler*" (painter). See Boll, p. 92.

27. Winzinger, 1952, p. 13.

28. Guild regulations of the painters' guild in Strassburg are known: two masterpieces were required, one Virgin executed in oil colors and one Crucifixion in tempera, both required to measure one *Elle.* See Hans Huth, *Künstler und Werkstatt in der Spätgotik,* 1923, p. 89. No similar regulations are known for Regensburg painters, nor is there any other data on the organization of guilds there before the mid-sixteenth century.

29. The ring with the seal was listed in the inventory of Altdorfer's effects at the time of his death. Eberhard Ruhmer, *Albrecht Altdorfer,* 1965, p. 6.

30. Gemeiner, p. 154, city council minutes, vol. 2, folio 86. The subject matter of Altdorfer's painting which was exhibited in St. Peter's was not recorded. The payment of 10 *gulden* (florins) corresponded to a three-month salary for the humanist Grünpeck. Nearly the same amount of money was paid to a fireworks specialist for a performance, p. 155. The house bought by Aventinus in 1531 cost 140 florins, the same price Altdorfer had paid in 1532 for his house with garden, Gumpelzhaimer, p. 803. On the other hand, the city's price for the head of a fugitive arsonist-murderer was 20 florins, Gemeiner, p. 125.

31. Altdorfer probably was responsible for all the designs on all the coins minted in Regensburg during these years. Winzinger, 1952, p. 96, plate 115.

32. Altdorfer was paid one *pfund* and six *schilling* for the curtain and five *schilling* and eighteen *pfennig* for the banner, Gemeiner, p. 318.

33. Altdorfer was one of several members of both the Inner and Outer Council delegated to negotiate in the Jewish Quarter the terms of the Jews' departure and the collection of all pawns left there by debtors. Gemeiner, p. 356.

34. Winzinger, *Albrecht Altdorfer, Graphik,* 1963.

35. See woodcut of the cult of the Beautiful Mary by Michael Ostendorfer, in Alfred Stange, *Malerei der Donauschule,* 1971, plates 34, 95. This is the most vivid extant account of the throngs of pilgrims and the wide range of states of devotion and ecstasy evoked in the devotees, and the vast variety and profusion of votive offerings.

36. The documents convey the city's continuous attempts until 1522 to stimulate the cult of the Beautiful Mary in order to keep the city's purse filled; see Gemeiner, pp. 386-87, 440, 475. The council and the bishop repeatedly quarrelled over the income from the chapel. Stories of miracles believed to have been wrought by the image of the Beautiful Mary were printed in two books and sold at the chapel.

37. Gumpelzhaimer, p. 700. The coin was minted in various sizes and metals. On the indulgence, see Gumpelzhaimer, p. 388.

38. This painting has been lost, and so has another one commissioned in 1515 by Bishop Peter Kraft for 80 florins; it must have been a sizeable altarpiece, Gemeiner, IV, p. 442; Gumpelzhaimer, p. 696; Winzinger, 1975, p. 28. Altdorfer's painting of the *Miracle Fountain in St. Florian* or the *Martyrdom of St. Florian* witness to his capacity of capturing life around him with vivid immediacy.

39. Winzinger, 1963, plates 137, 140, 87, 83, 88, 89, 90. Dürer owned a woodcut of the *Beautiful Mary* on the verso of which he had expressed himself with disgust against the idolatry which had "risen against the Holy Writ in Regensburg." See Erwin Panofsky, *Dürer,* 1945. p. 199.

40. Gemeiner, p. 406.

41. Ruhmer, p. 7. 1520-1525, municipal office to supervise all craftsmen working in the city.

42. From this time dates a miniature engraving depicting a *Baumeister* in the pose of Dürer's *Melancholia I;* see Winzinger, 1963, plate 152.

43. Widmann, p. 19.

44. Gumpelzhaimer, p. 765.

45. Compare documents in Winzinger, 1975, p. 148, no. 29, 30, 31; see also Leonhard Theobald, *Die Reformationsgeschichte der Reichsstadt Regensburg,* 1936, p. 187. Würzlburger was executed in October, 1528.

46. Gumpelzhaimer, p. 798.

47. Ibid. Altdorfer was also among those members of the city council who ordered *Amt, Vesper,* and *Salve* to be discontinued at the church of the Beautiful Mary and that the organist there be dismissed.

48. Ibid., pp. 807-8.

49. The letter of instruction for Altdorfer as to the exact duty of this mission is partially paraphrased in Boll, p. 96, note 16, and in Winzinger, 1975, p. 150, No. 44.

50. Lucas Cranach was city council member and mayor in Wittenberg; Hans Baldung Grien was city council member in Strassburg; Dieter Köpplin, *Lucas Cranach,* 1974, pp. 185-6.

51. Janssen, pp. 8, 18.

52. Reproduced in Baldass, p. 20. The miniature was painted by Hans Mülich who is probably identical with Altdorfer's apprentice the "dear servant Hans" whom he generously acknowledged in his will.

53. Josef Meder, "Albrecht Altdorfers Donaureise," *Mitteilungen der Gesellschaft für Vervielfältigende Kunst,* 1902. Compare Winzinger, 1952, plates 28, 29.

54. Ruhmer, p. 6. He assumes two Italian journeys, 1506-1510, and then again around 1520 without supporting his assumption with at least circumstantial evidence. See also Hans Hildebrandt, *Die Architektur bei Altdorfer,* 1908, p. 37, 54, 55. Winzinger, on the other hand, claims that Altdorfer knew Italian art and architecture solely on the basis of prints and through the Italian-inspired designs of the Augsburg architect Hans Hieber, Winzinger, 1952, pp. 47-8.

55. Peter Halm, "Eine Gruppe Architekturzeichnungen aus dem Umkreis Albrecht Altdorfers," *Münchener Jahrbuch der Bildenden Kunst,* 1951, p. 207.

56. Stange, pp. 82-83.

57. See, for example, *Meyers Künstler Lexikon,* 1872, Vol. I, p. 539.

58. Altdorfer's will is reprinted in its entirety in Boll, pp. 94-97.

59. Gailer von Kaisersberg's writings were put on the Index after 1540.

60. Boll, p. 95, Note 20.

61. See, for example, Craig Harbison, *Symbols in Transformation: Iconographic Themes at the Time of the Reformation,* 1969.

62. Gailer von Kaisersberg preached in 1508, ". . . it is not necessarily prayer when someone recites many *pater noster* with his mouth. . . ," Widmann, p. 117; ". . . he held in his hand a wooden, uncouth *pater noster* . . ."; a Nurnberg police regulation stated: "no citizen may carry a *pater noster* that is worth more than twelve Haller. . . ," Jakob Grimm, *Deutsches Wörterbuch,* 1886, Vol. 7, p. 1503.

63. These are: *Portrait of a Lady,* collection Thyssen; *Portrait of a Canon,* private ownership; and *Portrait of Peter Maurer,* donor of the St. Sebastian altarpiece, St. Florian.

64. Sandrart's drawing is in cod. icon. 366, Munich, Staatsbibliothek; it is also reproduced in Wolfgang Wegner, "Wie sah Altdorfer aus?" *Zeitschrift für Kunstwissenschaft,* 1952, no. 6, p. 81. L. v. Baldass, 1941, made the same suggestion. Sandrart had personal relationships in some of the vicinities of Altdorfer's activities, and several of Sandrart's sojourns to Regensburg are documented. Whether his drawing was based on a self-portrait by Altdorfer or on a portrait by a contemporary cannot be determined.

65. Luke even speaks of Pilate's triple assertion of Jesus' innocence, thereby also exonerating Pilate. Matthew's account, however, can be translated much more easily into dramatic visual imagery. See *The Interpreter's Dictionary of the Bible,* 1962, p. 811.

66. *The Interpreter's Dictionary,* p. 811. The Coptic church made Pilate both a saint and a martyr. Note K. Tscheuschner-Bern's study on Pilate's role in passion plays, "Die deutsche Passionsbühne und die deutsche Malerei des 15. und 16. Jahrhunderts in ihren Wechselbeziehungen," *Repertorium für Kunstwissenschaft,* Vol. 27, 1904.

67. See Winzinger, 1963. Altdorfer executed 23 designs for luxury goblets and decanters, and he owned a collection of at least 11 such objects. The St. Florian decanter is identical with a dragon-spouted design by Altdorfer. Winzinger, 1963, plate 202. Winzinger dates these etchings of luxury vessels around 1520-25.

68. Harbison, p. 373. For an excerpt of Luther's tract "Against the Heavenly Prophets in the Matter of Images and Sacraments" of 1525 see W. Stechow, pp. 129-30.

69. Widmann, p. 135, and Gumpelzhaimer, p. 805. When Augsburg became officially Protestant in 1537, all statuary and painted panels were removed from the churches and a great deal was destroyed. See Widmann, p. 143, and Gumpelzhaimer, p. 816.

70. See eyewitness accounts in Cicely Wedgewood, *The Thirty Years' War,* 1961, p. 492.

Chapter 2

1. W. H. Wackenroder, quoted in Andreas Müller, *Kunstanschauung der Frühromantik,* 1931, p. 67.

2. Erasmus called Dürer the "new Appeles," an equal to the great artists of Antiquity, because like them Dürer distinguished himself both as draftsman and as scholar and theoretician. Erasmus' ultimate praise was that Dürer depicted "what cannot be depicted." Erwin Panofsky, "Erasmus and the Visual Arts," *Journal of the Warburg and Courtauld Institutes,* XIV, 1951, p. 41 ff. Only the nineteenth century historians Gumpelzhaimer and Gemeiner who compiled the documents from the Regensburg municipal archives injected for Altdorfer adjectives such as "famous."

3. "... schön, lustig, kunstreich abgemahlet ..." Winzinger, *Altdorfer, Gemälde*, 1975, p. 151; Fickler's inventory, dated 1598, of the Duke of Bavaria's collection of paintings, contains a description of the *Battle of Alexander* which is void of any kind of interpretive remark. *Catalogue: Alte Pinakothek*, Munich, 1963, p. 205.

4. "Lustig in Verbingung mit dem Gesichtssinne ... lustiges Land, lustige Felder, lustige Bäume, lustige Wiesen—grün und lustig, grüne lustige Aue"—"Schöner lustiger Garten"; Aventinus: "solch züg gesehen von rauhen Landen in Fruchtbare und lustigere"; "das gelobte Land, das so lüstig sei, als hette es Gott selbs gepflanzt." Grimm, *Deutsches Wörterbuch*, 1885, Vol. 6, p. 1339.

5. Peter Halm, "Eine Altdorfer Sammlung des 17. Jahrhunderts," *Münchener Jahrbuch der bildenden Kunst*, Vol. XI, 1960, p. 162. He discusses the so-called Peuchel Band, cod. icon. 412 of the Staatliche Graphische Sammlung, Munich.

6. The panel represents Bathsheba's Bath. Halm attributed it to a close follower of Altdorfer. The painting is now in the Regensburg Municipal Museum. Halm, 1960, p. 163.

7. The copy of the *Birth of the Virgin* is by Georg Christoph Eimmart the Elder. Winzinger reports four copies of the Berlin *Crucifixion*, one dated 1633. Winzinger, 1975, p. 99.

8. The erroneous attribution of Altdorfer's work to Dürer was made by Jacob Sturm: "Historisch Poetisch Zeitverfassende Beschreibung der Stadt Regensburg aus dem Jahre 1663," in *Verhandlungen des Historischen Vereins Oberpfalz und Regensburg*, Vol. XXXI, 1875, p. 88.

9. Sandrart used Carl van Mander as a model although the latter did not include Altdorfer in his *Painters' Book*, 1604.

10. I saw the edition of Dr. A. R. Peltzer, *Sandrarts Teutsche Akademie*, 1925; see p. 333 for a description of the contents of Sandrart's own *Künstkammer*. Since family names were often toponyms, Sandrart seems to have assumed that Altdorfer's birthplace was Altdorf in Switzerland.

11. This motif cannot be found among Altdorfer's graphic work as compiled by Winzinger, *Altdorfer Graphik*, 1963. Either this print has since been lost or it has been attributed to someone other than Altdorfer. The theme of Abigail was related to the Marian virtues of *Sanftheit* and *Klugheit*. In the typology of the *speculum homanae salvationis* Abigail prefigured *Maria mediatrix nostra placat iram Dei contra nos*. See, for example, folio 42 recto in *Codex Cremifanensis 243*, 1972 (facsimile edition). The motif could well have occurred in Altdorfer's oeuvre in which the celebration of Mary occupies central importance.

12. I have given my own translation of Sandrart's original German in Peltzer: "... er malte am besten kleine Historien, sanne denselben emsig nach und wandte grossen Fleiss an, wie auch in allen eine geistreiche Invention und ungemeine Selzamkeit zu spüren ist, derenthalben ihm auch sonderbares Lob gebühret, denn obschon seine Werke etwas wild untereinander scheinen, so weil das hinterste nach selbiger Zeit Gewohnheit ebenso hart als das vorderste herauskommt, so ist dennoch ein tiefsinniger Verstand darinnen zu finden, besonders in seinem grossen Hieronymus, in der Kreuzigung und andern. Sehr zierlich ist auch sein grosser Fendrich in Holzschnitt, ingleichen sein Pyramus, Thysbe, Abigail und Passion, in der sich sehr schöne Affecte erzeigen. Kupfer und Holzschnitte, die allesamt in Ehren zu halten

seyen, und mit den Büchern unter den kleinen Kupferstichen oder Meistern gehalten werden, woraus seine Emsigkeit, Fleiss und sinnreicher Verstand bäster massen zu verspüren."

13. R. W. Lee, "Ut Pictura Poesis: The Humanistic Theory of Painting," *Art Bulletin,* XXII, 1940, p. 262. Sandrart himself wrote, "The artist must always shape that which he wishes to present in accordance either with some accepted formula, or according to his own idea and his own reason. Then he must consider and try to understand the age, feelings, and other qualities of the thing he wants to form that thereafter the image will show from the outset what it represents. And all the members must mutually correspond in true equality." Quoted from Waldijslav Tatarkiewicz, *History of Aesthetics,* Vol. III, 1974, p. 407.

14. Elizabeth G. Holt, *A Documentary History of Art,* Vol. II, 1963, p. 368.

15. Such buildings as the meathouse, rebuilt under Altdorfer's supervision in 1528, the church of the Augustinians where both he and his wife were buried, St. Emmeran where one could admire the painting of the *Two Sts. John.*

16. Walter Boll, *Regensburg,* 1963, p. 34.

17. See Hume's *History of England* (1754-62) quoted from Heinrich Lützeler, "Die Kunstkritik," *Jahrbuch für Aesthetik,* Vol. VIII, 1963.

18. "In einem anderen Zimmer ist Alexander des Grossen erste Schlacht wider Darium, von Albrecht Dürer im Jahre 1529 mit unglaublicher Arbeit gemalet. Man sieht auf diesem Stück viele tausend Menschen, an welchen man die Haare am Kopfe und Barte, die geringsten Fugen der Harnische und andere Kleinig keiten aufs deutlichste und zarteste ausgedrückt sieht, nach des Meisters Gewohnheit, die ihm von etlichen für übel genommen wird, da sie ihm übrigens das Lob einer netten Zeichnung nicht versagen können. Das gewöhnliche Zeichen seiner Arbeit ist folgender Zug: monogram D in A." Johann Georg Keyssler, *Neueste Reisen durch Deutschland,* 1751, p. 59.

19. Johann Georg Sulzer, *Allgemeine Theorie der Schönen Künste,* 1792 (Olms edition, 1967), pp. 607, 319, 253.

20. Reprinted in Martin, *Alexanderschlacht,* 1969, p. 27.

21. The *Battle of Alexander* (sometimes called the "Battle of Issus") was one of 72 paintings taken from Munich by Napoleonic military forces. Only it and Titian's *Crowning with Thorns* have since become famous. In 1814-15 the German delegation which occupied the Palace of St. Cloud found it there in the bathroom. This may have started the legend of Napoleon's fondness for this painting. This legend was taken most seriously by Sturge Moore who wrote the first English monograph on Altdorfer (1900) and who justified his appreciation on the basis of Napoleon's supposed enthusiasm for Altdorfer's *Battle of Alexander.* Cecil Gould has shown, however, that Napoleon himself had no visual appreciation of the arts, that his mentor Denon had no opinion of this picture and that Napoleon had not made the choice of those Munich pictures which he received. See Cecil Gould, *Trophy of Conquest,* 1965, p. 74.

22. Friedrich Schlegel, "Ansichten und Ideen von Christlicher Kunst," *Europa,* II, 1803, p. 111 ff.

23. Panofsky, 1951, p. 211.

24. Lee, 1940, p. 262. Schlegel compared Altdorfer's painting with the writing of Homer and Shakespeare.

25. Tatarkiewicz, 1974, p. 408.

26. My translation of the original: "... Das romantische Drama denke man sich hingegen als ein grosses Gemälde, wo ausser der Gestalt und Bewegung in reicheren Gruppen auch noch die Umgebung der Personen mit abgebildet ist, nicht bloss die nächste, sondern ein bedeutender Ausblick in die Ferne, und dies alles unter einer magischen Beleuchtung, welche den Eindruck so oder anders bestimmen hilft. Ein solches Gemälde wird weniger vollkommen begrenzt sein als die Gruppe, denn es ist wie ein ausgeschnittenes Bruchstück aus dem optischen Schauplatz der Welt. Indessen wird der Maler durch die Einfassung der Vorgründe, durch das gegen die Mitte gesammelte Licht und andere Mittel den Blick gehörig festzuhalten wissen, dass er weder über die Darstellung hinausschweife, noch etwas in ihr vermisse." Reprinted in Müller, *Kunstanschauung der Frühromantik*, 1931, pp. 303-304.

27. Müller, 1931, pp. 303-304.

28. Ibid., pp. 75-76. In his *"De Ludo Globi"* Nicolaus Cusanus developed the concept of infinity.

29. Venturi, *History of Art Criticism*, 1964, p. 170.

30. Friedrich Schlegel, *Collected Writings*, vol. 5, 1846, p. 187. The brothers Boisseré who studied with Schlegel in 1803-04 and who were instrumental in arousing Schlegel's interest in old German painting said of Schlegel's nationalism: "Zugleich war Schlegel von der treuesten Liebe zum deutschen Vaterland durchdrungen und er enterliess keine Gelegenheit, seinen Schmerz über dessen Erniedrigung, so wie seine Bewunderung über dessen ehemalige Grösse und Herrlichkeit auszudrücken. Diese doppelte Richtung, die ideelle und die nationale, ging bei Schlegel überhaupt in allen Ansichten durch ..." Quoted from Eduard Firmenich-Richartz, *Die Brüder Boisseré*, 1916, p. 49.

31. See Hans Mettke, ed., *von Hutten: Deutsche Schriften*, 1972.

32. In his preface to the *Bayerische Chronik* Aventinus wrote: "Es sind die Chronika von Anfand der Welt nit darum angefangen, dass sie jedermann gefallen sollen, sondern erdacht worden, dass man die Wahrheit abmale und an das Licht, an den Tag brächte und wie in einem Spiegel der Welt Lauf anzeige, den rechten Grund darlegte, wie und warum Land und Leute—Obrigkeit und Untertan in gutem Wesen—Frieden und Eintracht bleiben, erhalten, reich und selig miteinander werden mögen." Edition by Georg Leidinger, 1975.

33. Lützeler, 1963, p. 114.

34. "... er (F. Schlegel) verlangt im Kunstwerk die eigentümlichen Züge seines religiösen Kosmos wiederzufinden." Walter Benjamin, *Der Begriff der Kunstkritik in der deutschen Romantik*, 1973, p. 68.

35. Benjamin, 1973, p. 68.

36. See appendix for my own translation from Schlegel's German text, reprinted in Martin, *Alexanderschlacht,* 1969. I know of no English translation of the essay since E. J. Millington's edition of "Letters on Christian Art," *Schlegel's Aesthetic and Miscellaneous Works,* 1875, p. 113 ff. The paragraphs are my own. Schlegel's free-flowing prose is almost impressionistic, his style differs greatly from Goethe's Strassburg essay which is tightly structured and approximates poetry.

37. This is not an automatic consequence of Sandrart's own artistic activity. Oskar Kokoschka, himself a prolific painter, wrote a totally metaphysical essay on the *Battle of Alexander.* See Chapter 7.

38. John B. Halsted, ed., *Romanticism,* 1965, p. 42.

39. Millington, 1875, p. 113.

40. *Encyclopedia of Philosophy,* Vol. 7, 1967, p. 315.

41. H. H. Borcherdt has shown that classicizing costumes were not used in the theatre in Germany until 1566. That year a school production in Strassburg used classical dress because of the director's personal interest in classical antiquity. Before then contemporary dress was preferred because of its moralizing effect: the protagonists, especially the heroes in a dramatic performance, were to be *imagines vitae.* Heinz Heinrich Borcherdt, *Das Europäische Theater im Mittelalter und in der Renaissance,* 1930, p. 184. The armour depicted is very similar to that which Dürer had designed for Emperor Maximilian and which also occurs in Altdorfer's own miniatures of the *Triumphal Procession* commissioned by the same emperor. See Winzinger, 1975, Nos. 56-79.

42. Quoted from Holt, 1963, p. 67.

43. Madame de Stael-Holstein, *Germany,* 1879, p. 46; also René Wellek, *A History of Modern Criticism 1750-1950,* 1955, p. 226. Compare also A. Schlegel's lectures on literature and the fine arts discussed earlier in this chapter.

44. Wellek, 1955, p. 26.

45. See, for example, the *speculum humanae salvationis,* of the *Codex Cremifanensis,* 1972. The representation of Darius as *typus* of the *antitypus* Christ Crowned with Thorns is based the *Apocrypha,* Book 3, Esdras 4:29-30. The epic of Alexander was translated into German prose in the fifteenth century. Because of its moralizing and didactic character this work was widely known. See De Boor-Newald, *Geschichte der deutschen Literatur,* 1970, p. 58.

46. Hartmann Schedel, *History of the World,* 1493, folium LXXVI.

47. See, for example, *Codex Cremifanensis* 243.

48. Dieter Kopplin, "Das Sonnengestirn der Donaumeister," *Werden und Wandlung,* 1967, p. 100 ff.

49. Martin, *Alexanderschlacht,* 1969. pp. 29-30.

50. Aventinus, *Bayerische Chronik,* (Leidinger edition), 1975, p. 142.

51. This is a "typical" Renaissance phenomenon. Paulsen, for example, writes: "Shifting of the general interest from the future to the present world was not unconnected with a similar shifting of the general interest from the world of abstract ideas to that of concrete reality, from dialectical and conceptual philosophy to the study of the concrete phenomena of nature and history." Paulsen, 1912, p. 44 ff.

52. Köpplin, 1967, p. 79.

53. These commissions constituted a generous act of art patronage similar to that of the Emperor Maximilian a decade earlier. Other contributing artists and the subjects of their paintings are listed in Hans Tietze, *Albrecht Altdorfer,* 1923, pp. 160-61.

54. Frank L. Borchardt, *German Antiquity in Renaissance Myth,* 1971, p. 171. See also Gerald Strauss, *Historian in an Age of Crisis: The Life and Work of Johannes Aventinus,* 1963, pp. 128-29.

55. Compare, for example, with Jörg Kölderer's "Der grosse Venedigsch Krieg," Vienna, Albertina.

56. Cord Meckseper, "Zur Ikonographie von Altdorfers 'Alexanderschlacht,'" *Zeitschrift des Deutschen Vereins für Kunstwissenschaft,* XXII, 1968, p. 179.

57. Ruhmer, *Albrecht Altdorfer,* 1965.

58. This topographical tradition became one of the main components in the formative stage of modern landscape painting. The Emperor Maximilian, for example, ordered inventories of hunting and fishing grounds, and in these one also finds the employment of the high vantage point in order to show a specific geographical location. Otto Benesch, *German and Austrian Art of the Fifteenth and Sixteenth Century,* 1972, p. 343.

59. Hans Hildebrandt, *Die Architektur bei Altdorfer,* 1908, pp. 86-89.

60. Nicholas of Cusa treated questions of beauty and art in his treatises *De mente* and *De ludo globi,* and also in a small treatise devoted to the problem of beauty, *Tota pulchra.* But since he was read by theologians his thoughts on art did not enter the theory of art of those times. Evelyn Underhill, *The Vision of God,* 1960, p. XVI. See also Tatarkiewicz, 1974, pp. 60-64.

61. This explains convincingly why painters belonged to the guild of pharmacists and physicians, also in Regensburg. Johannes Paricius, *Regensburg,* 1753, pp. 130-69.

62. Dagobert Frey, *Gotik und Renaissance als Grundlagen der modernen Weltanschauung,* 1929, p. 121.

63. *Encyclopedia of Philosophy,* Vol. 6, 1967, p. 39.

64. Erwin Panofsky, *Dürer,* 1945, p. 164 ff.

65. The concept of motion is crucial in Nicholas of Cusa's ideas on artistic creativity. He writes, "firstly, he (the artist) tries to infuse his material with potency, that is, to make the material capable of receiving the form of art; when this is done he sees that only through movement can he transform potency into the form which he conceived in his mind." Quoted in Tatarkiewicz, p. 66.

66.   *Encyclopedia of Philosophy,* 1967, p. 315.

67.   Benjamin, 1973, p. 94 ff.

68.   Wellek, p. 14.

69.   Millington, p. 145.

70.   Halstead, ed., *Romanticism,* p. 43.

71.   Otto Mann, *Der junge Friedrich Schlegel,* 1932, pp. 108-109.

72.   Müller, p. 139. My own translation of *Ideen 86,* from "Fragmente" 10.

73.   Ibid., p. 128; also Benjamin, 1973, p. 70.

74.   Ibid., p. 135.

75.   Aventinus (Leidinger edition), p. 11.

Chapter 3

1.   Bernard Berenson, *Italian Painters of the Renaissance,* 1962, p. 5.

2.   The German title of Fiorillo's work is *Geschichte der zeichnenden Künste in Deutschland und den Vereinigten Niederlanden,* 9 volumes, 1815-1820. The work was modelled after Abatti Lanzi's *Storia pittorica dell'Italia,* 1785. While Lanzi's governing concept is that of the school, Fiorillo attempts to go beyond this to trace connections between schools.

3.   It was Fiorillo who had introduced the young Wackenroder to the history of Old German and Italian art.

4.   Johann Dominik Fiorillo, *Kleine Schriften artistischen Inhalts,* 1803-06.

5.   Bertold Hinz, "Säkularisation als verwerteter 'Bildersturm,'" in Martin Warnke, ed., *Bildersturm: Die Zerstörung des Kunstwerks,* 1973, p. 114. Before secularization in Cologne there were 83 churches and 33 chapels, afterwards there remained 4 main churches and 16 auxiliary churches.

6.   Fiorillo did not acknowledge Schlegel as his source. Friedländer, 1891, p. 101, credited Fiorillo for his citation of the *Battle of Alexander* as a major work by Altdorfer, not realizing that Fiorillo's contribuution was but a copy of Schlegel.

7.   The Vienna *Nativity* and the Vienna *Landscape with Tree* and the Munich *Susanna's Bath.*

8.   Johann Dominik Fiorillo, *Geschichte der Mahlerei,* Vol. II, 1815-20, p. 409, note "a."

9.   Nagler, *Künstlerlexikon,* 1830.

10.   "Am zugänglichsten aber für die Kunst ist in diesem Kreise die Liebe der Maria, die Mutterliebe, der gelungenste Gegenstand der religiösen romantischen Phantasie." Georg W. F. Hegel, *Aesthetik,* Vol. I and II, 1977 (first edition 1835 posthumously), pp. 594-95.

11. G.W.F. Hegel, *Aesthetics, Lectures on Fine Arts,* translated by T. M. Knox, Vol. I, 1975, p. 541.

12. Ibid., pp. 542-43.

13. *Thieme-Becker Künstlerlexikon,* Vol. 20, p. 78.

14. W. Waetzoldt, *Deutsche Kunsthistoriker,* 1921, p. 163, points out the influence of the great geographers and world travellers on art historians by causing a world-historical approach in the history of art at the beginning of the 1840s and by encouraging and strengthening an empirical viewpoint.

15. Franz Theodor Kugler, *Handbuch der Kunstgeschichte,* 1842, p. 465.

16. Ibid.

17. Ibid.

18. Grimm, *Deutsches Wörterbuch,* Vol. 7, 1889, pp. 1822-26.

19. Together with Rumohr, Kugler and Schnaase, Waagen was one of the individuals who had especially well treated the study of medieval and more recent art from a scientific viewpoint. In Heidelberg in 1818 he saw the Boisseré collection which influenced his scientific work significantly.

20. Ralph von Rettberg, *Nürnberger Briefe,* 1846, pp. 164-65.

21. Anton Springer, *Kunsthistorïsche Briefe,* 1857, p. 585.

22. Rettberg had used the term "child-like" (*kindlich*) to characterize Altdorfer's visionary approach, meaning those qualities which are most desirable in a child, such as purity of character, piety, religiosity, a directness in communication. Grimm, p. 769. But Springer used childish (*kindisch*), a term which has only negative connotations, meaning everything undesirable in a child, or an adult who behaves like a child. ". . . am wenigsten konnte Albrecht Altdorfer unter dessen Händen sich historische Scenen in ein buntes Puppenspiel verwandelten, den malerischen Formenreiz verwirklichen und die weltliche Kunst in Ansehen bringen." Springer, *Letters,* 1857, p. 593.

23. Anton Springer, *Handbuch der Kunstgeschichte,* 1909.

24. Springer, 1909, p. 107.

25. Waetzoldt, 1921, p. 108.

26. Achim von Arnim, *Die Kronenwachter,* 1857, pp. 188-89. The time between the revolutions of 1848-49 and the unification of Italy and Germany is dealt with here. The revolutions of 1848-49 failed to achieve national independence and unity through popular uprisings by the people. The *Fürstenstaaten* had repressed the national movement.

27. Ibid., pp. 188-89.

28. Ibid.

29. Ernst Förster, *Geschichte der deutschen Kunst,* Vol. II, pp. 314-15. Counted as his most significant work together with his *Denkmale deutscher Baukunst, Bildnerei und Malerei.*

30. *Thieme-Becker Künstlerlexikon,* Vol. 12, 1969, pp. 135-36, calls him a *Kunstschriftsteller* which is the not the same as a *Kunsthistoriker,* the term used for Kugler.

31. ". . . Travestien, die ungeachtet ihres kindlich geschmacklosen Vergnügens Ereignisse der Vergangenheit mit Verwischung jeder historischen Spur bis in die kleinsten Verhältnisse der Gegenwart umzusetzen, bald sehr beliebt wurden."

32. Waetzoldt, Vol. II, 1921, p. 119.

33. W. Engelmann, "Altdorfer," in Meyers, ed., *Kunsterlexikon,* Vol. I, 1872, pp. 536-53.

34. Ibid.

35. Ad. Rosenberg, "Die deutschen Kleinmeister," in *Künst und Künstler des Mittelalters und der Neuzeit,* ed. Robert Dohme, 1877, Vol. I, part I, pp. 35-44.

36. "Dilettant" refers to the *uomini universali* such as Leonardo, Michelangelo, Goethe, persons guided by the idea of completion and perfection of their humanity. In 1799 Goethe and Schiller devised an analysis of *Dilettantismus* and a study of its role. Alfred Mundhenk, *Über den Dilettantismus,* 1966, pp. 13, 19. See also *"Dielettantismus"* in Alois Riegl, *Volkskunst,* 1894.

37. Rosenberg, p. 40.

38. F. Lippmann, *Jahrbuch der Königlich Preussischen Kunstsammlungen,* Vol. VII, 1886, pp. 154-56.

39. *Liebhaber Bibliothek alter Illustrationen,* 1888.

40. Friedländer, 1891.

41. Ibid., p. 165.

42. Ibid., p. 102. In 1809 Hubert Janitschek rejected this view, recognizing the *Battle of Alexander* for its symbolic power and "pathos." Janitschek suggested that Altdorfer knew how to relate nature and its elements to the human spectacle. The art of the sixteenth century is seen here as having a kinship to the Romantic literature of the nineteenth century, for example, to Eichendorf. Janitschek claims that Altdorfer knew and was dependent on Grünewald: "Darlegung der Wirkungen eines kraftigen Lichtzentrums auf die Atmosphäre." He criticizes the art of Altdorfer's time because it reflects "Das Zuviel, die Unart der Zeit." Hubert Janitschek, *Die Geschichte der deutschen Malerei,* 1890, Vol. III, pp. 411-20.

43. Ibid., p. 119.

44. Franz von Reber, *Kurfürst Maximilian von Bayern als Gemäldesammler,* 1892, p. 25.

45. _____. *Klassischer Bilderschatz,* 12 volumes, 1893.

46. Ernst Buchner, *Albrecht Altdorfer und sein Kreis,* 1938.

47. Franz von Reber, *Geschichte der Malerei,* 1894.

48. Hildebrandt, 1908.

49. Sturge T. Moore, *Albrecht Altdorfer,* 1901, p. 12; all of Chapter II.

50. Ibid., pp. 8-9.

51. Hermann Voss, *Der Ursprung des Donaustils,* 1907.

52. Ibid., p. 174.

53. Karl Scheffler, *Verwandlunger des Barocks,* 1947, p. 40. Elsewhere it is stated, "Grundsatzlich war es im 16. Jahrhundert in Deutschland nicht viel anders als im 19. in ganz Europa," p. 10.

54. Walter Benjamin, *"Beschaulicher Historismus,"* 1977, p. 70.

55. Voss, p. 139.

56. Friedlander hesitatingly attributed it to Altdorfer in 1891, p. 119. Robert Stiassny published on it too, in "Aus einer Osterreichischen Klostergalerie," *Zeitschrift fur Bildenden Kunst,* 1891, pp. 256-96.

57. Voss, p. 192, "krankhaft."

58. Georg Dehio, "Die Krisis in der deutschen Kunst im 16. Jahrhundert," *Archiv für Kulturgeschichte,* XII, 1913. Dehio sees the crisis as a tragic conflict between Renaissance and Reformation.

59. Rosenberg, *Kunst und Künstler des Mittelalters und der Neuzeit,* 1877, p. 13.

60. Voss, p. 192. The notion of Altdorfer as a dilettant was to appear once more in Hans Tietze's monograph *Altdorfer,* 1923, p. 10, where he calls Altdorfer an "amateur," a word which implies "self-trained" whereas Goethe's or Lichtwark's use of the term dilettant implies a highly trained person. See also Alfred Mundhenk, 1966, for further discussion of the term.

61. A. Lichtwark, *Vom Arbeitsfeld des Dilettantismus,* 1897. Lichtwark's movement addressed itself to the wealthy burghers whereas the conscious revival of dilettantism in mid-nineteenth century England hoped to revive the arts in order to solve sociopolitical and national economic problems. John Ruskin's revival of English crafts aimed at a new dilettantism of the craftsman. Similar to it, Alois Riegl's *Volkskunst* had appeared in 1894.

62. Voss, p. 175.

63. Ibid., pp. 176-77. Theodor Hetzer argued also that Italian (Venetian) artists were receptive to "Northern" art, particularly so Tintoretto's reception of Altdorfer motifs relating to form, space and the figure. See Hetzer, *Das deutsche Element in der italienischen Malerei des 16. Jahrhunderts,* 1929, pp. 139-44.

64.   Johannes Janssen, *History of the German People,* 1896, Vol. I.

65.   Ibid., pp. 252 ff., 319-39.

66.   ". . . es trauert alles Laub und Gras, nun bieg dich Baum, nun bieg dich Ast, nun bieg dich Laub und grünes Gras . . ." Voss, p. 183, a song on the Passion of Christ.

Chapter 4

1.   Ludwig von Baldass, *Albrecht Altdorfer, Studien über die Entwicklungsfaktoren im Werk des Künstlers,* Vienna, 1923; E. W. Bredt, *Albrecht Altdorfer,* Munich, 1923; Max J. Friedländer, *Albrecht Altdorfer,* Berlin, 1923; Hans Tietze, *Albrecht Altdorfer,* Leipzig, 1923.

2.   C. Dodgson in his book review of H. Tietze's monograph, *Burlington Magazine,* XLV, p. 94.

3.   Tietze, p. 3.

4.   Ibid., p. 10.

5.   Ibid., p. 18.

6.   Ludwig Baldass, *Albrecht Altdorfer,* Vienna, 1941, p. 9.

7.   Ibid.. Compare the table of contents.

8.   Ibid., p. 208.

9.   Ibid., p. 210.

10.   Ibid., p. 219.

11.   Eberhard Ruhmer, *Albrecht Altdorfer,* Munich, 1965, p. 19.

12.   Ibid., p. 20.

13.   Ibid., p. 33.

14.   Ibid., p. 44.

15.   Personal communication with Franz Winzinger, Regensburg, April 13, 1977.

16.   Franz Winzinger, *Albrecht Altdorfer, Gemälde,* Munich, 1975, p. 5.

17.   Winzinger, *Albrecht Altdorfer, Zeichnungen,* Munich, 1952, p. 15.

18.   Ibid., 1952, p. 29.

19.   Ibid., 1975, p. 61.

20.   Ibid., pp. 5 and 28.

21. Ibid, p. 28.

22. Ibid., pp. 40 and 5: "Maler von Gottes Gnaden."

23. H. W. Janson, *The History of Art,* New York, 1977, plate 72. The related text on p. 475 is biased and remained unchanged from the first edition's ninth printing in 1966, p. 393. The time chart appears on p. 549.

24. Ibid., 1977, p. 724.

25. Exhibition Catalogue, Yale University Art Gallery: *Prints and Drawings of the Danube School,* 1969.

26. Charles Talbot, "Landscape from Incunabula to Altdorfer," *Gesta,* 1977, pp. 321-26. Charles Talbot wrote his dissertation in 1968 on "The Passion Cycle by A. Altdorfer at St. Florian: A Study of Program and Style," Yale University. The problems of correlation between content and style which Winzinger had also addressed (1975, pp. 37 and 63) are discussed here. He explains the stylistic discrepancies, which Baldass had called Altdorfer's versatility, between the panels of the *St. Florian legend* and *Susanna's Bath,* for example, on the basis of the nature of the commission. In the first case "plain painting" (*schlichte Malerei*) was specified; in the latter, the commission for the Bavarian court called for "precious painting" (*köstliche Malerei*). Altdorfer varied his style according to the nature of the commission.

27. William Walter Wolf III, "The Art of Albrecht Altdorfer, a Mirror of Society," unpublished dissertation, University of Missouri, Columbia, 1974.

Chapter 5

1. Kenneth Burke, *A Grammar of Motives and a Rhetoric of Motives,* 1962, p. 634.

2. Clifford Geertz, *The Interpretation of Cultures,* 1973, p. 232.

3. Eduard Firmenich Richartz, *Die Brüder Boisseré: Sulpiz und Melchoir Boisseré als Kunstsammler, ein Beitrag zur Geschichte der Romantik,* 1916, p. 1. I have translated into prose the following poem from this book.

Mir winkt ein alter schöner Saal,
Zwei Brüder haben ihn gebaut,
da hab ich in dem reinsten Strahl
Mein Vaterland geschaut.

Das war in jener trüben Zeit
Ein holder stiller Wallfahrtsort
Wo sich der Väter Herrlichkeit
Verbarg im sichern Port.

Der Märtyrer und Heil'gen Schar,
Viel Helden Gottes treu und kuhn,
die zarten Frauen mild und klar,
Die für den Heiland glühn.

Manch Bild der allerreinsten Magd,
Wie Gottes Engel ihr erschien,
bald wie sie um den Sohn geklagt,
bald wie die Weisen knien.

Was frommer Fleiss und keusche Kunst
gepflegt in alter deutscher Welt
Ward hier nach Gottes Rat und Gunst
gerettet aufgestellt.

Es kam wohl manches treue Herz
und sah die lieben Bilder an,
Gesegnet sei der tiefe Schmerz,
der da in ihm begann.

O Liebesbrunst zum Vaterland
und zu der alten Heldenzeit
Du bittre Lust und Gottes Hand
Habt uns vom Joch befreit.

Nun schauen wir euch ander an,
Ihr sprechet uns auch fröhlich zu,
Ihr Bilder, doch ein rechter Mann
Begehrt noch keine Ruh.

Ihr müsset erst an Künstler Hand
Durch unsre freien Länder gehn,
Man soll an keiner deutschen Wand
Mehr Heidenbilder sehn.

Ihr lieben Heil'gen, kommt heraus
Und segnet uns, wir flehen euch,
Ihr holden Mägdlein, schmückt das Haus,
Ihr Ritter, schützt das Reich.

Du steh' noch lange, Bildersaal,
Ihr Brüder, übet euer Amt,
Dass an der frommen Vorzeit Strahl
Sich manche Brust entflammt.

4.   Heinrich Wölfflin, *Gedanken zur Kunstgeschichte,* 1946 (first edition, 1940).

5.   Wölfflin, *Principles of Art History,* 1932 (first German edition, 1915), pp. 235-36.

6.   Wölfflin, *Italien und das deutsche Formgefuhl,* 1931. The English translation deletes the national element from the title, as *The Sense of Form in Art,* 1958.

7.   Wolfflin, *Gedanken,* 1946, pp. 130-31.

8.   Ibid., p. 24.

9. Ibid., *Italien,* 1931, p. 17.

10. Ibid., pp. 89 and 108.

11. Ibid., p. 67.

12. Ibid., p. 112.

13. Ibid., pp. 197-98.

14. Ibid., p. 222.

15. Ibid., p. 211.

16. Ibid., pp. 176-78.

17. Otto Pächt, "Zur deutschen Bildauffassung der Spätgotik und Renaissance," *Alte und Neue Kunst,* 1952, pp. 70-78, originally written in honor of Fritz Saxl's 25th anniversary at the Warburg Institute. The German text of the quotation is as follows:

". . . da ist einmal der Blick aus dem zur Wochenstube adaptierten dunklen Seitenschiff in das helle Mittelschiff und den Kirchenchor gegeben. Im Fluge dieses Ringelspiels—der Engel —erleben wir noch einmal den genzen Innenraum und spüren dabei seine hallende Weite noch anders als beim blossen ruhigen Hinschauen. . . . Altdorfers Bild gibt zu erkennen, was die Überwindung der flächigen Anordnung, die Eroberung der Bildtiefe dem deutschen Maler bedeutet: die Öffnung der Raumtiefe wird als Einladung aufgefasst, ins Innere des Bildraums einzutreten, den Hohlraum nach allen Richtungen zu durchwandern, nicht nur nach der einen . . . Davorstehen und Drinnensein, Schauen und Innehaben, die Verei- nigung dieser Haltungen bleibt der stete Anspruch, den die deutschen Maler an sich und an die Betrachter ihrer Werke stellen . . . Das Grundverhalten mit seiner Tendenz, zwei einan- der widersprechende, ja strenggenommen ausschliessende Einstellungen zu vereinigen, ist eine genuine künstlerische Problemstellung. Vollkommen konnten sie (die Lösungen) nur dort gelingen, wo wie bei Altdorfer über den Charakter der Darstellung als Traumgesicht und Märchen, über das Fiktive der Wunschtraumerfüllung kein Zweifel gelassen wurde. Dürer empfand das Problem als tragischen Widerspruch."

18. Theodor Hetzer, 1929, pp. 139-44.

19. Hanna Priebsch-Closs, *Magie und Naturgefühl in der Malerei von Grünewald, Baldung Grien, Lukas Cranach und Altdorfer,* 1936.

20. Ibid.

21. Ibid., p. 44.

22. Ibid.

23. Ibid., p. 39.

24. Ibid., pp. 43-44.

25. Hans Watzlik, *Der Meister von Regensburg, ein Albrecht Altdorfer Roman,* 1939. The novel continued in popularity after World War II, being re-edited in 1955. It is today found in many public libraries, according to W. Kehr, 1973, p. 15. The 1939 version was printed in Gothic letters, the 1955 edition in Latin letters.

26. A. Luther, *Deutsche Geschichte in deutscher Erzählung,* 1943, pp. 176-82, suggests that of the forty biographies published on early sixteenth century painters and sculptors, nine are on Dürer, seven on Grünewald, two on Cranach, and only one on Altdorfer.

27. The theme of the divided soul is mentioned directly in connection with the work *Rest on the Flight* ("Die Seele Altdorfers ist geteilt"), Watzlik, p. 244; also, "die eigene Seele schien ihm gespalten: Wie versöhne ich Stoff und Geist, wie das Vergängliche und das Ewige, das Begrenzte und Schwankende?", p. 310. Peter Halm also discusses the "gespaltene Seele" polarity in *Werk des Künstlers,* 1939-40, pp. 102-3.

28. Watzlik, p. 456.

29. Ibid., p. 217.

30. Ibid., p. 360.

31. "Majestät, es ist ein deutsches Werk"; and to Altdorfer, "Euer Werk steht hoch über der Laune der Gehörten, es bleibt ewiger Besitz der Nation und einst wird man in Deutschland sagen, welch ein Geist hat unter uns gewohnt." Watzlik, pp. 435-36.

32. Ibid., p. 6.

33. Ibid., pp. 139 and 406.

34. Karl Öttinger in *Altdeutsche Kunst im Donauland,* 1939, p. 14.

35. Wolfgang Kehr, *Projekt einer didaktischen Ausstellung zu Altdorfers "Alexander-schlact,"* 1973, p. 16.

36. Watzlik, pp. 426-27.

37. Ibid., p. 390.

38. Öttinger's preface specifically excludes the Church and by so doing serious falsifies historical facts.

39. *Münchener Zeitung,* July 12, 1938; *Königsberger Tageblatt,* June 2, 1938. To this day "Culture" substitutes for church in Germany on Sunday mornings. According to Peter Halm, 1939-40, pp. 101-2, the exhibit "Albrecht Altdorfer und sein Kreis" drew ca. 100,000 viewers from May to October, 1938, and was in other respects "eine der erfolgreichsten und der bedeutendsten Jubiläumsveranstaltungen der letzten Jahre—aus allen Schichten des Volkes."

40. In 1937, 417 paintings and prints by Oskar Kokoschka were confiscated; he escaped to England in 1938. Max Ernst was imprisoned in Paris in 1939, then emigrated to the States in 1941. Otto Dix lost his teaching position at the Academy in Dresden in 1938. Georg Grosz lived in emigration in the States since 1935.

41. See, for example, *Hannoverscher Kurier,* "Ein alter Meister tritt ins Neue Reich," May 4, 1938. ". . . Jene Zeit und jene Meister sind hingesunken; spätere Jahrhunderte haben die atemweite Lebensgemeinschaft, die ihnen Gegenwart war, mit Grenzrainen überwuchert. Heute aber ist der gemeinsame *Raum,* der politische Rahmen dieses *Raumes* wenigstens wieder hergestellt, und uns allen, jedem Schaffenden des grössren Reiches, fällt die Aufgabe zu, ihn *im alten Geist auszufüllen.* Österreich, das ist nicht Huld des Glücks, sondern das ist uns Aufgabe und Aufruf. Da kommt uns denn das Zeichen, das heute über den Königlichen Platz zu München hinleuchtet, für den Anbeginn dieser Aufgabe gerade recht; es ist uns *wie ein rufendes Feldzeichen* . . . die Ausstellung wendet sich an den deutschen Menschen schlechthin . . . Was diese Welt zur Zeugenschaft eines neuen Zeitalters erhebt . . . ist . . . dass in diesem Werk der urgermanische Genius eine Selbsterneuerung aus dem innersten Kern heraus feiert . . ."

42. Ernst Buchner, *Albrecht Altdorfer und sein Kreis,* 1938, p. 2.

43. Ibid.

44. Ibid.

45. Ibid.

46. *Hannoverscher Kurier,* May 24, 1938.

47. Buchner, p. 2.

48. *Altdentsche Kunst im Donauland,* 1939. The introductory note to this exhibition catalogue was written by the then Secretary of State, Dr. Kai Mühlmann.

49. Ibid.

50. Ibid.

51. In his 1907 *Ursprung des Donaustils,* H. Voss had rejected the work as Altdorfer's because it did not fit his concept of Altdorfer's "gentle, poetic style of quiet maturity."

52. Otto Benesch, *Pantheon,* Vol. XXI, 1938, p. 80 ff.

53. Ibid., p. 80 ff.

54. Ibid. The introduction of the 1939 Vienna exhibition catalogue also suggested hesitation or disfavor toward art commissioned by the courts. The demand for heroic representation and gallant splendor was thought to be alien to the natural talents of the race. *Altdeutsche Kunst,* p. 14.

55. Further discussion of the history of this painting's attribution is given by Achim Hubel, *Die Schöne Marie von Regensburg: Wallfahrten, Gnadenbilder,, Ikonographie,* 1977. This is the catalogue of an exhibition assembled by the Regensburg Bishopric in Regensburg, June 24 to August 15, 1977, to celebrate the 850th anniversary of the Kollegiatstift zu den Heiligen Johannes Baptist und Johannes Evangelist in Regensburg. The author rejects the thesis, now sanctioned by the church, that Altdorfer's panel of the Beautiful Mary was the miracle-working image of the pilgrimage chapel by the same name in Regensburg, and argues that it represents merely a copy of the actual miraculous image, executed for one of the more

wealthy pilgrims. See pp. 218-19. For a discussion of Byzantine mariological types in fifteenth and sixteenth century Europe in general see Regine Dölling, *Byzantinische Elemente in der Kunst des 16. Jahrhunderts,* 1957, p. 151.

56. Joseph Kagerer, "Die schicksalsreiche Geschichte der Schönen Maria," *Verhandlungen des historischen Vereins für Oberpfalz und Regensburg,* 1952, p. 118.

57. *Altdeutsche Kunst,* 1939.

58. Some of these may be given here, in abbreviated form, to illustrate their tone, as shown by our emphasis.

". . . *Urdeutsche* Künstler wie Altdorfer . . . ihre eigenständige Persönlichkeit ist oft *pflanzenhaft* der Landschaft eingebunden, und ihr Wesen lässt sich erst in ihrer Volks und Zeitverbundenheit erfassen. . . . Das Wesentliche an Altdorfers Kunst . . . ist ein unbändig kraftoolles Temperament voll Phantasie, mit einer schwer zu zugelnden, reichen und vielseitigen Begabung . . . Denn wenn das glühende Bemühen eines Grossen einen religiösen Inhalt in seine beste Form gebracht hat, dann kann uns keine kirchliche Sonderdeutung davon trennen; dann spricht *das Ewige* und Göttliche aus dem Werk zu uns." Karl Busch, "Erlebnis einer Ausstellung," *Das Bayerland,* Jg. 49, 1938, pp. 545-49.

Another commentator saw the *St. Florian Altarpiece* and the *Battle of Alexander* as the two opposite poles of the "genuine German character trait," the divided soul. The *St. Florian Altarpiece* is of a "wild, sometimes bizarre, bravery" (*Kühnheit*); the *Battle of Alexander* shows infinite patience of the most minute workmanship. Egon Kornmann, *Gesammelte Aufsätze: Kunst im Leben,* 1954, p. 88.

"Sein (Altdorfers) Erfinden war wie das Singen eines Vogels, das den Menschen in die Seele dringt." Ulrich Christoffel, "Albrecht Altdorfer," *Zeitschrift für deutsche Geisteswissenschaft,* 1938-39, p. 539. Elsewhere the author states that Altdorfer enriched German art in its repertory of figures, especially through his women, for example, the young *Bürgersfrau* who lifts her skirts to step into the water in the *Recovery of the Body of St. Sebastian.* The *St. Florian Altarpiece* is called an *idyll,* it emphasizes reconciliation even in tragic moments and recognizes in each individual fate the return of *eternally* flowing life. p. 534.

"The *St. Florian Altarpiece* is Altdorfer's most extensive accomplishment, twelve large and four smaller panels. Of German passion cycles, this polyptych is the last before the Reformation. The conception is entirely changed from the traditional one; Christ merely is the pretext for a colorful narrative. The story of His passion has become a composition, a scene, a popular play. Herein lies the novelty and the fascination of this passion cycle which harbors the germ of the whole range of effects of Bavarian baroque art." Hans Jantzen, *Das Werk des Künstlers,* 1939, pp. 42 ff. Jantzen's comments contain slight hints of National Socialist ideology, but one passage is striking in this regard. He puts down the Christian content of the *St. Florian Altarpiece* by saying: ". . . Der Christus der Altdorferschen Passion, eine vergleichsweise unansehnliche Figur mit kleinen Mausaugen und grämlichem Ausdruck, ist nur noch 'Anlass' für ein farbenfrohes Bildgeschehen, das den Betrachter vor allen Dingen kunstlerisch von der optischen Seite her fesselt," pp. 43-44. But in fairness to Jantzen, he then proceeds into a very valid investigation of the role of light and color in the altarpiece.

A professional botanist responded to the "Altdorfer Year 1938" by carefully analyzing Altdorfer's use of trees, the fir and the willow appearing most frequently. "Altdorfer geht

über das zufällig Beobachtete mit Zutaten einer phantasievoll geführten Feder gern hinaus
. . .Vorliebe für abwärts gerichtete Zweigspitzen und hängende Äste, für lotrecht herab-
hängende Laubbaumzweige; Vollends frei von dem, was sorgfältige Naturbeobachtung
hätte geben können, sehen wir Altdorfer in denjenigen Drucken und Zeichnungen sich zei-
gen, auf welchen die Vegetationen zur Erde sprühen wie Kaskaden oder Wasserfälle." Ernst
Küster, "Bäume und Baumkronen in Altdorfers Kunst," *Forschungen und Fortschritte,*
Nr. 35-36, 1938, pp. 408-09.

59. William Pinder, "Die Romantik in der deutschen Kunst um 1500," in *Das Werk des Kun-
stlers,* I, 1939-40, pp. 3-41. Pinder published this material for the first time in 1935 in the
journal *Völkische Kultur,* the title giving away the emphasis both of the times and the
author.

60. Ibid., p. 7.

61. Ibid., p. 41; "Das Volk hat seine Romantik auf zwie verschiedene Zeiten verteilt. Im geschicht-
lichen Anblick treten sie weider zusammen. . ."

62. Ibid., p. 27.

63. Ibid., p. 30.

64. Ibid., p. 30; ". . . ein ungeheures Getöse verkündet das Herannahen der Sonne" (Goethe);
". . . Die Chöre der Morgenröten schlugen jetzt wie Donner einander entgegen mit Tönen
statt Farben" (Jean-Paul).

65. *Albrecht Altdorfer und die Kunst der Donauschule in Oberösterreich,* 1947. Exhibition
Catalogue.

66. From the preface, *Kunst der Donauschule.*

67. Ibid.

68. Ibid., p. 8.

69. Adolf Laube, Max Steinmetz, Günter Vogler, eds., *Illustrierte Geschichte der Frühbürgerlichen Revolution,* 1974.

70. Ibid., p. 79.

71. Ibid., pp. 301-2.

72. Ibid., pp. 309-10.

73. Ibid., p. 77.

74. Ibid., p. 261.

75. Ibid., p. 310; Albrecht Dürer designed a monument to the defeated peasants in his book *Un-
terweisung der Messung mit dem Zirkel und Richtscheit,* 1525. Titled "Crown him with a
mourning peasant who is pierced by a sword," the motif is a direct transferance of his

Christus in der Rast woodcut from the Small Passion of 1511, and is repeated in his *Melancolia I.*

76. Klaus Sliwka, *Aspekte zum Unterrichtsfeld Bildende Kunst—Visuelle Kommunikation,* 1972, pp. 20-28.

77. This is but a small step removed from a model for adult education, devised by the director of the Museumspädagogisches Zentrum of the Alte Pinakothek in Munich, which proposed to teach *Bundeswehr* officers "attack and defense" and "the battle piece as political method" through Altdorfer's *Battle of Alexander.* I owe this information to Wolfgang Kehr, *Altdorfers "Alexanderschlacht" im Unterricht,* 1973, p. 71.

78. Kehr, *Projekt einer didaktischen Ausstellung,* 1973. The topic of the conference was "Problems of the Perception (*Rezeption*) of works of art in museums and churches."

79. Ibid.

80. To stage an unconventional exhibition seemed appropriate for the Munich art association which had been founded 150 years earlier as a protest against the classicism which had become established at the Academy, according to Laszlo Glozer, "Mit der 'Alexanderschlacht' ans neue Ufer," *Süddeutsche Zeitung,* 19-20 January, 1973.

81. Wolfgang Kehr, *Curriculum—Gesamtschule. Fach: Kunsterziehung,* 1973, p. 77.

Chapter 6

1. Otto Benesch, *Albrecht Altdorfer,* 1939.

2. Arthur Schnitzler, *Paracelsus,* 1920.

3. Craig Harbison, 1969, p. 33.

4. *Encyclopedia of Philosophy,* Vol. 6, 1967, p. 39.

5. Paracelsus, *Sämtliche Werke:* Vol. IV, *Fragment über die Imagination, IV.* Edition of Bernhard Aschner, 1926-28.

6. ". . . Dann sind also die Elementischen Cörper / das keine perfect Farben mit nammen mag genennet werden. Was aber von ihnen kommt / das hat seine deutliche verstendige und namhafftige Farben. Wann die Elementen also nicht perfect Farben haben / sondern wie gemelt ist. Dann nicht eine Farben wachst von ihnen / sondern viel Farben. Darumb seind sie componiert von viel Farben / in so viel / so viel von ihnen gehend." Paracelsus, *Dess Buchs Meteorum,* Caput I, cited in Benesch, 1939, p. 5.

7. Benesch, p. 7.

8. ". . . Menschen: denn es hat sein Haut / und ist die Rinden / hatt sein Haupt und Haar / ist die Wurtzen / sein Figur und zeichen / sein Sinne / hatt sein empfindlichkeit in seim Stammen darein sein letzung folgt dass es stirbt: Sein Laub / Blumen und Frucht sein Zierde / im Menschen das gehör / Gesicht und redende Arth." Paracelsus, *Philosophiae Liber III: De Elemento Terrae,* cited in Benesch, p. 8.

9. Benesch, p. 9.

10. Ibid., p. 12.

11. ". . . Nun auff solches hat Gott gefallen / dass er ein Element Wasser machte / und vom selbigen schüffe für und für in die gebärung die Mineralien, damit das dieselbigen täglich wüchsend / und dem Menschen nutz werend zu seinem Gebrauch. Und hat also das Wasser geschafen / dass es soll ein Mutter sein der Ertz / und in demselbigen die drei Ersten / Feur / Saltz und Mercurium: und dermassen geordnet / mit einem unterschied / aus dem Element Wasser zu werden die Metallen / Gestein / Stein und Ertz. Und obgleichwol die Frucht widerwärtig sey der Mutter: also hats Gott geschafen / ein jegliches in sein art. . . . Diese Ding alle seind dem Gewalt Gottes zugestellt / der also sein Willen verbracht hat. Nun wissen am ersten / das dass Element Wasser ein Mutter ist / aller Mineralien und ist ihm gar nicht gleich: Dann also ist auch die Erden Holtz / und ist nicht Holtz / und Holtz wird von ihr. Also wird auch der Stein / das Eysen / usw. vom Wasser. Das Wasser wird / das es selbs nicht ist / die Erden auch / das sie selbs nicht ist: Also muss auch der Mensch werden das er selbs nicht ist. Was soll in sein letzt Materiam gehen / dass muss anders werden / dann der Angang ist . . . Anders ist der Metall / anders der Stein / anders der Straal anderst der Regenboden . . . Also auch im Erdrich / anderst das Holtz / anderst das Kraut / anderst die Blum / anderst der Schwamm. Also hat sich ein Künstler lassen sehen / ein Meister über all / dass ihms niemands mag nachthun: Er ists allein / alles in allem / er ist *Rerum Prima Materia,* er ist *Rerum ultima Materia,* er ist der alles ist." Paracelsus, *De Generatione Metallorum: Mineralium zwen Tractat,* in Benesch, p. 13.

12. ". . . Nun aber weiter von den Farben zu reden / sag ich / dass aller rechten / vollkommenen Farben nicht mehr dann sechs sind: Nemlich Schwartz / Weiss / Gelb / Roth / Grün / und Blau. . . Also ist es auch mit anderen Beyfarben und vermischten Farben zu verstehen / wie mir dann alle Mahler zeugniss müssen geben / dass man aus diesen sechs Farben über dreissig Farben machen kann / und doch keine der anderen gleich ist." Paracelsus, *Liber de imaginibus,* in Benesch, p. 25.

13. Benesch, 1939, p. 30.

14. ". . . Und das solt ihr wissen und mercken / dass der Chiromantie vielerley sind / und nicht allein die / so in Händen der Menschen zustehen / darnach den Menschen zu urtheilen / warzu er geneigt sey / und was im begegnen / und gutts und böss widerfahren werde: Sondern es seind der Chiromantiae noch mehr: Ein Chiromantia der Kreutter / ein Chiromantia des Laubs an dem Bäumen / ein Chiromantia des Holtzs / ein Chiromantia der Landschaften / durch die Strassen und Wasserflüss." Paracelsus, *Liber de imaginibus,* Cap. VII, in Benesch, p. 33.

15. G. F. Hartlaub, "Paracelsisches in der Kunst der Paracelsuszeit," in *Nova Acta Paracelsica,* Band 7, 1954, p. 139.

16. Benesch, 1939, p. 13.

17. Lottlisla Behling, *Die Pflanze in der mittelalterlichen Tafelmalerei,* 1957, pp. 125-31, citing Paracelsus, *Labyrinthus* (Aschner edition), Vol. I, p. 519.

18. Ibid., p. 127, citing Albertus Magnus.

19. In Albertus Magnus' words, ". . . folia dormire faciunt comesta, et *permutant rationem* . . . ," in Behling, p. 127.

20. Ibid., p. 129.

21. Paracelsus, *Labyrinthus,* Vol. 4, p. 366 ff.

22. André Chastel and Robert Klein, *Die Welt des Humanismus,* 1963, pp. 207-8.

23. Erwin Gradmann, "Phantastik und Komik: Versuch einer Deutung des Phantastischen," *Schriften der schweizerischen Geisteswissenschaftlichen Gesellschaft,* I, 1957, pp. 207-8.

24. "Formwerdung und Formauflösung sind die beiden Komponenten Altdorferscher Empfindung . . ." Examples given by Gradmann of the Altdorfer approach are "Steigen, Spriessen, Blähen, Treiben, Quellen, Fallen, Tropfen, Hängen, Spiralen, Zacken, Girlanden."

25. Gradmann, p. 46.

26. Hartlaub, pp. 132-33.

27. Alexander Friedrich, *Handlung und Gestalt des Kupferstichs und der Radierung,* 1931.

28. Ibid., p. 49 ff.

29. Alfred Stange, "Die Kunst der Donauschule," in *Alte und Moderne Kunst,* 1966, p. 2.

30. Ibid., *Malerei der Donauschule,* 1971, pp. 30-34 for discussion of *devotio moderna.*

31. Ibid., 1971, p. 31.

32. "Ihr Bestes aber gaben die Donaumaler in stilleren Bildern." The word quiet or a synonym thereof occurs eleven times within three pages of Stange's discussion.

33. Stange, 1971, p. 77.

34. Ibid., pp. 38-39.

35. Ibid., p. 80.

36. Benno Ulm, "Die Devotio moderna und die Architektur der Donauschule in Österreich," in *Alte und Moderne Kunst,* 1966, pp. 3-4.

37. Ulm, p. 5, refers to the "Raudnitzer Bewegung" at the Augustinian *Stifte* Durnstein and St. Dorothea in Vienna.

38. Franz Lipp, "Volksart und Volksfrömmigkeit als Triebkräfte der Kunst der Donauschule," in *Katalog der Ausstellung "Werden und Wandlung: Kunst der Donauschule,"* 1967, pp. 20-35.

39. Ibid., p. 24.

40. Ibid., p. 31.

41. Nicolo Rasmo, "Donaustil und Italienische Kunst der Renaissance," in *Werden und Wandlung,* 1967, p. 115 ff.

42. Ibid., p. 117.

43. Ibid., p. 121.

44. "Diese Atmosphäre, die den Farben tonale Leuchtkraft verleiht, der besinnlich-getragene Stimmungseinklang von Mensch und Natur, die Beseelung der Landschaft zu einer vielstimmingen, von lebendigen Spannungen erfüllten Wesenheit: Das sind die grundlegenden Erkenntnisse, die Altdorfer der venetianischen Malerei verdankt." Rasmo, p. 123.

45. Rasmo, p. 124.

46. Ibid., pp. 124-25.

47. Carl Linfert, *Albrecht Altdorfer. Die Enthüllung der Landschaft* (The Unveiling of Landscape), 1938, p. 17. ". . . Sie lockt heran, und bleibt doch wunderlich, unvertraut und fremd."

48. Ibid., p. 16, "Naturbegierde."

49. ". . . Die Himmel kreisen im Feuer oder entweichen in ätherisches, luftloses Eis; und beidemal erliegt man der Illusion, dass auch sie—wie der rauchende Erdkreis—von oben erblickt seien. Was aber von der Erde zu sehen ist, legt sich wie ein Rand von Geröll und Gestrüpp an den unverlässigen *Krater* dieses Himmels. Nicht mehr überwölbt der Himmel die Erde oder begrenzt sie ruhig in der Ferne. Mit Ruhe ist kaum hineinzufinden in das Bild, jedoch, aus dem *Sonnenkrater* kommend, landet der Blick wie an einem Ufer. Eine Landkarte mehr als ein Bild! Aber eine Karte von Ereignissen, nicht von Orten. Und der Himmel ist ein Meer, worin die Wege nicht mehr festzulegen sind, weder für Gott noch für Menschen. Im Schatten unten kämpfen die Menschen ihre Schlacht. Hier herrscht der präzise und nüchterne Zugriff, die unbekümmerte irdische Anordnung der Machtmittel und gute Benützung des Sieges. So unentscheidbar kurz vorher noch alles was, hier ist nichts von dem katastrophalen Rätsel des Lichtkampfes oben. Die Schlacht ist ein Ergebnis der Sorgfalt wie nur irgendein stiller Zustand bei dem Zeltlager oder in der fernen Stadt. Hier beginnt nun aber zugleich die eigentliche Merkwürdigkeit Altdorfers. Selbst in den abgelegenen Winkeln der 'Idylle' ist noch der funkelnde, glimmende, Schein von dem *kreisenden Ausbruch* in den Wolken." Linfert, pp. 21-23.

50. Linfert, p. 25.

51. "Vielgehöhlte Form des nordischen Mittelalters ist noch bewahrt," Linfert, p. 27.

52. Ibid., p. 31.

53. ". . . jener Krater erkaltet zur Zuflucht, und der schützende Ort wiederum verliert nicht alle Gefahr . . . was wie Krater aussieht ist nicht nur Feuerstrahl, auch schöner See, Lichtlockung und strahlender Sturm . . . die Zuflucht der Menschen in ihre trümmerhaften Häuser, zeigt noch Flucht. Aus dem harten Steinboden kommen heftige Extreme: Feuer und Wäl-

der. Jédes hat bei Altdorfer die Form des Strahls, jene eigentümlich ziehende Linie, als ob Strahlen und Wachsen von gleicher Natur wären. Die Menschen verwachsen darin auf eine Art, die einzig in der Natur der deutschen Kunst, keiner anderen, je gelegen hat." Linfert, pp. 32-33. This is singular to German art, and this perception of nature, he suggests, cannot be perceived or interpreted as an idyll. The harshness of minute multiplicity, the endlessness, is more significant.

54. Linfert, pp. 36-37.

55. *Encyclopedia of Philosophy,* Vol. 6, 1967, p. 39.

56. Karl Öttinger, "Laube, Garten und Wald. Zu einer Theorie der Suddeutschen Sakralkunst, 1470-1520," in *Festschrift für Hans Sedlmayr,* 1962, pp. 201-28.

57. ". . . Wie der Wald dem Mann, dem Jäger gehört, so der Garten der Frau. Die Laube ist ihr Symbol; weiblich ist die Heiligkeit des Gewächses, das atmende Gedeihen." Öttinger, p. 223. Compare Gerhart B. Ladner's essay on "Vegetation Symbolism and the Concept of the Renaissance," in *De Artibus Opuscula,* Millard Meiss, ed., 1961, Vol. I.

58. Öttinger, pp. 225-26.

59. ". . . eine neue Weltmalerei entsteht, die den Wald erschliesst und in der Landschaft und Mensch protopantheistisch eins werden." Öttinger, p. 227.

60. Ibid.

61. Ibid., where the author refers to Dürer's woodcut illustration of Philosophy in Celtis' "Quattuor Libri" and to Celtis' tombstone in Vienna.

62. Bernhard Saran, "Der Maler Albrecht Altdorfer als Humanist in seiner reichsstadtischen Umwelt," in *Die Humanisten in ihrer politischen und sozialen Umwelt,* 1976, pp. 131-39.

63. Ibid., pp. 135-36. Winzinger refrained from interpreting the iconographical meaning of this painting, but established the Italian prototypes for Altdorfer's fountain. See Winzinger, 1975, p. 76.

64. Ibid., p. 139. See also Ovidius's description of the Golden Age in *Metamorphoses of Ovid,* trans. by Mary M. Innes, London, 1955, p. 34.

65. A. G. Roth, *Die Gestirne in der Landschaftsmalerei des Abendlandes,* 1945; W. Schone, *Uber das Licht in der Malerei,* 1954.

66. Dieter, Köpplin, "Das Sonnengestirn der Donaumeister, zur Herkunft und Bedeutung eines Leitmotivs," in *Werden und Wandlung,* 1967, pp. 78-114. Dürer had provided the motif of the rising sun first in the woodcut of the Resurrection in the *Small Passion* (1509). Altdorfer proceeded to transform his raw material from Dürer already in his own Resurrection woodcut (1512) where he interprets the miracle in dynamic terms as a total eruption of light. Examples of the motif of the sun in Altdorfer's paintings are: The *Resurrection* of the St. Florian altarpiece; *Mary Magdalene at the Tomb;* the *Recovery of the Body of St. Florian;* and the *Battle of Alexander.*

67. Ibid.

68. Ibid.

Chapter 7

1. Albrecht Dürer, *Entwürfe zur Einleitung des Lehrbuchs der Malerei,* quoted in Herbert von Einem, *Das Auge, der edelste Sinn,* Sonderdruck aus dem *Wallraf-Richartz Jahrbuch,* Band XXX, 1968, p. 283.

2. Karl Schwarz, *Augustin Hirschvogel, Ein deutscher Meister der Renaissance,* 1917; Annegrit Schmitt, "Hans Lautensack," in *Nürnberger Forschungen,* Band IV, 1957.

3. Heinrich Weizsäcker, *Adam Elsheimer,* 1952, dates the "Holy Family with Angels" to be of Elsheimer's Venetian sojourn, ca. 1598-1600. Saran, 1976, p. 138, suggests that Altdorfer's *Rest on the Flight* was conceived if not executed during a stay in Venice.

4. Rheinisches Landesmuseum, Bonn. Copper, 26 x 19.7 cm.

5. Personal communication with Wolfgang Pfeiffer, director, Landesmuseum Regensburg, April 13, 1977; see also Weizsäcker, 1952; *Adam Elsheimer: Werk, künstlerische Herkunft und Nachfolge,* 1967, pp. 15, 16, 25; *Katalog der Gemäldegalerie, Berlin,* 1975, p. 143.

6. Stange, 1971, p. 80; Benesch, 1939, p. 49.

7. Agricola was born (1667) and died (1719) in Regensburg, but traveled extensively in Germany, England, the Netherlands, and France and lived mostly in Naples and Augsburg. Especially important for the present analysis are the Kassel landscapes which include his *Evening Landscape with Praying Turks,* in small format, and the *Discovery of a Statue* and *Landscape with Men Who Erect a Tomb.* See *Katalog der Ausstellung* (Schwerin), *Malerei des 18. Jahrhunderts,* n. d., pp. 36, 73, plates XXIV, XXV; see also *Thieme-Becker Künstlerlexikon,* Vol. I, pp. 135-36.

8. Andreas Andresen, *Die deutschen Maler als Kupferstecher,* Vol. 5, 1878, pp. 344-51.

9. Herbert von Einem, "Die Symbol-landschaft der deutschen Romantik," special publication in *Klassizismus und Romantik in Deutschland,* Katalog Deutsches Nationalmuseum Nürnberg, 1966, p. 22.

10. von Einem, p. 22. For the frequency of the theme "Cross-in-a-Landscape," see Helmut Börsch-Supan and Karl Wilhelm Jähnig, *Caspar David Friedrich,* 1974-75, plate 6 (*Das Kreuz im Gebirge,* Dresden), plate 11 (*Kreuz in der Ostra,* Berlin, 1815), plate 13 (*Morgen im Riesengebirge,* 1810-11, Berlin); see also pp. 236, 242, 251, 258, 283, 291, 293, 322, 385.

11. William Pinder, "Die Romantik in der deutschen Kunst um 1500," in *Das Werk des Künstlers,* I, 1939-40, pp. 3-41.

12. From comments by Max Ernst in *View,* Vol. I, pp. 7-8, made shortly after his emigration to the United States from Nazi-occupied France. The fact that Ernst does not mention Dürer

is interesting. In a similar comment below, Picasso mentions Cranach and Altdorfer as occasional exemplars, but not Dürer. See also *Katalog der Kestner Gesellschaft,* 4, n.d., "Ausstellung Max Ernst," p. 11.

13. Georg Grosz, "Unter anderem ein Wort für deutsche Tradition," *Das Kunstblatt,* 1931, pp. 79-84. Grosz concludes this satiric piece with the expression, "Ugh, Ich habe gesprochen," a quote from Karl May, the phrase with which all Indian chiefs in May's work conclude every utterance.

14. Grosz, p. 84.

15. Reference to French artists is amplified by a drawing in the article showing an artist wearing blinders over his eyes, and having a parrot's cage as chest; before him is an artist's easel with a cubist painting on it. Grosz, p. 84.

16. Grosz, p. 6.

17. Hans Hess, *Georg Grosz,* 1974, p. 159.

18. Ibid., p. 179.

19. Ibid., p. 181.

20. Ibid., p. 197.

21. Ibid., plate 177.

22. Ibid., plate 184.

23. Ibid., plate 182.

24. Ibid., plate 185.

25. Ibid., plate 190.

26. Ibid, plate 186; another apocalyptic scene by Grosz is his "Cain" (1944), depicted in *Ausstellungs Katalog,* Akademie der Kunste, Dortmunc, 1963.

27. Fritz Löffler, *Otto Dix, Leben und Werk,* 1967, p. 96.

28. *Katalog der Ausstellung Otto Dix,* Galerie der Stadt Stuttgart, 1971, p. 182; see also Löffler, p. 98.

29. Löffler, pp. 103-4.

30. Ibid., p. 107; plates 160-65.

31. ". . . gegen ästhetisierende Schönmalerei. Dix wollte 'unmalerisch malen,' objektiv, nüchtern, unbeschönigt, unsentimental, Horror vor dem Pathos. Das 'Unmalerische' fand er bei

den Alten . . . er benutzt ihre Themen, Titel, Kompositionsschemata, und ihre Lasurtechnik." Otto Conzelmann, *Ausstellungskatalog "Otto Dix,"* Galerie der Stadt Stuttgart, 1971, p. 16.

32. Franz Roh, "Altdorfer," *L'Oeil,* 5, 1955, pp. 28 and 38.

33. Heribert Hutter, *Picasso Katalog,* 1968.

34. "C'est que c'est bien, Altdorfer! Tout y est: une petite feuille par terre, une brique fendue, pas comme les autres! Il y a un tableau avec une sorte de petit balcon fermé—des cabinets, je l'appelle. Tous ces details sont integres. C'est beau. On a perdu tout ca, plus tard. On est allé jusqu'à Matisse—la couleur! Peut-être est-ce un progrès mais c'est d'autre chose. On devrait faire copier ces choses, comme autrefois. Mais je sais bien, on ne comprendrait pas." Roh, p. 37.

35. Hutter, 1968.

36. Oskar Kokoschka, "Das Auge des Darius," *Schweizer Monatschefte,* 1956-57, pp. 32-36.

37. Werner Hofmann, "Oskar Kokoschka," in *Wort in der Zeit,* No. 3, 1956, pp. 1-11.

38. Oskar Kokoschka, "Altdeutsche Malerei," in *Das schriftliche Werk,* Vol. III, 1975, pp. 81-83.

39. ". . . Mit Altdorfer endlich wölbt sich der Abend uber eine Welt, die so viel Erbarmen hatte mit den Trägern der heiligen Handlung. Nun haben wir ein Bild wie die 'Bergung der Leiche des Heiligen Florian;' mit Sonnenuntergang kehrt ein Landmann aus der Donaugegend, müde von seinem Tagewerk, vom Felde heim. Auf der Strasse hält man ihn an, damit er einen Toten auf seinen Wagen nehmen soll. Wer könnte einen armen Toten den Raben und Wölfen der Nacht zur Beute überlassen! Der Heilige Florian ist ein Mensch wie unsereins." Kokoschka, 1975, pp. 81-83.

40. Hofmann, 1956, p. 6.

41. ". . . Eine komplizierte, viel-raümige Architektur, mit den Mitteln der Renaissance-perspektive dargestellt, droht das Geheimnis des Marienlebens ganz zu überwuchern in Altdorfers "Mariae Geburt." Doch eben in dieser Freude uber eine neue Entdeckung ist der Künstler unschuldig wie ein Kind. In einer kuhnen Vision bringt er einen Riesenkranz von schwebenden Engeln in den geometrischen Raum, wo sie um so seltsamer wirken und um so glaubhafter von einer himmlischen Höhe, die ausserhalb der Möglichkeiten der Mess—und Errechenbarkeit einer Konstruktion liegt, die Glorie der Ewigkeit verkünden. Singen nicht dieselben Engel in der Krönungsmesse des späten Landsmanns des Altdorfer, Anton Bruckner?" Kokoschka, 1975, p. 82.

42. Oskar Kokoschka, *My Life,* 1974, p. 210.

43. Ibid., pp. 198-99.

44. Ibid., p. 210.

45. Ibid., pp. 81-82.

46. Ibid., 1974, p. 198.

47. See Appendix for Kokoschka's "The Eye of Darius" in Hans Maria Wingler, *Oskar Ko-koschka: The Work of the Painter,* 1958, pp. 79-90.

48. Kokoschka, 1974, p. 210; see also Benno Reifenberg, "Alte Pinakothek," an essay which expresses the same idea of works of art as statements of continuity, while contemplating the *Battle of Alexander.* This reflection leads also to a strong feeling of the immutability of death, on the part of a lonely visitor to the Pinakothek while a storm rages outside. In Reifenberg, *Das Abendland gemalt: Schriften zur Kunst,* 1950, pp. 430-41.

49. Kokoschka had experienced Rembrandt similarly, particularly Rembrandt's last self-portrait in London. Rembrandt's courage to face his own imminent death gave Kokoschka, an exile on the fringe of existence, renewed courage to continue the struggle of life. Kokoschka, 1974, p. 210. Wingler's English translation, 1958, does less than full justice to the original ideas by Kokoschka of identification with those who had courage in the face of adversity.

50. Kokoschka notes that he had been fascinated by Greek art and thought since his high school days, and particularly by the writings of Johann Bachofen (1815-1887) and his pupil Briffault on the Greek ideas Eros and Thanatos as counterparts of progress and enlightenment. Kokoschka, 1974, pp. 15 and 26.

51. Kurt Martin, *Die Alexanderschlacht,* 1969, p. 15.

52. Gilbert and Kuhn, *A History of Esthetics,* 1972, p. 62.

53. Ibid., pp. 62-63.

54. Ibid., p. 66.

55. Ibid., p. 86.

56. Kokoschka, 1974, p. 17.

57. Ibid., p. 19.

58. Given the circumstances of the commission of the *Battle of Alexander,* this could hardly have been Altdorfer's interpretation. Friedrich Piel has called the memorial tablet surrounded by billowing red cloth a *"tabula velata"* which in Christian iconography signifies the "headband" of Christ, a white cloth with a red seam. Piel probably means the loincloth of Christ when he refers to *velum* here; an observation about the obvious if one recalls the same figurations of the loincloth of the crucified Christ. Wolfgang Kehr, 1973, p. 21. According to Schramm, the red cloth could have reference to the *lorum,* purple cloth which designated the Byzantine emperors in all book illuminations. This interpretation would suggest that the red cloths of the memorial tablet announce the two emperors in this painting. P. E. Schramm, *Herrschaftzeichen und Staatssymbolik,* 1954, p. 26, cited from Kehr, 1973.

59. Lincoln Diamant, "Introduction" to *Aristotle's Politics and Poetics,* 1971, p. xiii. This interpretation of the *Battle of Alexander* in terms of tragedy may also be found at the time of the approaching end of World War II in A. G. Roth, *Gestirne in der Landschaftsmalerei des Abendlandes,* 1945, p. 65.

60. Oskar Kokoschka, "Non-objective art?" in Wingler, 1958, pp. 75-78.

61. This triptrych was originally destined for the student restaurant (*mensa*) of the University of Hamburg. In 1953 he prepared eight sketches and the triptych was finished in the fall of 1954.

62. Wingler, 1958, description opposite plates 28-30.

63. Kokoschka, *Das schriftliche Werk,* 1975, pp. 321-25.

64. Ibid., p. 322.

65. Wingler, 1958, pp. 62-63.

66. Ibid., p. 63.

Chapter 8

1. José Ortega y Gasset, "In Search of Goethe from Within," in *The Dehumanization of Art,* second printing 1972, p. 174.

2. Ibid., p. 174. He refers to Goethe, the personified classic. I have taken the liberty to change the reference to Goethe, "him," to "it."

3. J. P. Hodin, 1966, p. 19.

4. Kenneth Clark, *Landscape into Art,* 1940, pp. 36-43.

5. Erwin Panofsky, "Die Perspektive als 'symbolische Form,'" in *Vorträge der Bibliothek Warburg,* 1924-25, p. 257 ff, reprinted in *Aufsätze zu Grundfragen der Kunstwissenschaft,* 1964, pp. 124-125.

6. Frank Winzinger, "Albrecht Altdorfer und die Miniaturen des Triumphzugs Kaiser Maximilian I," in *Jahrbuch der Kunshistorischen Sammlungen in Wien,* Bd. 62, 1966.

7. Friedrich Piel, *Altdorfers Alexanderschlacht,* Buchhandlung Bernsdorf, Munich, 1970. This study was not available to me because Piel had withdrawn it from the book market by spring of 1977. My reference is based on a personal communication in July 1977.

8. Herbert Achternbusch, *Die Alexanderschlacht,* 1972.

Appendix A

Friedrich Schlegel's Essay on
Albrecht Altdorfer's *Battle of Alexander*

Would I be permitted to select but few from all the paintings which I have seen this one would be among them because of its great perfection and its delicacy. And yet, it is far surpassed by a small painting by Altdorfer which shows figures only one or two inches tall. Should I call it a landscape, or a historical painting, or a battle piece? All of these (labels) do not quite suit, the painting is all of these together and yet much more; it is a new type of painting, a species of its own whose concept we have yet to establish. How should I describe the astonishment which seized me as I first saw this miraculous work? I felt like someone who until this moment only knew the graceful, charming poetry of the Italians as the only poetry there was and who, unprepared, suddenly sees unfolding before his eyes the figures of Shakespeare's magic world. That is exactly how I felt.

But this comparison describes only the abundance, wealth and depth of Altdorfer's painting or poetry. It (the comparison between Italian and Shakespearean poetry) does not characterize the spirit of chivalry which dominates it to such an extent that one could designate it a "painting of chivalry." It represents the victory of Alexander the Great over Darius but not in the matter which imitates antiquity, rather in the manner of the poems of the Middle Ages as the most exalted adventure of chivalry. The costume is thoroughly (clearly) German and knightly. Man and horse clad in armour and iron, in gilded and embroidered coats of arms, spikes on the foreheads of the horses, the shining lances and stirrups, the variety of weapons, all of this combines to indescribable splendor and richness.

Nowhere is there blood or gore, nor limbs thrown about nor distortions; only if one looks very carefully at the nearest foreground does one see several rows of cadavers—as if to symbolize the foundation of this world of war and weapons, of shining iron and of even brighter glory and chivalry—under the hoofs of the cavalry which are just advancing from both sides against each other. Indeed this is a world, a small world of few feet; immeasurable, uncountable are the armies which flow against each other from all directions, and the view in the background leads to the infinite. It is the cosmic ocean (*Weltmeer*), a historical error if you like, but one which contains a significant and true allegory. The cosmic ocean, high mountain rocks, between those an island of cliffs, distant battleships and fleets of ships; then, to the left, the glistening moon, to the right the rising sun, a distinct and a great symbol of the historical event which is represented.

By the way, the multitudes of armies are ordered into neat rows and they lack totally the grandeloquent positions, contrasts and distortions which one normally finds in so-called battle pieces; how was this possible in view of the immeasurable profusion of figures? It is the straightness, the severity—or if you will—the stiffness of the old style. But on the other hand the characterization and the execution of the small figures is so marvelous that a Dürer would not have had to be ashamed of them.

Once and for all it should be noted that the thoroughness of the craftsmanship in this painting—even though it seems to have been damaged not little—is superior to that of the old Italian school and can be found only in the paintings of the zenith of the old German school. And what variety, what expression do we see not only in the characterization of the individual warrior, knight, but also in that of whole troops; here pours forth from a mountain a whole row of black archers with the ferocity of a swelling river, and there are more and more who push on; on the other side one sees on a high cliff a scattered group of fugitives turning in a hollow path. One does not see anything of them but their helmets reflected in the sun, and yet, even in this distance everything is very clear. The decision, the focal point of the whole brilliantly emanates from the center. Alexander and Darius both are shining in golden armor. Alexander on Bucephalus rushes far in advance of his men, his lance at the ready, toward the fleeing Darius whose charioteer already has fallen onto the white horses as Darius turns to his victor with the tragic glance of a defeated king. One ought to step back from the painting so that nothing else is recognizable; then this group still stands out clearly and is deeply moving.

This small painted Iliad could teach through its language of color that thoughtful painter who strives for new and great subjects—who, for instance, would abandon the holy cycle of catholic images and would seek to produce a truly romantic painting—what the spirit of chivalry means and what it signifies. If there are (in Munich) still more pictures of this great quality then German painters ought to make a pilgrimage there as they do to Rome or Paris.

Appendix B

Oskar Kokoschka: "The Eye of Darius"

. . . What is reality? Where does it begin and end? It was a Sunday midday and rain was pouring down, when I reached Munich on the last day of my journey back to London. Munich looked dead; it had been heavily bombed. And so I turned my steps toward the pictures of the old masters in the Pinakothek in that "bomb proof house of art" built by Hitler, where the famous collection was housed, and which had in fact survived the bombing. What I had in mind was to stand before the *Alexanderschlacht* by Altdorfer, and once again try to guess the answer to the riddle: What is reality? To think that Altdorfer could have been taken for one of the minor masters of humanistic historical painting! Why should the *Alexanderschlacht* not have been recognized rather as the earliest baroque painting? One becomes acutely aware of this after two world wars have razed to the ground so many important centers of baroque art. A chapter of European history was saved with Altdorfer's picture: "eppure si muove." The earth ball really turns in this picture which was painted before Galileo taught how it moves. Its movement is seen at the first glance—the turning of the sun's fire, space circling round the pregnant earth that brings reality into existence. More than a hundred years after this picture was painted human shapes were to wander through these airy spaces and Christian saints together with Olympian gods were to plunge in cascades out of the painted ceilings of the baroque art in the interiors of cathedrals and palaces.

The *Alexanderschlacht* was commissioned in Munich at the time that the Turks were besieging the neighboring city of Vienna. The picture broke with the classic practice of Italy and the Netherlands, where the Catholic world order dictated the content of a picture, but where, nevertheless, in Books of Hours, perhaps at first in the backgrounds, plants, rocks, water, animals, towns, castles and genre scenes were making a shy appearance. Further, the painter makes no use of the perspective with one focus which was at that time coming into fashion in Italy and Flanders. Since the Renaissance this so-called horseback perspective has served painting as a crutch to enable the painter, with the help of an artificial perspective of a theoretical depth and distance, to give to each figure its appropriate place and recession according to its importance. The figures representing biblical or secular themes are as actors playing their assigned parts.

I should call the *Alexanderschlacht* a work of absolute painting. It grips one as if the curtain had been torn aside from an abyss—not from a peepshow. It lays bare the other side of reality, not a transcendental one, but a side that only one who had gained insight into things can see. One is amazed at the power of this picture. It transforms the imagination of the beholder, and the memory of its impact remains with him long afterwards, by force of the growth and sprouting of the vegetation of the raging of water, the shattering of stones and rocks, the hurricane-like tension and breaking of tension of the atmosphere, which is that of nature herself in catastrophic mood. But strip the picture of all that may be expressed in language, everything that today is called "subject matter," and then the individual life of the composition, its formal existence, really begins. A harmony lies over the whole, though it is not the harmony of those masters from van Eyck to Titian, in whose creations divine majesty has sanctioned a second act of creation. Here on the contrary it is material that becomes form and shape, which brings to mind the viewpoint of Aristotle, for whom formless material was a notion unthinkable and devoid of sense.

In Altdorfer's work there is something that struggles to become form, as in a fugue; nevertheless it is a product of absolute visual experience, and opens up regions of reality other than those presided over by the illustrious painters mentioned above. The duration of time in which the separate motifs struggling one with the other come to their harmonious reconciliation in the musical fugue is the *content* of Altdorfer's picture.

Let us study the subject of the picture in the light of the descriptions presented to us by the best authorities. Here is the flight of the battlefield, the flight of the Persian army before the Greeks; here a troop of cavalry, momentarily jammed in a narrow pass, break out in the open country which is cut in two by the river Isus; over the bridge the way leads to a burning town ringed around by towers and hills, and out of the town the defenders venture a sortie which breaks upon the foot soldiers of the besiegers spread out fanwise. Single combats are taking place between the two armies. Is not all this a contrapuntal theme preparing the way for a closing effect, which, in view of the giant strides of the meteor-like sun across a vast, featureless tract of land and water, might be anticipated by the over-hasty beholder? The intention of the picture is to glorify the great victory of Alexander; but the sound judge will not neglect to point out as a secondary theme the moving contrast presented by the fear-stricken princesses in the train of Darius, hurried along by the fleeing, defeated army of the Persian King of Kings.

And yet, strangely enough, something has always escaped the notice of the beholders of this picture. They are in general willing to pay their tribute of praise to its expression of a romantic mood of nature, but they tend to look upon the human element as a childish game, as if it were a sort of battle of toy soldiers! Perhaps, in order to better understand a picture motif in which for some judges the reckoning is at fault, we might go back to our chosen example of the Beethoven fugue. Think of the absurdity of that famous passage, consisting of individual, obstinately maintained beats, in that fugue which is the crown of European music. In that passage with the shortest, most elementary sounds in music, eternity reveals itself. One needs, as it were, two modes of thought, two standards of value, two attitudes of mind, one of thinking and the other of seeing (which our time, having lost possession of the visual faculty, will find unimaginable) to discover at last—an antinomy—in the middle distance of the picture the pivot upon which the essential action of this world drama turns. It sounds like a paradox to say that what has escaped the eye of the connoisseur is a monumental miniature right in the middle of the picture! It is not easy, even after intensive searching, to find that gem, hardly as big as a pin, which is the face of Darius in the tumult of ten thousand men in flight. And it is still harder to catch a glimpse of the expression of defeat on the averted face of the King of Kings fleeing in his war chariot. Alexander the Great on his battle charger Bucephalus is much more easily picked out on account of his silvery shining armour, belonging to the period of Dürer's designs made for the Emperor Maximilian. But let us first run our eye over the whole composition—up to the red colour ribbons holding a memorial tablet, the only red in the picture, and from these downwards over the ice blue sky to the world stage where the bloody decision fell in favour of the West; high above mountain peaks, above the sea, above the victors and the vanquished hangs the memorial tablet. Upon it in big Roman characters and Roman numerals the triumph of the great Alexander is proclaimed and the numbers of the victors and the vanquished are given. In reading the names of the great men and of the dates and the victories as history has recorded them, who would not think: What is man, and even if all the kingdoms and glories of the world were laid at his feet? If in so few short words and figures all could be summed up of what remains of man in his history and in his brief existence—brief as that of the ant heedlessly trodden under foot—then the picture might as well be as empty of men as the world was on the third day of creation, as that moment is pictured in the grisaille outer wing of the altarpiece by Hieronymus Bosch in Madrid: *The Kingdom of a Thousand Years*. In this picture, painted in a period of chiliastic hope of the millenium, the eye of God rests with satisfaction, as if contemplating a still life, on His creation, which had so far separated into water, dry land and light. If man were not more than a mere cipher, a coefficient in the calculations of physical world happenings, then the world would have no need of a single picture more. Mathematical symbolism is inhuman, objectless, condemned to a single track. No simultaneous act of seeing and thinking is needed for the flight into the beyond.

"I will not bow down! I cannot perish." Thus speaks a human look, the look in the eye of Darius, a coloured speck in the middle distance of Altdorfer's cosmic picture. Pitifully small as that face may seem to us, small the whole figure, small even the army of ten thousand men and that of the Greeks as well, yet what stands forth as our vivid experience in the monotony of human history is the deeply sad look on the face of a man consciously turning his eye away from the glory of the setting sun. He knows that he is defeated; and yet, in spite of that, life affirms itself, monotonously and stubbornly like the single beats in the Beethoven fugue. And this affirmation is hurled in the face of the metaphysical beyond! This look of Darius took me unawares, and waked me out of that daydream which others call their everyday life. On a flight through time this look on the face of the vanquished king stopped me and opened my eyes.

Plate 1. Albrecht Altdorfer, *The Two Sts. John,* ca. 1513-15, panel, 133 ,6:173, 2 cm, Regensburg, Municipal Museum (W. G. 27).

Plate 2.   Albrecht Altdorfer, *Birth of the Virgin,* ca. 1520, panel, 140, 7:130 cm, Munich Alte Pinakothek (W. G. 44)

Plate 6.   Albrecht Altdorfer, *Susanna's Bath,* 1526, panel, 74, 8:61, 2 cm, Munich,
        Alte Pinakothek (W. G. 49)

Plate 8.   Albrecht Altdorfer, *St. George,* 1510, parchment on wood, 28, 2:22, 5 cm,
                 Munich, Alte Pinakothek (W. G. 6)

Plate 9. Max Ernst, *The Last Forest*, 1960-69, ©Estate of Max Ernst, SPADEM, Paris/ VAGA, New York, 1980

Plate 10. Otto Dix, *St. Anthony in the Forest,* 1941, mixed media on panel, Aachen, private collection (Fritz Löffler, *Otto Dix, Leben und Werk,* pl. 166)

Plate 11.   Pablo Picasso, *Recovery of the Body of St. Florian,* 1953, lithograph
(Franz Roh, "Picasso and Altdorfer," *L'Oeil,* 1955, p. 37)

Plate 12. Pablo Picasso, *Kneeling Woman,* after Altdorfer, 1953, lithograph
(Franz Roh, "Picasso and Altdorfer," *L'Oeil,* 1955, p. 37)

Albrecht Altdorfer, "Darius," enlarged detail from the *Battle of Alexander,* 1529, panel, Munich, Alte Pinakothek (Kurt Martin, *Die Alexanderschlacht*)

Plate 14. Oskar Kokoschka, *Thermopylae*, central panel, 1954, tempera on canvas, 225:300 cm, Villeneuve, private collection

Bibliography

Books

Achternbusch, Herbert. *Die Alexanderschlacht.* Frankfurt, 1972.

Allgemeines Lexikon der Bildenden Kunst. Von der Antike bis zur Gegenwart. 37 vols. Ulrich Thieme and Felix Becker, eds. Leipzig, 1908—.

Andresen, Andreas. *Die deutschen Maler als Kupferstecher.* Vol. 5. Leipzig, 1878.

Aristotle's Politics and Poetics. New York, 1971.

Arnim, Achim von. *Die Kronenwächter.* Berlin, 1857.

Aventinus (Turmair), Johannes. *Bayerische Chronik.* Georg Leidinger, ed. Köln, 1975. (First edition 1572, manuscript ca. 1527-33.)

Baldass, Ludwig. *Albrecht Altdorfer.* Vienna, 1941.

Behling, Lotlisla. *Die Pflanze in der mittelalterlichen Tafelmalerei.* Weimar, 1957.

Benesch, Otto. *Der Maler Albrecht Altdorfer.* Vienna, 1939.

———. *Collected Writings, Vol. III: German and Austrian Art of the Fifteenth and Sixteenth Century.* New York and London, 1972.

Benjamin, Walter. *Der Begriff der Kunstkritik in der deutschen Romantik.* Frankfurt, 1973.

———. *Das Kunstwerk im Zeitalter seiner technischen Reproduzierbarkeit: Drei Studien zur Kunstsoziologie.* Frankfort, 1977.

Berenson, Bernard. *Italian Painters of the Renaissance.* London, 1962.

Börsch-Supan, Helmut, and Jähnig, Karl Wilhelm. *Caspar David Friedrich.* Munich, 1974-75.

Boll, Walter. *Regensburg.* Deutscher Kunstverlag, 1963.

Borchardt, Frank L. *German Antiquity in Renaissance Myth.* Baltimore, 1971.

Borcherdt, Heinz Heinrich. *Das Euopäische Theater im Mittelalter und in der Renaissance.* Leipzig, 1930.

Burger, Heinz Otto. *Renaissance, Humanismus und Reformation.* Verlag Dr. Max Gehlen, 1969.

Burke, Kenneth. *A Grammar of Motives and a Rhetoric of Motives.* Cleveland and New York, 1962.

Chastel, André, and Klein, Robert. *Die Welt des Humanismus.* Munich, 1963.

Clark, Kenneth. *Landscape into Art.* London, 1940.

De Boor, Newald. *Geschichte der deutschen Literatur.* Munich, 1970.

Deutsches Wörterbuch. 16 vols. Jakob and Wilhelm Grimm, eds. Leipzig, 1854—.

Diehl, Gaston. *Max Ernst.* New York, 1973.

Dölling, Regine. *Byzantinische Elemente in der Kunst des 16. Jahrhunderts.* Sonderdruck. Berlin, 1957.

von Einem, Herbert. "Das Auge, der edelste Sinn." *Wallraf-Richartz Jahrbuch.* Band XXX. Sonderdruck. 1968.

Encyclopedia of Philosophy. 8 vols. Paul Edwards, ed. New York, 1967.

Englemann, W. "Altdorfer." *Allgemeines Künstlerlexikon.* Vol. I. Julius Meyer, ed. Leipzig, 1872-85.

Fiorillo, Johann Dominik. *Kleine Schriften artistischen Inhalts.* 2 vols. Göttingen, 1803-1806.

————. *Geschichte der zeichnenden Künste in Deutschland und den Vereinigten Niederlanden.* 9 vols. Hanover, 1815-1820.

————. *Geschichte der Mahlerei.* Vol. II, n.p., 1798-1820.

Firmenich-Richartz, Eduard. *Die Brüder Boisseré.* Vol. I. Jena, 1916.

Forster, Ernst. *Geschichte der deutschen Kunst.* Vol. II. 2nd edition. Leipzig, 1860.

Friedländer, Max J. *Albrecht Altdorfer, der Maler von Regensburg.* Leipzig, 1891.

Friedrich, Alexander. *Handlung und Gestalt des Kupferstichs und der Radierung.* Essen, 1931.

Geertz, Clifford. *The Interpretation of Cultures.* New York, 1973.

Gemeiner, Carl Theodor. *Regensburgische Chronik.* Munich, 1971 (first edition 1803).

Gilbert and Kuhn. *A History of Esthetics.* New York, 1972 (first edition 1939).

Gould, Cecil. *Trophy of Conquest.* London, 1965.

Gumpelzhaimer, Christian Gottlieb. *Regensburgs Geschichte, Sagen und Merkwürdigkeiten.* Vol. 2, 1486-1618. Regensburg, 1837.

Hable, Guido. *Geschichte Regensburgs, Eine Übersicht nach Sachgebieten.* Regensburg, 1970.

Hegel, Georg W. F. *Aesthetics, Lectures on Fine Arts.* Vol. I. Translated by T. M. Knox. Oxford, 1975.

————. *Vorlesungen uder die Aesthetik.* Stuttgart, 1977.

Heinse, Wilhelm. *Ardinghello und die glückseligen Inseln.* Max L. Baeumer, ed. Stuttgart, 1975 (first edition 1787).

Hess, Hans. *George Grosz.* London, 1974.

Hetzer, Theodor. *Das deutsche Element in der italienischen Malerei des 16. Jahrhunderts.* Berlin, 1929.

Hildebrandt, Hans. *Die Architektur bei Altdorfer.* Strassburg, 1908.

Hodin, Josef Paul. *Oskar Kokoschka: the Artist and His Time; a Biographical Study.* New York, 1966.

Holborn, Hajo. *A History of Modern Germany, the Reformation.* New York, 1959.

Holt, Elizabeth Gilmore. *A Documentary History of Art.* Vol. II. New York, 1963.

Huth, Hans. *Künstler und Werkstatt in der Spätgotik.* Augsburg, 1923.

von Hutten, Ulrich. *Deutsche Schriften.* Heinz Mettke, ed. Leipzig, 1972.

Illustrierte Geschichte der Frühbürgerlichen Revolution. Adolf Laube, Max Steinmetz, and Gunter Vogler, eds. VEB Verlag, 1974.

The Interpreter's Dictionary of the Bible. Vol. 3. "Pontius Pilate." New York, 1962.

Janssen, Johannes. *History of the German People at the Close of the Middle Ages.* Vol. I. London, 1896.

Jay, Martin. *The Dialectical Imagination, a History of the Frankfurt School and the Institute of Social Research, 1923-1950.* Boston and Toronto, 1973.

Kehr, Wolfgang. "Probleme der Gemäldeinterpretation, dargestellt am Beispiel von A. Altdorfers Alexanderschlacht." *Curriculum-Gesamtschule. Fach: Kunsterziehung. Stand: Dez. 72.* Nürnberg, 1973.

Keyssler, Johann Georg. *Neueste Reisen durch Deutschland.* N.p., 1751.

Klassischer Bilderschatz. 12 vols. Franz von Reber and Ad. Bayersdorfer, eds. Munich, 1893.

Klein, Ulrich. "Rezeption." *Handlexikon der Literaturwissenschaft.* Diether Krywalski, ed. Munich, 1976, pp. 409-413.

Kokoschka, Oskar. *My Life.* New York, 1974.

————. *Das schriftliche Werk.* Vol. III. Hamburg, 1975.

Köpplin,, Dieter. *Lukas Cranach, Gemälde, Zeichnungen, Druckgraphik.* Bd. 1. Kunstmuseum Basel, 1974.

————. "Das Sonnengestirn der Donaumeister." *Werden und Wandlung, Studien zur Kunst der Donauschule.* Linz, 1967, pp. 78-114.

Kornmann, Egon. *Gesammelte Aufsätze: Kunst im Leben.* N.p., 1954.

Kugler, Franz Th. *Handbuch der Kunstgeschichte.* Stuttgart, 1842.

Levin, Harry. *Contexts of Criticism.* Cambridge, 1957.

Liebhaber Bibliothek alter Illustrationen. 1888.

Linfert, Carl. *Albrecht Altdorfer. Die Enthüllung der Landschaft.* Mainz, 1938.

Lipp, Franz. "Volksart und Volksfrömmigkeit als Triebkräfte der Kunst der Donauschule." *Werden und Wandlung, Studien zur Kunst der Donauschule.* Linz, 1967.

Löffler, Fritz. *Otto Dix, Leben und Werk.* Dresden, 1967.

Luther, A. *Deutsche Geschichte in deutscher Erzählung.* N.p., 1943.

Mann, Otto. *Der junge Friedrich Schlegel.* Berlin, 1932.

Martin, Kurt. *Die Alexanderschlacht.* Munich, 1969.

Moore, Sturge T. *Albrecht Altdorfer.* New York and London, 1901.

Muller, Andreas. *Kunstanschauung der Fruhromantik.* Leipzig, 1931.

Mundhenk, Alfred. *Über den Dilettantismus.* Düsseldorf, Staatliche Kunstakademie, Hochschule für Bildende Kunste, 1966.

Nicolaus, Cusanus, Cardinal. *The Vision of God.* Introduction by Evelyn Underhill. New York, 1960.

Öttinger, Karl. "Laube, Garten und Wald. Zu einer Theorie der Süddeutschen Sakralkunst, 1470-1520." *Festschrift für Hans Sedlmayr.* Munich, 1962.

Ortega y Gasset, José. *The Dehumanization of Art and Other Essays on Art, Culture, and Literature.* Princeton, 1972 (first edition 1925).

Ovidius Naso, Publius. *The Metamorphoses of Ovid.* Translated and Introduction by Mary M. Innes. London, 1955.

Panofsky, Erwin. *Albrecht Dürer.* Princeton, New Jersey, 1945.

_____. "Die Perspektive als 'symbolische Form.'" *Aufsatze zu Grundfragen der Kunstwissenschaft.* Berlin, 1964.

Paracelsus (Theophrastus von Hohenheim). *Sämtliche Werke.* Bernhard Aschner, ed. Jena, 1926-1928.

Paricius, Johannes. *Regensburg.* Regensburg, 1753.

Paulsen, Friedrich. *German Education Past and Present.* Translated by T. Lorenz. New York, 1912.

Peuchel-Band. Cod. icon. 412. Staatliche Graphische Sammlung. Munich.

Piel, Friedrich. *Altdorfers Alexanderschlacht.* Munich, 1970.

Priebsch-Closs, Hanna. *Magie und Naturgefühl in der Malerei von Grünewald, Baldung Grien, Lukas Cranach und Altdorfer.* Bonn, 1936.

Rasmo, Nicolo. "Donaustil und Italienische Kunst der Renaissance." *Werden und Wandlung, Studien zur Kunst der Donauschule.* Linz, 1967.

Reber, Franz von. *Kurfürst Maximilian von Bayern als Gemäldesammler.* Munich, 1892.

_____. *Geschichte der Malerei, vom Angang des 14. bis zum Ende des 18. Jahrhunderts.* Munich, 1894.

Reifenberg, Benno. *Das Abendland gemalt: Schriften zur Kunst.* Frankfurt, 1950.

Rettberg, Ralph von. *Nürnberger Briefe.* Hannover, 1846.

Romanticism, Definition, Explanation and Evaluation. John B. Halsted, ed. Boston, 1965.

Rosenberg, Ad. "Die deutschen Kleinmeister." *Kunst und Künstler des Mittelalters und der Neuzeit.* Robert Dohme, ed. Vol. I. N.p., 1877, pp. 35-44.

Roth, A. G. *Die Gestirne in der Landschaftsmalerei des Abendlandes.* Bern, 1945.

Ruhmer, Eberhard. *Albrecht Altdorfer.* Munich, 1965.

Sandrart, Joachim von. *Teutsche Academie der Edlen Bau-, Bild- und Mahlerey-Künste.* A. R. Peltzer, ed. Munich, 1925 (first edition Nurnberg, 1674).

Saran, Bernhard. "Der Maler Albrecht Altdorfer als Humanist in seiner reichsstädtischen Umwelt." *Die Humanisten in ihrer politischen und Sozialen Umwelt.* Otto Herding and Robert Stuyzerick, eds. Haroldt and Boldt Verlag, 1976.

Schedel, Hartmann. *Weltchronik.* Nürnberg: Anton Koberger, 1493.

Scheffler, Karl. *Verwandlungen des Barocks in der Kunst des 19. Jahrhunderts.* Vienna, 1947.

Schlegel, Friedrich von. *Gesammelte Werke.* Band 5. Vienna, 1846.

_____. *The Aesthetic and Miscellaneous Works of Friedrich von Schlegel.* Translated by E. J. Millington. Long, 1875.

Schöne, Wolfgang. *Über das Licht in der Malerei.* Berlin, 1954.

Schwarz, Karl. *Augustin Hirschvogel, ein deutscher Meister der Renaissance.* N.p., 1917.

Sliwka, Klaus. *Aspekte zum Unterrichtsfeld Bildende Kunst—Visuelle Kommunikation; Über die Inhalte Mensch und Gesellsahft.* Kohn, 1972.

Speculum humanae salvationis. Codex Cremifanensis 243. Facsimile edition. Graz, 1972.

Springer, Anton. *Handbuch der Kunstgeschichte.* N.p., 1909 (first edition 1855).

_____. *Kunsthistorische Briefe.* Prag, 1857.

Stael-Holstein, Madame de. *Germany.* Boston, 1879.

Stange, Alfred. *Malerei der Donauschule.* Munich, 1971.

Stechow, Wolfgang. *Northern Renaissance Art, 1400-1600, Sources and Documents.* Englewood Cliffs, New Jersey, 1966.

Strauss, Gerald. *Historian in an Age of Crisis: The Life and Work of Johannes Aventinus.* Cambridge, 1963.

Sulzer, Johann Georg. *Allgemeine Theorie der Schönen Künste.* Facsimile edition. Georg Olms Verlagsbuchhandlung, Hildesheim, 1967 (first edition 1792).

Tatarkiewicz, Waldijslav. *History of Aesthetics.* Vol. III. Paris, 1974.

Theobald, Leonhard. *Die Reformationsgeschichte der Reichsstadt Regensburg.* Bd. I. Munich, 1936.

Tietze, Hans. *Albrecht Altdorfer.* Leipzig, 1923.

Venturi, Lionello. *History of Art Criticism.* New York, 1964.

Voss, Hermann. *Der Ursprung des Donaustils.* Leipzig, 1907.

Waetzoldt, Wilhelm. *Deutsche Kunsthistoriker.* 2 vols. Leipzig, 1921.

Warnke, Martin. *Das Kunstwerk zwischen Wissenschaft und Weltanschauung.* Gütersloh, 1970.

Watzlik, Hasn. *Der Meister von Regensburg, ein Albrecht Altdorfer Roman.* Leipzig, 1939.

Wedgewood, Cicely Veronica. *The Thirty Years' War.* New York, 1961.

Weizsäcker, Heinrich. *Adam Elsheimer.* Berlin, 1952.

Wellek, René. *A History of Modern Criticism 1750-1950.* New Haven, 1955.

Widman, Leonhard. "Regensburger Chronik." *Die Chroniken der deutschen Städte vom 14. bis 16. Jahrhundert.* Band 15. Göttingen.

Wingler, Hans Maria. *Oskar Kokoschka.* Salzburg, 1958.

Winzinger, Franz. *Albrecht Altdorfer, Zeichnungen.* Munich, 1952.

———. *Albrecht Altdorfer, Graphik.* Munich, 1963.

———. *Albrecht Altdorfer, die Gemalde.* Munich, 1975.

Wölfflin, Heinrich. *Italien und das deutsche Formgefühl.* Munich, 1931.

———. *Gedanken zur Kunstgeschichte.* Basel, 1946.

———. *Principles of Art History.* Dover Publications. N.d. (first German edition 1915).

———. *The Sense of Form in Art: A Comparative Psychological Study.* New York, 1958.

Ziegler, Theobald. *Geschichte der Pädagogik.* Munich, 1909.

Periodicals

Benesch, Otto. *Pantheon.* Vol. XXI, 1938, p. 80 ff.

Boll, Walter. "Albrecht Altdorfers Nachlass." *Münchener Jahrbuch der bildenden Kunst.* 1938-39, p. 91.

Busch, Karl. "Erlebnis einer Ausstellung." *Das Bayerland.* Jg. 49, 1938, pp. 545-49.

Christoffel, Ulrich. "Albrecht Altdorfer." *Zeitschrift für deutsche Geisteswissenschaft.* 1938-39.

Dehio, Georg. "Die Krisis in der deutschen Kunst im 16. Jahrhundert." *Archiv für Kulturgeschichte.* XII, 1913.

Ernst, Max. "My Favorite Poets and Painters." *View.* I, 7-8, 1941.

Gradmann, Erwin. "Phantastik und Komik: Versuch einer Deutung des Phantastischen." *Schriften der schweizerischen Geisteswissenschaftlichen Gesellschaft.* I, 1957.

Grosz, Georg. "Unter anderem ein Wort für deutsche Tradition." *Das Kunstblatt.* 1931, pp. 79-84.

Halm, Peter. "Eine Gruppe Architekturzeichnungen aus dem Umkreis Albrecht Altdorfers." *Münchener Jahrbuch der bildenden Kunst.* 1951.

———. "Eine Altdorfer Summlung des 17. Jahrhunderts." *Münchener Jahrbuch der bildenden Kunst.* Bd. XI, 1960.

Hartlaub, G. F. "Paracelsisches in der Junst der Paracelsuszeit." *Nova Acta Paracelsica.* Band 7, 1954.

Heckscher, William S. "Petits Perceptions." *The Journal of Medieval and Renaissance Studies.* Vol. 4, No. 1, Spring 1974.

Hofmann, Werner. "Oskar Kokoschka." *Wort in der Zeit.* No. 3, 1956, pp. 81-83.
Janitschek, Hubert. *Die Geschichte der deutschen Malerei.* Vol. III. Berlin: G. Grote, 1890.
Jantzen, Hans. "Albrecht Altdorfers Passionsaltar aus St. Florian." *Das Werk des Künstlers.* 1939, pp. 42-59.
Kagerer, Joseph. "Die schicksalsreiche Geschichte der Schönen Maria." *Verhandlungen des historischen Vereins für Oberpfalz und Regensburg.* Bd. 93, 1952, pp. 89-120.
Kokoschka, Oskar. "Das Auge des Darius." *Schweizer Monatschefte.* 36, 1956-57, pp. 32-36.
Küster, Ernst. "Bäume und Baumkronen in Altdorfers Kunst." *Forschungen und Fortschritte.* Nr. 35-36, 1938, pp. 408-9.
Ladner, Gerhart B. "Vegetation Symbolism and the Concept of the Renaissance." *De Artibus Opuscula XL, Essays in Honor of Erwin Panofsky.* 2 vols. Millard Meiss, ed. New York, 1961.
Lee, R. W. "Ut Pictura Poesis: The Humanistic Theory of Painting. *Art Bulletin.* XXII, 1940.
Lippmann, F. "Albrecht Altdorfers Farbenholzschnitt 'Die Madonna von Regensburg.'" *Jahrbuch der Königlich Preussischen Kunstsammlungen,* Vol. VII, 1886, pp. 154-56.
Lützeler, Heinrich. "Die Kunstkritik." *Jahrbuch für Ästhetik.* Band VIII, 1963.
Meckseper, Cord. "Zur Ikonographie von Altdorfers Alexanderschlacht." *Zeitschrift des Deutschen Vereins für Kunstwissenschaft.* XXII, Berlin, 1968.
Meder, Josef. "Albrecht Altdorfers Donaureise im Jahre 1511." *Mitteilungen der Gesellschaft für Vervielfältigende Kunst.* 1902.
Pächt, Otto. "Zur deutschen Bildauffassung der Spätgotik und Renaissance." *Alte und Neue Kunst.* 1952.
Panofsky, Erwin. "Erasmus and the Visual Arts." *Journal of the Warburg and Courtauld Institutes.* XIV, 1951, p. 41 ff.
Pinder, William. "Die Romantik in der deutschen Kunst um 1500." *Das Werk des Künstlers.* I, 1939-40, pp. 3-41.
Roh, Franz. "Altdorfer." *L'Oeil.* Nr. 5, Mai 1955, p. 28.
_____. Picasso et Altdorfer." *L'Oeil.* Nr. 5, Mai 1955, p. 37.
Schmitt, Annegrit. "Hans Lautensack." *Nürnberger Forschungen.* Band IV, 1957.
Stange, Alfred. "Die Kunst der Donauschule." *Alte und Moderne Kunst.* 1966.
_____. "Das Bildnis im Werke Albrecht Altdorfers." *Pantheon,* 1967.
Stiassny, Robert. "Aus einer österreichischen Klostergalerie." *Zeitschrift für Bildenden Kunst.* Leipzig, 1891, pp. 256-296.
Sturm, Jacob. "Historisch Poetisch Zeitverfassende Beschreibung der Stadt Regensburg aus dem Jahre 1663." *Verhandlungen des Historischen Vereins Oberpfalz und Regensburg.* Band XXXI, 1875.
Tscheuschner-Bern, K. "Die deutsche Passionsbühne und die deutsche Malerei des 15. und 16. Jahrhunderts in ihren Wechselbeziehungen." *Repertorium für Kunstwissenschaft.* Band 27, 1904.
Ulm, Benno. "Die Devotio moderna und die Architektur der Donauschule in Österreich." *Alte und Moderne Kunst.* 1966.
Wegner, Wolfgang. "Wie sah Altdorfer aus?" *Zeitschrift für Kunstwissenschaft.* Nr. 6, 1952.
Winzinger, Franz. "Albrecht Altdorfer und die Miniaturen des Triumphzugs Kaiser Maximilian I." *Jahrbuch der Kunsthistorischen Sammlungen in Wien.* Bd. 62, 1966.

Exhibition Catalogues

Albrecht Altdorfer und sein Kreis. Text: Ernst Buchner. Munich, 1938.
Albrecht Altdorfer und die Kunst der Donauschule in Oberösterreich. Linz, 1947.
Altdeutsche Kunst im Donauland. Staatliches Kunstgewerbemuseum. Vienna, 1939.
Berlin-Dahlem, Katalog der Gemäldegalerie. Staatliche Museen Preussischer Kulturbesitz, Berlin, 1975.
Cranach-Picasso. Text: Heribert Hutter. Albrecht Dürer Gesellschaft, 1968.
The Danube School: Prints and Drawings from the Danube School. Yale University Art Gallery, 1969.
George Grosz. Dortmund, Akademie der Künste, 1963.
Klassizismus und Romantik in Deutschland. Deutsches Nationalmuseum Nürnberg, 1966.

Malerei des 18. Jahrhunderts. Schwerin, n.d.

Otto Dix. Text: Otto Conzelmann. Galerie der Stadt Stuttgart, 1971.

Die Schöne Maria von Regensburg: Wallfahrten, Gnadenbilder, Ikonographie. Text: Achim Hubel. Regensburg, 1977.

Symbols in Transformation: Iconographic Themes at the Time of the Reformation. An Exhibition of Prints in Memory of Erwin Panofsky. Text: Craig Harbison. The Art Museum, Princeton University, Princeton, 1969.

Ephemera

Kehr, Wolfgang. "Altdorfers 'Alexanderschlacht' im Unterricht." Photocopied typescript. Munich: Akademie der bildenden Künste, 1973.

_____. "Projekt einer didaktischen Ausstellung zu Altdorfers 'Alexanderschlacht.'" Photocopied typescript of a paper given at the Tagung der Evangelischen Akademie in Tutzing über "Probleme der Rezeption von Kunstwerken in Museum und Kirche." May 1973.

Index

Achternbusch, Herbert, *Die Alexander-schlacht* (novel), 107
Agricola, Christoph Ludwig, 92, 137 n.7
Agrippa von Nettesheim, Heinrich Cornelius, *De Occulte Philosophia,* 34-35
Alchemy: art as, 78, 81; etching and, 82
Alberti, Leon Battista, 24
Albertus Magnus (bishop), 80-81
Alexander the Great, 32, 104
Altdorfer, Albrecht: Anabaptism, 17, 21; artistic origin, 14, 111 n.26; birth, 9, 110 n.2 and n.3, 115 n.10; Chinese landscape painting, 59; death, 19; Dilettant, 46, 50; and Dürer, 1, 17, 23, 25-26, 41, 43, 45, 48, 50, 55-58, 66; estate, 19, 111 n.21; in fiction, 66-69; folksong of sixteenth century Germany, 51; as "Little Master", 46; and northern Humanism, 13, 56, 77, 87-89 *(see also* Sodalitas Danubiensis); ideologies, 61, 63, 68-69, 73-74; and Italian art, 5, 65, 84-85, 104; leitmotif, 89-90, 93, 136 n.66; and medicinal plants, 80-81; as mystic, 50; and nature, 42; self portrait and portrait of, 19, 114 n.64 and n.66; as "True Master", 55; and Protestantism, 17, 19; public offices, 15-18; and Reformation, 113 n.43 and n.47; salaries, 111 n.20, 112 n.30 and n.32; and 'Storm and Stress', 49, 56; travels, 18, 113 n.54; treatment of space, 48, 58, 64, 106; and Venetian painting, 135 n.44; will, 18-19; works commissioned by city of Regensburg, 15-16, 57; workshop, 18
Altdorfer's works, drawings:
Armed Robbery in a Woods, 10
Christ in the Garden of Gethsemane, 71
Dead Pyramus, 81
Deathly Leap of Marcus Curtius, 86

Early drawings of wild men and witches, 88
Knight and Foot Soldier, 10
Maximilian's Prayerbook, 58
Pyramus and Thisbe, 25
Vita Frederici et Maximiliani, 13
Altdorfer's works, engravings:
Saint Christopher, 89-90, 94-95
Altdorfer's works, landscape etchings, 82; *Fir Tree and Castle,* 73
Two Views of the Synagogue in Regensburg, 15
Altdorfer's works, woodcuts:
The Beautiful Mary, 44-46, 112 n.39
Fall and Redemption of Man, 25-26, 40, 46
Monk Praying Before A Virgin and Child Enthroned, 50, 82-83
Standard Bearer, 25
Triumphal Arch, 13, 58, 61
Triumphal Procession, 14, 18, 57, 61, 69
Woodcuts for the Benedictine Monastery at Mondsee, 14
Altdorfer's works, paintings:
Adoration of the Kings (Frankfurt), 86
The Battle of Alexander, 23, 27, 49, 58-59; and alchemy, 81; as Baroque art, 100; commercial use of, 1-2; didactic use of, 73-75, 132 n.58; as Dürer's, 2, 26; in fiction, 67-68; German spirit of, 85; iconography of, 32-33, 140 n.58; and Kokoschka, 96-102, 104-5; as *Kunstkammer-stück,* 71; and Napoleon, 116 n.21; and Paracelsian thought, 79-80, 83, 132 n.58; reception of, 45-48, 66, 70, 72, 86, 105-6; and *Rezeptionsgeschichte,* 4; and Schlegel, 4, 16, 27, 30-31, 34-36, 104-5; structuralist

analysis of, 107; and Wölfflin, 65
The Beautiful Mary of Regensburg, 44,
    71, 85; motif of, 16; cult of, 11,
    15, 17, 50, 83, 112 n.35-36, 129
    n.55
The Birth of Mary, 47, 71; as Dürer's,
    24, 71; and Bramante, 85; and
    Kokoschka, 97, 106; and Wölfflin,
    64-65; as "urgermanisch", 129 n.41
Crucifixion (Berlin), 47, 56, 72; and
    Caspar David Friedrich, 92; and
    devotio moderna, 83-84
Crucifixion (Nürnberg), 47, 72; and
    devotio moderna, 83
Emperor's Bath (frescoes in the Bishop's
    Palace, Regensburg), 20, 85 (see also
    Dossi and Romanino)
Finding of the Body of St. Florian, 43,
    47; and Kokoschka, 97; and
    Rembrandt, 106
Finding of the Body of St. Sebastian (St.
    Florian altarpiece): and Picasso, 95-
    96, 107
Gethsemane (St. Florian altarpiece), 57,
    70-71; and Bellini, 85
Holy Family with St. John (Virgin
    Between St. Joseph and John
    Evangelist), 82; and Bellini, 85
Leavetaking of Christ from His Mother,
    40-41; and devotio moderna, 83
Lot and His Daughters, 56; and George
    Grosz, 95, 106; and Titian, 85
Madonna and Child in Glory, 43, 47;
    and Altdorfer's devotion, 83; and
    Kokoschka, 97
Martyrdom of St. Catherine, 78
Martyrdom of St. Florian: and Venetian
    painting, 85
The Miraculous Fountain in St. Florian:
    and devotio moderna, 84
Landscape With Trees (Waldstrasse), 43,
    66
Nativity (Bremen), 14, 71, 78; and
    George Grosz, 94; and Leonardo
    Da Vinci, 85; nature as threat in,
    86
Nativity (Berlin), 86
Nativity (Vienna), 18; nature as threat,
    86
Portrait of a Canon (St. Florian altar-
    piece), 83
Rest on the Flight to Egypt, 47, 49, 71;
    and Benesch, 79; and Elsheimer,
    91; iconography of, 81, 88-89
Satyrfamily, 14; and Bellini, 85
Saint Florian Altarpiece, 14, 18, 20, 49,

    106; and nationalist ideology, 79,
    130 n.58
Saints Francis and Jerome, 78
Saint George, 14, 71, 88; and Bellini,
    85; and Max Ernst, 93
Saint John the Baptist and Saint John
    the Evangelist (The Two Saints
    John), 23-24, 58, 80, 90, 106; and
    Benesch, 79
Separation of The Apostles, 83, 87-88,
    92
Susanna's Bath, 18, 45, 47-48, 67, 71,
    81, 84, 86-88
Wild Man, 71
Altdorfer, Erhard, 35
Altdorfer, Ulrich, 13-14
Altichiero, 45
Amberg, 9, 13
Aristotle, 99
Art: and Aristotle, 99; as collective expres-
    sion, 44; as exempla virtutis, 30; as
    imitation of nature, 45; and Paracelsus,
    78. See Romanticism
Athenaeum, 35
Augsburg, 11
Augustinian Order: and devotio moderna,
    83; monastery in Regensburg, 13, 19
Austria: and Altdorfer's artistic origin, 14,
    69; and ideology, 72, 81
Avanzo, Jacopo, 45
Aventinus, Johannes (Turmair): and The
    Battle of Alexander, 33; definition of
    God, 36; in fiction, 67; History of
    Bavaria, 13, 24, 29, 115 n.4, 117 n.32

Baldass, Ludwig von, 56-57, 59
Baldung Grien, Hans, 65, 80, 95
Baroque: Kokoschka's definition of, 98-
    100
Bavaria: and Altdorfer's artistic origin, 14;
    topography of, 23
Beauty: Schlegel on, 36; Kugler on, 42;
    Ruskin and Morris, 48
Beckmann, Max, 101
Beethoven, Ludwig van: Fugue in B major
    op. 133 and The Battle of Alexander,
    99
Behling, Lottlisla, 80, 106
Bellini, Giovanni, Allegory, Mount of Olives,
    Martyrdom of Saint Peter, 85
Bemmel, Peter von, 92
Benesch, Otto, 56, 70-71; on Paracelsus,
    77-80, 82-84, 87, 95, 106
Benjamin, Walter: theory of Rezeptions-
    geschichte, 2-3, 49, 107

Berlin: nineteenth-century art historians, 55
Boisseré, Melchior and Sulpiz, 61-62
Bosch, Hieronymus, 42, 94
Bramante, Donato, 85
Brueghel, Pieter, 59, 94
Breydenbach, Bernhard von, 59
Bruckner, Anton, 97
Buchner, Ernst: *St. Florian altarpiece*, 70
Burckhardt, Jacob, 3, 58
Burke, Kenneth, 61

Caravaggio, Michelangelo Merisi da, 98
Celtis, Konrad: *sodalitas danubiensis*, 87-88; *Quattuor Libri Amorum*, 11-12, 111 n.14
Chastel, André, 81
Clark, Kenneth, 5, 106
Cologne School, 42, 61
Cornelius, Peter, 45
Correggio, Antonio, 26, 59
Counter reformation, 20, 25
Cranach, Lukas, 35, 65, 80, 93, 96; and *devotio moderna*, 84
Cusanus, Nicolaus (Nicolas of Cues): and Altdorfer, 34; on art, 119 n.60 and n.65; definition of God, 106, 58, 82

Dante, Aleghieri, 32
Danube, 10, 18, 69, 70
Danube School (Donauschule): and Altdorfer, 1, 4; ambivalence of, 90; exhibits of, 4, 59, 68, 72; and *devotio moderna*, 82-84; origin of, 48-50
Darius (Persian king), and iconography of *The Battle of Alexander*, 32-33
Degenerate Art, exhibit of, 68
Deutsch, Nikolas Manuel, 93
Devotio Moderna (New Devotion), 77. *See also* Danube School
Dilettantism, 46, 50, 123 n.60 and n.61
Dix, Otto, 95-96, 107
Dohme, Robert, 50
Douvermann, Heinrich: *Altar of the Seven Pains* (Kalkar), 80
Dresden Academy, 95
Dossi, Dosso, and Romanino: frescoes in the Castello of Trient, 85
Dürer, Albrecht: and Altdorfer, 14, 24, 26, 40, 44, 63; on artist's role, 17; and *devotio moderna*, 84; Kokoschka on, 96-97; and Nürnberg, 10
Dvorak, Max, 59, 106

Von Einem, Herbert, 92
Elsheimer, Adam: *Holy Family With Angels*, 91; *Three Maries At The Tomb Of Christ*, 92
Enlightenment, 29
Erasmus of Rotterdam: on art, 27; on Dürer, 23
Ernst, Max: *La Foresta Imbalsamata, The Last Forest, The Horde*, 93-94, 96
Etching, 82. *See also* Alchemy

Fantastic in art: definition of, 42-43; Kugler, Waagen, Springer, Kant, 43, 81
Fiorillo, Johann Dominik, 39-40, 120 n.2
Florence, 11
Förster, Ernst, 45, 47
Fondaco Dei Tedesci, Venice, 10
Francis of Assisi, Saint, 85
Franconia. *See* Altdorfer's artistic origins
Friedlander, Max J., 25, 47-49, 55, 57
Friedrich, Alexander, 82. *See also* Alchemy; Etching
Friedrich, Caspar David, 72; *Tetschener Altarpiece*, 92-93, 94
Furtmayr, Berthold: *Missal for Bishop Von Rohr of Salzburg*, 14

German Art: characteristics of, 47, 59, 62, 65-66, 70, 105, 135-136 n.53; education, 75; eighteenth century, 26; fifteenth century, 42, 86; language, 13, 29; Old German School, 93-95, 97-98; Romantic philosophy of, 27-28; seventeenth century, 26; sixteenth century, 48, 56-57, 71, 85, 88, 118 n.41; in the Third Reich, 4, 55, 62-63, 66-70, 72, 96, 104, 128 n.40
Giorgione, 50
Goethe, Johann Wolfgang, 26-27, 29, 72, 77, 103
Göttingen, 39. *See also* Fiorillo
Greco, El (Domenico Theotocopoulos), 98
Grosz, George: *Christ With Gasmask, Central Park At Night, Hansel And Gretel, Rocks And Ferns At Bornholm, Rocks And Moon, No Let Up, Apocalyptic Landscape*, 93-96, 107
Gradmann, Erwin, 81. *See also* Fantastic in art
Grünewald, Mathis Neithardt-Gothardt, 25, 57, 65, 80, 93
Grünpeck, Joseph: *Vita Frederici Et Maximiliani*, 13, 35
Guild: Regensburg, 17-18; regulations, 111 n.28

Hamann, Richard, 87
Harbison, Craig, 5, 106
Hartlaub, G. F., 80, 106. *See also*
    Altdorfer; Paracelsus
Hegel, Georg W. F., 40-42, 45
Heinse, Wilhelm, 2. *See also Rezeptions-*
    geschichte
Herder, Johann Gottfried, 2, 29. *See also*
    Rezeptionsgeschichte
Herodotus, 101-2
Hetzer, Theodor, 65. *See also* Altdorfer
    and Italian art
Hildebrandt, Hans, 48
Hirschvogel, Augustin, 91
Hitler, Adolf, 68
Holbein, Hans (the Younger), 44, 57
Homer, 32, 105
Honthorst, Gerhard, 24
Humboldt, Alexander von, 41
Hume, David, 26
Huber, Wolf, 35; and *devotio moderna,*
    84, 94
Humanism: definition of, 88; in Italy, 58-
    59; ideal of, 82; Kokoschka's, 105;
    Northern humanism, 77; *Sodalitas*
    Danubiana, 11, 13, 56, 87
Hutten, Ulrich von, 10, 29

Iconoclasm, 20, 114 n.69
Ideology: definition of, 61; nationalist,
    61; National Socialist, 63, 67, 69-70

Janson, Horst W., 58
Janssen, Johannes, 51
Jauss, H. R., 4. *See also Rezeptions-*
    geschichte
Jean Paul: *Flegeljahre,* 72

Kahnweiler, Daniel Henry, 95
Kaisersberg, Gailer von: *Das Buch Vom*
    Guten Tode, 18
Kant, Emanuel, 43. *See also* Fantastic in
    art
Kaulbach, Wilhelm von, 45
Kehr, Wolfgang, 4, 106
Keyssler, Johann Georg, 26
Klein, Robert, 81
Koepplin, Dieter, 89-90, 106
Kokoschka, Oskar: *Thermopylae,* 96,
    101-2; and Altdorfer's art, 4, 55, 59,
    91, 96-102, 104-7, 139 n.39 and n.41;
    The Eye of Darius, 145-48; intellectual
    influences on, 140 n.50; and
    Rembrandt, 140 n.49

Krafft, Adam: *Sakramentshaus* (St. Lorenz,
    Nürnberg), 80
Krakau, 11. *See also* Konrad Celtis
Kugler, Franz Theodor, 41-43, 47
Kunstwollen, 57

Landscape: ambiguity of, 92; as genre,
    73; as image of genesis, 86-87; transi-
    tion from garden to forest, 88; reflect-
    ing human soul, 85; *Stimmungsland-*
    schaft, 66
Lautensack, Hans, 91
Lech (river), 69
Leipzig, 55
Leitha (river), 69
Leonardo Da Vinci, 26, 59, 85
Lessing, G. E., *Laokoon,* 27, 29
Lichtwark, A., 50. *See also* Dilettantism
Liliencron, Rochus, Baron von, 50
Linfert, Carl, 85-87, 90, 106. *See also*
    Landscape
Linz, 4, 72
Longinus, 26
Lorraine, Claude, 92
Lübeck, 11. *See also* Konrad Celtis
Luther, 29

Mainz, 11. *See also* Konrad Celtis
Memlinc, Hans, 42
Mannerism, 56
Master HL: Breisach High Altar, 80
Maulbertsch, Franz Anton, 96, 100
Maximilian I (emperor), 10, 50; patronage
    of Altdorfer, 11, 29
Meyer, Julius: *Künstlerlexikon,* 46-48
Michelangelo Buonarroti, 26, 96
Middle Ages: Romanticism and, 31-32;
    and Chivalry, 30-32, 102, 105
Mondsee (Benedictine monastery), 14
Moore, Sturge, 5
Morris, William, 48. *See also* Beauty
Mülig, Adelphus (physician in Strassburg):
    Bukolika, 89
Müller, Johann Georg, 45
Multscher, Hans, 94
Munich, 55-56; Altdorfer exhibitions in,
    57, 68, 74; exhibit of Degenerate Art in,
    95; catalogue of Hofgarten Collection
    in, 27; and Kokoschka, 98

Nab (river), 67
Nagler: *Künstlerlexikon,* 40
Nietzsche, Friedrich, 45

Northern Renaissance: the fantastic, 42;
infinite space, 56; and nature, 34
Novalis, 35

Öttinger, Karl, 87-88, 106. *See also*
Landscape
Ortega y Gasset, José, 103-4

Pacher, Michael: *Saint Wolfgang Altarpiece,*
14
Pächt, Otto, 65
Padua: frescoes by Altichiero and Alvanzo
in the Oratorio S. Giorgia, 45
Panofsky, Erwin: Altdorfer and space, 106
Pantheism, 58, 68, 81
Paracelsus (Theophrastus von Hohenheim),
34-35, 77; alchemy of art, 78-79, 81;
nature as pharmacy, 80; God as physi-
cian, 80; principles of genesis, 82, 87;
theory of chiromancy, 79
Paricius, Johannes: *History of Regensburg,*
26
Parmigianino, Francesco, 59
Patinir, Joachim, 43
Peasant Uprising, 72-73
Petrarca, 58
Peuchel, Georg Abraham: *Peuchel Band,*
24
Picasso, Pablo, 5, 59, 95-96; *Guernica,*
101, 107; and Dürer, 137-38 n.12
Piel, Friedrich, 107, 140 n.58. *See also*
Altdorfer's works, paintings: *The
Battle of Alexander*
Pinder, Wilhelm, 71-72, 87, 93
Pirckheimer, Wilibald, 10
Poussin, Nicolas, 92
Priebsch-Closs, Hanna, 66, 69
Protestantism, 17, 20

Raphael, 26, 40, 45-46
Rasmo, Nicolo: Altdorfer and Italian art,
5, 84-85, 104
Raselius (chronicler), 23-24, 27
Ratgeb, Jörg, 17
Reber, Franz von, 47-48
Reformation, 10, 17, 72
Regen (river), 10, 67
Regensburg: Altdorfer's civic role, 88, 92;
Benedictine monastery of St. Emmeram,
23; Burgher-Books, 13; charter-book
(Freiheitsbuch), 17; City Council of,
13; guild of illuminators, 14; expulsion
of Jews, 11, 15, 20, 50; and humanism,
13; industry and trade, 10-11; and

Napoleon, 19; patronage of arts, 12,
26; Saint Peter's Cathedral, 12;
schools, 12-13; social conditions, 10-12
Rembrandt van Ryn: compared to
Altdorfer, 43, 45; Kokoschka on, 96,
98
Renaissance: Altdorfer and Italian Renaissance, 77; characteristics of, 119 n.51;
Germany's own, 57, 62; and
Kokoschka, 97-98
Rettberg, Ralph von, 43, 47; on Altdorfer
and Rembrandt, 106
Reuwich, Erhard: *Bernhard von Breyden-
bach's Journey to The Holy Land,* 59
Rezeption (reception), 46, 56, 91; of
Altdorfer in the United States, 58;
creative, 107; definition, 2; dialectic,
104; errant, 104; and ideology, 3, 55-
56; objectivity of, 104, 107; primary,
4; secondary, 4; and semiotics, 4;
theory of, 2; twentieth century
Altdorfer reception, 105. *See also* W.
Benjamin; J. G. Herder; H. R. Jauss;
Ortega y Gasset
Rezeptionsgeschichte. See *Rezeption*
Riemenschneider, Tilman, 17
Romanticism: aesthetics, 30; critical
categories, 28; definition of "romantic"
35-37 *(see also* Friedrich Schlegel);
German Romanticism, 49, 71; of the
nineteenth and sixteenth century, 6;
romantic movement, 39; taste, 40
Roth, A. G., 89. *See also* Iconography
Rousseau, Jean Jacques, 49
Ruhmer, Eberhard, 56-59
Ruisdael, Jacob van, 59
Runge, Philipp Otto: *Rest On the Flight To
Egypt,* 93
Ruskin, John, 48

Sadler, Aegidius, 24
Saint Florian (town, location of Altdorfer's
Saint Florian altarpiece), 49
Sandrart, Joachim von: on Altdorfer, 24-
25, 115 n.12; on art, 116 n.13; com-
pared with Schlegel, 30, 44, 106;
portrait of Altdorfer, 19
Saran, Bernhard, 90, 106. *See also*
Humanism
Schadow, Wilhelm von, 45
Schedel, Hartmann: *Pictorial World His-
tory,* 11-12, 39, 59, 111 n.13
Schenkendorf, Max von, 61
Schiller, Friedrich, 35
Schlegel, August Wilhelm, 28, 35, 117 n.25.
See also Romanticism

Schlegel, Friedrich: Altdorfer's individualism, 36, 106; and *The Battle of Alexander*, 4, 27, 39-40, 43, 44, 48, 61, 104-6, 143-44; definition of "romantic", 31, 35; *Letters On Christian Art*, 29-30; and the Middle Ages, 31-32; nationalism, 117 n.30; philosophy of art, 28, 35-36
Schnitzler, Arthur: on Paracelsus, 77
Schöne, Wolfgang, 89
Sodalitas Danubiana. *See* Humanism; Johannes Stabius
Spalding, Jack, 5
Speculum Humanae Salvationis, 32
Springer, Anton, 43-44, 47
Stabius, Johannes, 13. *See also* Regensburg and humanism
Stael-Holstein, Anne Louise Germaine (Necker) Baronne De, 31-32. *See also* Romanticism
Stange, Alfred, 82-84. *See also* Humanism; *Devotio Moderna*
Sulzer, Johann Georg: *General Theory of The Fine Arts*, 26
Synaesthesie, 71, 72

Tacitus: *Germania*, 88
Talbot, Charles, 5, 59
Thieck, Ludwig, 35. *See also* Athenaeum
Thomas à Kempis, 82
Tietze, Hans, 55-59
Tintoretto, Jacopo, 65
Titian, 26, 85, 96

Trient, Castello of: frescoes by Dossi and Romanino, 85

Uffenbach, Philipp, 91
Uhland, Ludwig, 51

Vasari, G., 24
Venice, 50, 91, 92. *See also* Fondaco Dei Tedesci
Verona, 18
Vienna: Altdorfer in, 18; College of Mathematics, 13; College of Poets, 13; Kokoschka in Vienna, 105
Voss, Hermann, 48-50

Waagen, Gustav Friedrich, 43; on Altdorfer and Rembrandt, 106
Wackenroder, W. H., 23, 28-29; *Effusions From the Heart Of An Art-Loving Monk*, 31; on Dürer, 31. *See also* Romanticism
Warnke, Martin, 3. *See also* Rezeption
Watzlik, Hans: Altdorfer novel, 66-69
William IV (Duke of Bavaria), 16, 33, 50
Winzinger, Franz, 4, 23, 56-59
Witten, Hans, 80
Wölfflin, Heinrich, 3, 55, 62-65, 77, 106
Wolgemut, Michael, 59

Zürich, 63